This book is dedicated to
Philip S. Reisman,
who, for over 95 years,
seized every day.

Perspectives on Productive Aging
Social Work with the New Aged

Lenard W. Kaye, Editor

NASW PRESS

National Association of Social Workers
Washington, DC

Elvira Craig de Silva, DSW, ACSW, *President*
Elizabeth J. Clark, PhD, ACSW, MPH, *Executive Director*

Cheryl Y. Bradley, Publisher
Schandale Kornegay, Manager, Publications
Marcia Roman, Managing Editor
Gail Martin, Copyeditor
Marcia Roman, Proofreader
Bernice Eisen, Indexer

Cover design by Eye to Eye Design Studios, Bristow, VA
Interior design by Cynthia Stock, Electronic Quill, Silver Spring, MD
Printed and bound by Victor Graphics, Baltimore, MD

Library of Congress Cataloging-in-Publication Data

Perspectives on productive aging: social work with the new aged/Lenard W. Kay, editor

    p. cm.
Includes bibliographical references and index.
ISBN 0-87101-377-0
1. Social work with the aged. I. Kaye, Lenard W.
HV1451.P47 2004
362.6—dc22

                                        2003025746

Contents

Foreword   ix
Robert N. Butler

Introduction   xi
Lenard W. Kaye

Acknowledgments   xv

Part 1
Setting the Stage

1   The Emergence of the New Aged and a Productive Aging Perspective   3
    Lenard W. Kaye

2   The Demographics of Productive Aging   19
    Charles F. Longino, Jr., and Don E. Bradley

3   Conceptualizing Productive Aging   37
    Nancy R. Hooyman

Part 2
Dimensions of Productive Aging

4   Labor Force Participation   61
    Michàl E. Mor-Barak and Steve Wilson

Contents

5 Volunteerism, Philanthropy, and Service   83
Nancy Morrow-Howell, Melinda Carden, and Michael Sherraden

6 Family Life   107
Roberta R. Greene

7 Personal and Individual Growth   123
Helen Q. Kivnick

8 Spiritual and Religious Growth   149
James W. Ellor

9 Education and Learning   163
E. Michael Brady

10 Activism   177
Sandra S. Butler

11 Physical Activity, Exercise, and Recreation   195
Melonie D. Grossman

12 The Potential of Productive Aging: A Personal Perspective
and Reference Point   215
T. Franklin Williams andCarter Catlett Williams

Appendix A
Resources for Practitioners to Facilitate Productive Aging   225
Jennifer Campbell and Fontaine H. Fulghum

Appendix B
Strengths Assessment Interview Guide   241

Subject Index   243

About the Editor   253

About the Contributors   255

List of Tables and Figures

Tables

1-1. Predictors of Successful Aging from the AARP Foundation Project on Successful Aging and Adaptation with Chronic . . .

1-2. Alternative Perspectives of Geriatric Social Work Practice

1-3. Human Service Programs with an Orientation toward Productive Aging

1-4. Challenges of Productive Aging for Older Adults and the Roles Social Workers Can Assume to Deal with Them

1-5. Productive Aging with Social Worker Skill Sets

1-6. The Multiple Dimensions of Productive Aging

2-1. Productive Persons Ages 65–75

2-2. A Profile of Productive Aging

4-1. Benefits, Barriers, and Social Work Interventions with Older Workers

5-1. Selected Senior Civil Service Programs

5-2. Selected Innovations in Senior Service

6-1. Geriatric Social Work with Older Adults and Their Families: Major Investments

Figures

4-1. Number of Persons 55 Years or Older

4-2. Labor Force Participation of Adults Ages 55 and Older . . . 1991–2000

4-3. Labor Force Projections to 2008

6-1. Components of Successful Aging

6-2. The Levels of Ecological System

6-3. Five Continua for the Elderly

7-1. Psychosocial Framework of the Life Cycle

Foreword

Robert N. Butler

Productive aging is defined as the capacity of an older individual or population to continue to work in a paid or voluntary capacity. It expresses the valuable contributions that older people make to the family, to the community, and to national life. For example, the foundation world has calculated that billions of dollars of equivalent contributions have come from older people who do volunteer work. In addition to contributing to society, evidence suggests that productivity encourages health in the same way that health supports productivity. Studies begun in 1955 by the National Institutes of Health have demonstrated that older people who have goals and structure are likely to live longer.

The extent to which an older person can remain productive depends on a variety of personal factors, including physical and emotional well-being, motivation, attitude, education, and experience, and societal factors, including changes in technologies, attitudes, and structures. The interplay between personal issues and societal norms has an important influence on both paid and unpaid productive activities.

Having a sense of purpose, goals, and structure is advantageous to both the individual and society. Today, however, many older people do not recognize the importance of constructive purpose, and society has few stabilized institutions that support genuine social, cultural, and productive roles for older people. Unfortunately, the important topic of productive aging is lacking in the social work literature.

We have no time to waste. Before the 21st century ends, biological and societal advancement in gene-based and regenerative medicine will further extend longevity. The demographic changes will necessitate new work patterns, including significant roles for older Americans, both in the paid and in the voluntary sectors. As baby boomers (those born between 1946 and 1964) age, it is increasingly apparent that they will continue to work. It is difficult to imagine 69 million talented and experienced baby boomers spending 20 to 30 years in retirement, collecting social security, and using Medicare rather than contributing to society.

Productive aging is in the best interest of society and the individual. Social work's role will be to help older individuals and society prepare for the growing numbers of older people as the 21st century becomes the century of productive old age.

Introduction

Perspectives on Productive Aging is a response to the argument that the professional literature in the field of aging and gerontological social work is exceedingly biased. Gerontological practice emphasizes the problems, crises, and losses experienced by individuals as they age. At the same time, discussions of social work intervention with older adults center inevitably around strategies for dealing with those problems, crises, and losses. We have been inundated with research reports that detail the physical and mental decline associated with aging. We have available practice texts that address social work and other professional interventions with Alzheimer's victims, abused elderly people, incapacitated elderly people in need of caregiving support, the institutionalized and homebound older adults, and other subgroups of older adults in similar states of incapacity, vulnerability, and decline. Lost in the shuffle are the creative and important functions and roles that social workers could more frequently assume as they serve the expanding cohort of the "new aged"—older adults who are more mobile, active, healthy, economically secure, educated, and politically sophisticated than older persons in any previous generation.

Bias toward the aging population has led to a scarcity of material that probes positive, successful, independent, and productive aging experiences in the context of the family, the workplace, volunteering, social and recreational performance, personal growth, and social and political activism. This widespread and unfortunate vacancy in gerontological social work exists at the research, policy, program development, and clinical practice levels.

This volume aims to fill the gap in the literature by providing readers with a different frame of reference for examining the aging experience and by exploring a new, expanded set of professional functions social workers must acquire now and in the future. This book highlights the assets, resources, capacities, and skills of older adults rather than their problems, deficiencies, and needs. The arrival of the new millennium is an appropriate time to promote such an expansion in our professional perspective toward the aging experience and the roles and functions that social workers can legitimately assume in their work with older adults.

Considering the significant numbers of gerontological social workers and allied health professionals in public, nonprofit, and proprietary agencies and organizations serving older adults and their families, this book should have a broad readership. Geriatric care managers, retirement planners, senior center personnel, community and group work specialists, leisure time and recreational workers, and aging services planners and administrators will all find the content relevant as they plan, design, and deliver services to older adults. Students preparing for careers in gerontological counseling and administration, care management, and adult recreational and leisure services are also appropriate audiences for this book.

The Responsibility of Contributors

Contributors to this volume were asked to review the scope and breadth of productive practices, behaviors, and contributions by older adults in various domains of daily life. They were also encouraged to draw on one or more theoretical perspectives to help them describe, explain, and predict the nature of older adult engagement in a particular life domain. Finally, contributors to the volume were expected to discuss a combination of macro, mezzo, and micro social work practice roles and methods to reinforce meaningful participation by older adults in a particular domain. In discussing social work practice functions, contributors have highlighted examples of innovative programs and model demonstrations that emphasize the promotion of productivity among older adults.

Readers will note that authors have used conceptual frameworks that recognize the personal resources, capacities, and abilities older adults can bring to bear in meeting the challenges of active engagement in particular domains of functional and instrumental performance. They have also considered the impact of such variables as culture, race, ethnicity, health, gender, age, and economic well-being on productive lifestyles.

The Book's Content

The content of this book is divided into two main sections. In the first section, entitled "Setting the Stage," the reader is presented with conceptual, demographic, and theoretical perspectives of productive aging. In chapter 1, Lenard W. Kaye considers alternative definitions of "productive aging" and offers an alternative paradigm for framing social work practice with older adults. Social work's role in promoting productive aging is considered here as well. In chapter 2, Charles F. Longino, Jr., and Don E. Bradley develop a detailed demographic profile of the "new aged" fully documented by the literature. Chapter 3 by Nancy R. Hooyman presents a series of analytical perspectives for conceptualizing productive aging and interpreting it in different life contexts. Variables that can be expected to influence conceptualizations of productive aging, including culture, race, ethnicity, health, economic security, gender, and, of course, age, are considered in the discussion.

In the second section, entitled "Dimensions of Productive Aging," the productive aging experience in various domains of daily living is explored, including the roles and responsibilities of social workers engaged in work with these individuals. Dimensions considered include the workplace (chapter 4 by Michàl E. Mor-Barak and Steve Wilson); volunteerism and service (chapter 5 by Nancy Morrow-Howell, Melinda Carden, and Michael Sherraden); family life (chapter 6 by Roberta R. Greene); personal growth (chapter 7 by Helen Q. Kivnick); spiritual and religious life (chapter 8 by James W. Ellor); education and lifelong learning (chapter 9 by E. Michael Brady); activism (chapter 10 by Sandra S. Butler); and physical activity, exercise, and recreation (chapter 11 by Melonie D. Grossman). In chapter 12, T. Franklin Willams and Carter Catlett Williams present a unique and compelling personal and professional perspective on the productive aging experience from the vantage point of two highly respected professionals, husband and wife, and pioneers in social work and medicine.

This volume includes a specially prepared appendix by Jennifer Campbell and Fontaine H. Fulghum that provides practitioners with special resources to facilitate productive aging, including listings of special programs and demonstration projects, directories of special interest professional and disciplinary associations and membership groups that emphasize productivity in later life, and professional and scholarly journals that focus on aspects of productivity in old age.

LENARD W. KAYE

Acknowledgments

I wish to thank, first and foremost, my contributors for the outstanding work they carried out to prepare the chapters for this volume. Their expertise and professionalism were most impressive and made the task of editing this volume virtually painless. It is noteworthy that they were asked to think a good bit differently about social work practice with older adults than is commonplace and they did it in superb fashion. They were also most patient given the delay that I am responsible for in moving this project to completion. Preparation of this book occurred during an unanticipated change in venue for me both professionally and personally. While the move that was undertaken by my family and myself from our prior home in Pennsylvania to our new home in Maine during the past year was exciting, it was also unexpected, unavoidably disruptive and inevitably timeconsuming. Joining a new faculty and establishing a new center on aging at the University of Maine in Orono has been, of course, challenging as well. Thus completion of this project ended up being about six months behind schedule.

Thanks are due the members of NASW's Publications Committee for approving this project. I am also very much appreciative of Cheryl Y. Bradley, Publisher, and Marcia Roman, Managing Editor, at NASW Press for their expert assistance as the manuscript was readied for publication.

Finally, I wish to thank both Lisa Marie Parent and Elizabeth W. Downey at the UMaine Center on Aging for their skilled editorial and stylistic assistance in readying the chapters for publication.

Part 1

Setting the Stage

1

A Social Work Practice Perspective on Productive Aging

Lenard W. Kaye

What does productive aging mean?[1] For that matter, what is successful, vital, meaningful, or satisfying aging? Is the absence of disease or infirmity, the accumulation of wealth, engagement in employment, or expression of philanthropic spirit to be equated with productivity in old age? Can a good diet, regular physical exercise, or a strong informal network of family, neighbors, and friends guarantee a productive old age?

The Difficulty in Defining Terms

The popular and professional literature offer a myriad, if not always consistent, answer to these questions. In the early

1980s, the John D. and Catherine T. MacArthur Foundation funded a group of scholars to research the factors behind improved old age. In reporting on the findings, Rowe and Kahn (1999) underscored the importance of health, mental acuity, vigor, and independence. They found that good mental, social, and physical habits expressed in the maintenance of strong social ties and connections, intellectual and mental creativity, good nutrition, and plenty of exercise were more important than genetic background. They also determined that the public needed to discard stereotypes and myths about old age and longevity, including the presumption that to be old is to be sick; that old people cannot learn new things; that poor lifestyle choices need not be altered because the damage cannot be reversed; that longevity genes are key to successful aging; and that old people lack sexual interest, attraction, and performance capacity.

Perls, Silver, and Lauerman (1999), reporting on the New England Centenarian Study, investigated the lives of

[1]For additional discussion on productive aging, see Kaye L. W. (2002). Productive aging and social work: Helping elders meet the challenges of a vital old age. *Social Work Today*, 2(13), 16–19; and Kaye, L. W., Butler, S. S., & Webster, N. M. (2003). Toward a productive aging paradigm for geriatric mental health. *Ageing International*, 28, 200–213, for a modified version of this chapter.

people at least 100 years old and discovered that avoiding the major diseases associated with old age was key to a long life and to reaping the benefits of a genetic predisposition to longevity. For them, income level, eating habits, ethnic and racial background, and education levels were less important to predicting longevity than the ability to maintain good mental and physical health over the long term. Continuing to learn, avoiding obesity, maintaining a steady weight throughout life, avoiding heavy drinking, and not smoking in late life were also important. In their research, survivors tended not to be neurotic, were rather charismatic, and were almost never loners. In fact, survivors attracted many friends and significant others and were respected and liked by many. They displayed excellent coping strategies and remained calm and collected when confronted with stressful situations and crises. Survivors also exhibited great adaptability to their circumstances, and they were often religious or spiritual.

Dychtwald's (1999) vision of healthy aging stressed taking advantage of opportunities that make life meaningful such as engaging in service and leadership activities. In his view, personal development and productivity—giving back to society and to the community that which has been gained over a lifetime in experiences—are the keys to a contented old age. These concepts were developed by Erik Erikson (1978, 1994); Erikson and Erikson (1998); and Erikson, Erikson, and Kivnick (1994). The importance of a spiritual life stage, called "gero-transcendence," in which individual interests shift from a materialistic and rational perspective to a more transcendent and cosmic perspective, was also underscored.

Klein and Bloom (1997) found that incorporating primary prevention strategies into the lifestyles of older adults provided an "advantage" in the aging process. They referred to a "learning and earning" process in which living wisely and well through mature adulthood, recognizing one's own role in the aging process, and engaging actively in that process maximized the likelihood of experiencing an advantaged old age.

George Vaillant (1995, 2003), director of the Harvard Study of Adult Development, reported on data drawn from 50 years of following individuals as they aged and wrote about the components of vital and interesting old age. Vaillant found that an adaptive and flexible coping style, a stable marriage, and regular exercise are considerably less important than are low cholesterol intake and ancestral predisposition to a long life. Intergenerational relationships, not smoking cigarettes, and avoiding alcohol were also important to happy older adulthood. These observations also held true for advantaged and inner-city males and gifted females.

Although McKhann and Albert (2002) recognized the inevitable physical changes in the brain, they argued that healthy aging is closely tied to mental and physical exercise programs. Eating a well-balanced diet, getting adequate sleep, and seeking timely medical assistance for depression, urinary and sexual problems, and hearing and vision loss are equally important.

Geriatric specialist David Lipschitz, author of *Breaking the Rules of Aging* (2002), emphasized the importance of vigorous exercise, sexual activity, avoiding obsessive concern with weight loss, minimizing invasive surgery for most cases of coronary disease when symptoms are absent, and avoiding overmedication.

Rosenblatt (2000) posted 56 rules for realizing a satisfying old age, most of which address behaviors and activities that should be avoided. This lighter take on the subject emphasizes the importance of looking out for one's well-being while not becoming overly engaged in self-examination. A satisfying life, according to Rosenblatt, is not tied to exercise, to vitamin consumption, or to drug and alcohol abstinence, but, rather, to realizing that you are responsible for your own destiny because others inevitably do not much care.

A series of five studies completed in 2001 and supported by the American Association of Retired Persons (AARP) Andrus Foundation (now the AARP Foundation) nicely summarized many factors that have played a role in predicting successful aging (see Beilenson, Sprouse, & Villarreal, 2002; Poon, Gueldner, & Sprouse, 2003). These studies were all part of the project "Successful Aging and Adaptation with Chronic Diseases in Older Adults." Major findings are summarized in Table 1-1. Although one of the AARP studies performed by Strawbridge and Wallhagen (2003) emphasized that successful aging is best likened to active aging (physically, intellectually, and socially), they suggested that differences in perception of successful aging existed for women compared with men. For women, successful aging was more closely associated with spiritual growth, involvement with friends and groups, and engagement in activities with others. For men, successful aging likely en-

tailed continued expression of athletic ability and opportunities to enjoy sexual intimacy. These researchers pointed out that definitions of successful old age varied, to some degree, from person to person; would change over time on the basis of the challenges individuals faced; were not restricted to the most robust; and could be realized as long as a person was alive. Most important, they suggested that good health alone does not predict perceptions of a successful old age (Strawbridge & Wallhagen, 2003).

To appreciate the variety of factors that are important to predicting or promoting a productive aging experience, consider these headlines from the popular media:

- "Protesting May be Good for Your Health" (*Reuters Health*, Monday, December 23, 2002)
- "Aging: Brain Boosts, from the Other Side" (*The New York Times*, November 19, 2002)
- "Can Brain Exercises Help You Stay Sharp?" (*The Boston Globe*, December 10, 2002)
- "Aromatherapy 'May Alleviate Dementia'" (based on an article from the *British Medical Journal*, December 6, 2002)
- "Tea May Help Your Bones" (*Health and Age News Alert*, No. 91, http://healthandage.com, July 19, 2002)
- "Milk Benefits More Than Bones" (*Health and Age News Alert*, No. 94, http://healthandage.com, August 30, 2002)
- "An Aspirin a Day . . . " (*Health and Age News Alert*, No. 94, http://healthandage.com, August 30, 2002)

Table 1-1

Predictors of Successful Aging from the AARP Foundation Project on Successful Aging and Adaptation with Chronic Diseases in Older Adults

Research Project Team	Factors Promoting Successful Aging in Elderly People with Chronic Impairments
Penrod, Gueldner, and Poon	• Feeling challenged to overcome impediments and accomplish tasks • Working through challenges and engaging in proactive planning • Monitoring personal status by reflecting on one's condition and challenges • Making choices among available options
Rakowski, Clark, Miller, and Berg	• Reciprocity (the ability to give care or attention to others as well as receive it) • Engagement with others • Intellectual stimulation
Seeman and Chen	• Exercise and other forms of physical activity • Higher levels of emotional support • Lowered levels of social conflict and stress
Strawbridge and Wallhagen	• Not smoking • Not being obese • Feeling very satisfied with personal relationships • Having little or no hearing impairment • Staying physically active • Volunteering often
AARP Foundation Projects, National Institute on Aging, and other sources	• Do not smoke • Drink in moderation • Stay physically active • Eat a balanced diet • Avoid obesity • Protect vision and hearing • Get regular health care and vaccinations • Maintain a vibrant social network and strong personal relationships • Stay active in professional, community, or other activities • Plan for your financial well-being

ADAPTED FROM: Beilenson, J., Sprouse, B. M., & Villarreal, R. (2002). *Aging successfully: Findings from research sponsored by the AARP Foundation*. Washington, DC: Author; Poon, L. W., Gueldner, S. H., & Sprouse, B. M. (Eds.). (2003). *Successful aging and adaptation with chronic diseases*. New York: Springer.

- "Moderate Drinking Reduces Diabetes Risk" (*Health and Age News Alert*, No. 93, http://healthandage.com, August 16, 2002)
- "Some Foods May Cut Alzheimer's Risk" (*The Associated Press*, June 26, 2002)
- "Natural Protein May Influence Aging" (*The Associated Press*, January 4, 2002)

According to these stories, a healthier, satisfying, successful old age, both physically and mentally, is more likely when older people take part in protests and demonstrations; make an effort to draw information from both sides of the brain; engage in mental exercises; apply sweet-smelling oils, such as lemon balm and lavender oil; drink tea regularly; consume lots of dairy products; take a small daily dose of aspirin; consume moderate amounts of alcohol; eat more nuts, leafy green vegetables, and other foods rich in antioxidants such as vitamin E; and control the activity of protein.

Given the multiplicity of meanings that might potentially be associated with a vital old age, is there any reason to think that a definition can be constructed that everyone will accept? Indeed, is not the idea of productivity defined differently depending on an individual's personal values and priorities and those of the society in which the individual [lives]?

Narrowing the Boundaries

Social workers and other human services professionals are interested in the concept of productive aging from sociological, economic, and psychological vantage points. For these individuals, a productive old age centers on participating in the work world and on engaging in compensated employment. For others, productivity may mean volunteering, namely, serving one's nation or community. For others, the focus may be on self-development, introspection, and personal insight and growth. Of course, some people would avoid labeling life as productive or unproductive because such normative prescriptions connote desirable and undesirable behavior.

At the risk of receiving criticism from some scholars on the subject, this volume uses the terminology of productivity but avoids narrow prescriptions of its meaning. Rather, the editor and the various contributors, taken together, provide an array of definitions and examples of productive aging. Contributors to this volume do not subscribe to a single definition of a productive old age. And that is good. Indeed, it is argued that productivity can be most usefully defined as either or as both an internal and external response to the aging experience. It is hoped that a broad definition of aging will both encourage social workers to explore alternative methods for intervening with older adults and will recognize the many ways in which social workers can effectively intervene to encourage and preserve productive lifestyles in older adults.

An Alternative Perspective for Working with Older Adults

An alternative practice paradigm for working with older adults that reflects a productive orientation to life is suggested. As reflected in Table 1-2, such a paradigm is closely aligned with a

Table 1-2

Alternative Perspectives of Geriatric Social Work Practice

The Traditional Perspective	A Productive Aging Perspective
Nihilistic	Hopeful
Deterioration	Growth and development
Disability and dysfunction	Illness prevention, health, and wellness
Dependence	Autonomy, independence, and interdependence
Rigid resistance to change	Receptive to change
Unable to learn	Intellectual stimulation
Vulnerability/passivity	Empowerment
Quality of life (one dimensional)	Quality of life (multidimensional)
Societal disengagement	Societal engagement
Community isolation	Community integration
Denial and avoiding challenges	Confronting challenges
Needs, deficits, opportunities lost	Strengths, abilities, desires, opportunities
The past and what might have been	The future and what can still be
The micro environment	The micro, mezzo, and macro environments
"Age-appropriate" behaviors	Age-neutral behaviors
Therapeutic stock taking	Therapeutic enhancement
Sedentary lifestyles	Activity and activism
Receiving	Giving, volunteering, and exchange

strengths-based perspective to geriatric social work practice. This perspective embraces growth and capacity, potential yet to be realized, and the continuing aspirations and enhancements of people over time, regardless of their relative age and health. It dwells less on consolidating and coming to terms with past accomplishments or failures, but rather it integrates present-day and future-oriented perspectives.

Defending the Productive Aging Emphasis

Several arguments might be posed that question the need to construct a practice focal point that builds a professional capacity for working with the productive elderly, given the scarcity of human services resources (Kaye, Butler, & Webster, 2003). Why dwell, one might ask, on such matters, given the severity of other needs, problems, and deficits expressed either explicitly or implicitly by older adults, including the devastating effects of poverty, ageism, chronic disease, and extreme isolation? Indeed, gerontological social workers have been rightly concerned with the negative circumstances that can and do arise during the course of aging. Yet, it is argued that gerontological social workers can maintain a productive aging perspective, an orientation, and a set of values even under these circumstances by promoting the elder voice and helping older people stay engaged in the community, advancing their personal control and mastery over their environment.

It could also be argued that social workers would have great difficulty identifying and reaching out to actively engaged older adults (that is, those experiencing a productive old age) because these adults are less likely to be associated with or even familiar with the social welfare system. Granted, these older adults may not be common beneficiaries of the traditional network of deficit-oriented health and human services (unless they are experiencing significant incapacity), but they can be expected to be associated with the mainstream health care system, where they consume routine care and participate in various community programs for active elders. Either way, it is argued that social work would do well to be geared explicitly to promoting productive behaviors and preventing nonproductive behaviors and that such a philosophy can and should permeate the world of routine health and social service programming.

Social workers, it is maintained, have a more explicit role to play in a variety of nontraditional settings, including retirement planning, travel and recreational programming, employment training and counseling, volunteer services, self-help programming, exercise programs, and continuing and lifelong learning programs. Such programs emphasize active engagement in community life and societal interaction. Increased social work involvement in these fields of practice will translate into more direct contact with and, ultimately, longer-term engagement of active elders in the very programs that

reinforce and reward productive older-adult behaviors. Table 1-3 summarizes the range of nontraditional social work programs referred to here.

A productive aging perspective may also be viewed as having greater relevance to financially secure and physically robust older adults. To the contrary, it is believed that a productive aging perspective has universal relevance. All older persons will benefit enormously from a philosophy that promotes choice, opportunity, creativity, and personal development regardless of financial well-being or health status. Regardless of the degree of physical, functional, and emotional health, all persons, as they age, are challenged to sustain a high quality of life, set genuine goals for themselves, structure their daily lives meaningfully, and remain engaged in community and family life. It is crucial that we remember that the manner in which active engagement is framed can vary dramatically

---

Table 1-3

Human Service Programs with an Orientation toward Productive Aging

---

- Volunteer and community service programs
- Continuing education and lifelong learning
- Retirement planning
- Elder mentor–tutor programs
- Social action programs
- Job training and workforce retooling
- Gero-therapy and counseling
- Self-help groups
- Intergenerational programs
- Health and wellness promotion projects
- Travel and elder hostelling programs
- Recreation and exercise programs

from one person to the next. Furthermore, the ability to remain productive and vital will be determined by a host of personal factors, including but not limited to attitude, physical and emotional well-being, motivation, education and experience, and changing societal attitudes and expectations. For this reason, work with productive elders can and must take place in traditional settings in which a large proportion of geriatric social workers are already employed (for example, long-term care facilities, adult day care, senior citizen centers, hospices, chronic and acute care hospitals, and in-home programs). In these settings, the capacity of social workers to identify, to reinforce, and to help preserve those dimensions of older adult capacity that reflect a productive aging philosophy is particularly crucial.

The Demographic Mandate

As adults in their forties and fifties edge toward retirement, they will carry with them a broadened set of expectations concerning the availability of services and programs that reinforce their continued engagement in the livelihood of our communities.

Increased social work attention to the productive dimension of aging is not solely an act of altruism. As a society, we have much to gain from the greater participation of older persons in many walks of life. Retirees buttress the economic and social infrastructure through travel, recreation, employment, and community service, and older adults also tend to pursue jobs that are less popular among younger workers, including part-time, tempo-rary, and contract employment (Alexander & Kaye, 1997).

Because reimbursement for wellness and prevention programs has been limited at the federal, state, and local levels and through private insurers, some may conclude that a discussion about working with productive elders is little more than an endeavor in utopian thought. Yet, it is suggested that more positive perspectives on the aging experience both at the societal and professional levels will eventually translate into alternative philosophies regarding funding and reimbursement patterns. Furthermore, funding streams (especially local and private foundation sources) are already beginning to support this changed philosophy, which is reflected in foundation support for such initiatives as the development of healthy, integrated, elder-friendly communities; intergenerational programming; and consumer-controlled programs that give older adults a voice.

Challenges Confronting Vital Older Adults

Active engagement in a vital old age can be expected to revolve around interaction in the lives of others rather than disengagement from the external environment. That may entail a desire on the part of the older person for paid employment. In these instances, engagement entails participating in activities that are not only genuine, meaningful, and emotionally satisfying, but also compensated. Achieving a vital old age, in this case, may mean older persons successfully negotiating the world of work, including job retraining, skills building, job interviewing, and salary negotiation even in the face of significant physical and functional impairment.

Another elder may seek social, emotional, and intellectual stimulation. Challenges for the older adult seeking this type of vital lifestyle may include maintaining an intellectually challenging and contemplative state of mind; successfully nurturing a robust, informal support network of some combination of family, friends, and confidants; or identifying community volunteer activities that will be meaningful and, therefore, personally satisfying. In both cases, older adults will need to be prepared to deal with the various shapes and forms of age discrimination. Relatives, neighbors, prospective employers, and the public continue to subscribe to outmoded conceptions of what constitutes age-appropriate behavior. Older adults may face additional challenges; they may need to overcome physical barriers in the environment that affect maneuverability and impede access to a vital lifestyle and learn to function in a technologically altered environment.

Geriatric social workers will need to assume a range of nontraditional roles as they respond to the challenges of productive old age, such as career or workplace counselors, volunteer service planners, retirement planners, public educators, and environmental change and adaptation specialists (see Table 1-4). These roles will likely be novel and unfamiliar to most social workers and may require additional on-the-job training and education.

Adoption of a diverse skill set and intervention perspective will also be relevant for a productive aging orientation to social work practice, given the need for the worker to delve into issues, fields of service, and client interests not traditionally addressed. These include a proactive orientation to intervention (that is, intervening before problems and challenges have surfaced or risen to crisis proportions); creative problem solving; interdisciplinary team playing (working with educators, travel agents, recreation therapists, and so

Table 1-4

Challenges of Productive Aging for Older Adults and the Roles Social Workers Can Assume to Deal with Them

The Challenge for the Older Adult	The Social Work Response
Financial insecurity	Financial planning
Labor force infiltration	Career counseling
Participation in meaningful community activities	Volunteer activity planning
Maintaining productive family relations	Family counseling
Adapting to a changing world	Adaptation counseling; lifelong learning and retooling
Overcoming public and professional discrimination and stereotyping	Public education and advocacy; gero-therapy
Remaining productive while living with long-term disability	Technology utilization training; gero-therapy

on); comfort working at multiple practice levels (that is, micro, mezzo, and macro); and familiarity with nontraditional community resources and services (for example, recreational, travel, educational, and exercise programs; see Table 1-5).

Much of what social workers do does not require additional layers of bureaucracy of aging-related services delivery. Rather, the astute social workers will be able to modify existing programs to subscribe to a vital engagement philosophy. To accomplish this, social workers will want to think creatively. They might work with town managers to determine ways to increase citizen participation in community affairs. They might counsel employers on how to recognize the benefits of older workers as opposed to the liabilities. Social workers will need to enlighten communities, governments, businesses, and individuals about the benefits they will accrue by creating opportunities for older adults to contribute to their well-being and the well-being of others. Re-

Table 1-5

Productive Aging Social Work Skill Sets

- Client empowerment strategies
- Strengths-based counseling
- Knowledge of traditional and nontraditional community resources
- Proactive (early) outreach and intervention activities
- Interdisciplinary team building and assessment
- Creative problem solving
- Engagement in micro, mezzo, and macro client issues
- Expansive perspectives on the life course

education extends to elders themselves because some may doubt their potential for growth and personal discovery or they question their inclination to be engaged in the lifeblood of their neighborhoods and communities.

What Is a Productive, Vital Old Age? Defining Terms

As implied earlier, "productive aging" is commonly defined as the capacity of an older individual to continue to work in a paid capacity (a perspective underscored, in part, by Robert Butler in the preface). This definition highlights the important contributions that older adults make to the economic well-being of the nation. Indeed, many older adults continue to work in paid part-time or full-time employment well into their advanced years. Yet, there may be normative limitations in a definition tied to a finite set of young-adult and midlife behaviors, such as employment, because a nonworking elder may be perceived as someone who does not subscribe to a productive or vital lifestyle.

Alternatively, a broad array of additional behaviors that reflect vital, active, and productive aging are recognizable. From a more personal perspective, productive aging can refer to behaviors that take the form of noncompensated community and family support, paid employment, and explicitly inner-directed behaviors that are personally meaningful and satisfying to the older person but may or may not directly benefit others. Such a perspective reflects the three dimensions of the productive or vital aging construct: (1) an internal, affective view that emphasizes personal or growth philosophies positively affecting one's own well-being and quality of life; (2) an internal, utilitarian perspective that focuses on more functional areas of growth and well-being; and (3) an external, utilitarian view that emphasizes concrete societal contributions made to individuals, families, groups, organizations, or communities (see Table 1-6). It is clear that activities designed to serve others offer personal rewards as well.

From a theoretical perspective, these three levels of potential vital behavior draw on a broadened definition of the basic tenets of activity theory (Havighurst, 1963, 1968). Although activity theory recognizes that active engagement presumably enhances self-esteem, life satisfaction, self-concept, and adjustment (Bengtson, 1969), such behavior (and its accompanying rewards) can be realized through engagement in a wide range of activities (both concrete and reflective) that are presumably shaped by many factors, including personality, socioeconomic status, health, and lifestyle. Unlike with

Table 1-6

The Multiple Dimensions of Productive Aging

Dimension	I. Inner (Affective)	II. Inner (Utilitarian)	III. Outer (Utilitarian)
Focus and activity	● Wellness promotion ● Gero-therapy (proactive) ● Life review ● Self-help ● Self-improvement ● Social interaction	● Retirement planning ● Travel ● Recreation ● Physical exercise and enhancement ● Education	● Job training ● Employment ● Volunteer service ● Family support
Primary impact	● Self	● Self	● Others and self
Specific outcomes	● Increased personal enhancement and growth ● Self-discovery ● Self-actualization ● Improved mental health ● Reduced isolation	● Increased financial security ● Heightened intellectual stimulation ● Increased fitness and health ● Increased life security ● Increased knowledge and improved skills	● Increased financial well-being ● Continued socialization ● Maintained identity and purpose ● Continued structure ● Enhanced community well-being ● Heightened philanthropic expression
General outcomes (all dimensions)	● Enhanced self-esteem ● Heightened morale ● Higher quality of life ● Increased life satisfaction ● Heightened emotional and physical well-being		

activity theory, the activities referred to here need not be carried out to preserve prior statuses or to subscribe to roles performed earlier in life (Hooyman & Kiyak, 2002). Nor do they need to be directly tied to engagement in compensated or charitable efforts in the community. This definition of productive aging assumes that productive older persons engage in activities that can positively affect themselves or the lives and circumstances of others.

The productive aging lifestyle can be illustrated by a number of facts such as the following:

- Tomorrow's elders will live and work longer and insist on doing interesting work. Many older adults remain in the labor force after leaving their primary jobs. In the United States, 62 percent of women over 65 continue to work part time, as do 30 percent of men (U.S. Administration on Aging, 1999). Twenty-three percent of older workers are self-employed; this is more than three times the rate of younger workers (National Academy on an Aging Society, 2000).
- The percentage of older adults with at least a bachelor's degree increased from 4 percent in 1950 to almost 15 percent in 1998 (Federal Interagency Forum on Aging Related Statistics, 2000). Older adults are increasingly seeking intellectual pursuits such as Elderhostel and academic coursework (Hooyman & Kiyak, 2002).
- The rate of disability among older adults is on the decline (Manton & Gu, 2001).

- The majority of elders consider their health to be good to excellent (National Center for Health Statistics, 1999).
- More than one-third of older adults do volunteer work (Hooyman & Kiyak, 2002), and they tend to invest more hours in their volunteer work than do younger volunteers (Van Willigen, 2000). Older volunteers contribute 36 billion hours of voluntary service to organizations, valued at about $15.3 billion to society (Fischer & Schaffer, 1993).
- More than four out of five older adults reported getting together with friends and neighbors in the preceding two weeks. About one-third of adults in their seventies had attended a movie, sports event, club, or other group in the past two weeks, and nearly one-seventh of persons ages 85 and older had done so (Federal Interagency Forum on Aging Related Statistics, 2000).

These facts, in many respects, contradict conventional wisdom and the underlying premises of much of current geriatric practice in general and social work practice in particular. They emphasize engagement by older adults in a variety of sectors of daily life. These facts show older adults as having direction, structure, and purpose in life; as engaging in activities; and as accomplishing tasks that have both personal and societal benefits. It is not surprising that many older adults served by health and human services professionals are incapacitated to varying degrees and unable to perform many activities of daily living associated with persons who are employed or engaged in voluntary activities. These individuals may still be living productive lives despite their infirmities. Too often in practice, the practitioner downplays or overlooks a vital aging perspective because he or she is focused on assisting others. This may explain why the literature on geriatric social work practice has rarely focused on productive aging.

Conclusion

Americans are not only living longer but are doing so more vigorously than ever before. Most older Americans take care of themselves without the assistance of family, friends, or health care professionals. And the prospects for the future are bright in terms of increasing life expectancy and years lived in the absence of severe disability and impairment. Disability is on the decline because older adults are more educated, take better care of themselves, and take advantage of new medical knowledge and technology (Recer, 2001). Although such elders have the capacity to live exceedingly productive lives, there is no assurance that they will do so. Sound health cannot be equated with a positive aging experience.

Conversely, even in the presence of persistent infirmities and challenges, older adults have the ability to live their lives in meaningful, satisfying, and productive ways. Feeling a sense of vitality, productivity, and satisfaction with one's aging need not and should not be determined by one's physical or functional capacity. Social and emotional losses, decline in energy levels, and many other acute and chronic challenges need not significantly diminish quality of life.

Some portion of the professional social work community is already committed to turning away from traditional problem-based and deficit-oriented practice dimensions to take a productive aging stance. Few, however, have succeeded in thoroughly divesting themselves of all the negative baggage of needs-based gerontological practice. Sadly, ageism and age-related stereotyping remain significant barriers for professional practice, especially for those who have not benefited from quality training in work with older adults.

One of the last challenges confronting social workers is for them to ensure that productive lifestyles in old age are encouraged and realized. To accomplish this, social workers must appreciate the meaning of productive aging, the various ways in which it manifests itself, and the range of interventive strategies available to the profession to promote its practice. That is the charge of this volume.

References

Alexander, L. B., & Kaye, L. W. (1997). *Part-time employment for the low-income elderly: Experiences from the field*. New York: Garland.

Beilenson, J., Sprouse, B. M., & Villarreal, R. (2002). *Aging successfully: Findings from research sponsored by the AARP Foundation*. Washington, DC: AARP Foundation.

Bengtson, V. L. (1969). Cultural and occupational differences in level of present role activity in retirement. In R. J. Haivghurst, J.M.A. Munnicks, B. C. Neugarten, and H. Thomas (Eds.), *Adjustments to retirement: A cross-national study*. Assen, The Netherlands: Van Gorkum

Dychtwald, K. (1999). *Age power: How the 21st century will be ruled by the new old.* New York: Penguin Putnam.

Erikson, E. H. (Ed.). (1978). *Adulthood.* New York: W. W. Norton.

Erikson, E. H. (1994). *Identity and the life cycle.* New York: W. W. Norton.

Erikson, E. H. & Erikson, J. M. (1998). *The life cycle completed.* New York: W. W. Norton.

Erikson, E. H., Erikson, J. M., & Kivnick, H. Q. (1994). *Vital involvement in old age.* New York: W. W. Norton.

Federal Interagency Forum on Aging Related Statistics. (2000). *Older Americans 2000: Key indicators of well-being.* Washington, DC: Government Printing Office.

Fischer, L. R., & Schaffer, K. B. (1993). *Older volunteers: A guide to research and practice.* Newbury Park, CA: Sage Publications.

Havighurst, R. J. (1963). Successful aging. In R. Williams, C. Tibbits, and W. Donahue (Eds.), *Process of aging* (Vol. 1). New York: Atherton Press.

Havighurst, R. J. (1968). *Personality and patterns of aging. Gerontologist, 38,* 20–23.

Hooyman, N. R., & Kiyak, H. A. (2002). *Social gerontology: A multidisciplinary perspective* (6th ed.). Boston: Allyn & Bacon.

Kaye, L. W. (2002). Productive aging and social work: Helping elders meet the challenges of a vital old age. *Social Work Today, 2*(13), 16–19.

Kaye, L. W., Butler, S. S., & Webster, N. M. (2003). Toward a productive aging paradigm for geriatric practice. *Ageing International, 28,* 200–213.

Klein, W. C., & Bloom, M. (1997). *Successful aging: Strategies for healthy living.* New York: Plenum Press.

Lipschitz, D. A. (2002). *Breaking the rules of aging.* Washington, DC: LifeLine Press.

Manton, K. G., & Gu, X. (2001). Changes in the prevalence of chronic disability in U.S. black and nonblack population above age 65 from 1982 to 1999 [Electronic version]. *Proceedings of the National Academy of Sciences of the United States, 98*(11), 6354–6359.

McKhann, G. M., & Albert, M. (2002). *Keep your brain young: The complete guide to physical and emotional health and longevity.* New York: John Wiley & Sons.

National Academy on an Aging Society. (2000). *Who are younger retirees and older workers?* [Data profile]. Washington, DC: Author.

National Center for Health Statistics. (1999). *Health, United States.* Hyattsville, MD: Author.

Perls, T. T., Silver, M. H., & Lauerman, J. F. (1999). *Living to 100: Lessons in living to your maximum potential at any age.* New York: Basic Books.

Poon, L. W., Gueldner, S. H., & Sprouse, B. M. (Eds.). (2003). *Successful aging and adaptation with chronic diseases.* New York: Springer.

Recer, P. (2001, May 8). Americans over 65 enjoying more vigorous old age, latest research indicates. Associated Press wire service.

Rosenblatt, R. (2000). *Rules for aging: Resist normal impulses, live longer, attain perfection.* New York: Harcourt.

Rowe, J. W., & Kahn, R. L. (1999). *Successful aging: The MacArthur Foundation Study.* New York: Dell.

Strawbridge, W. J., & Wallhagen, M. I. (2003). What can be learned about successful aging from those experiencing it. In L. W. Poon, S. H. Gueldner, & B. M.

Sprouse (Eds.), *Successful aging and adaptation from chronic diseases*. New York: Springer.

U.S. Administration on Aging. (1999). *Profile of older Americans: 1999*. Washington, DC: Author.

Vaillant, G. E. (1995). *Adaptation to life*. Boston: Harvard University Press.

Vaillant, G. E. (2003). *Aging well: Surprising guideposts to a happier life from the landmark Harvard study of adult development*. New York: Little, Brown.

Van Willigen, M. (2000). Differential benefits of volunteering across the life course. *Journal of Gerontology, 55B*(5), S308–S318.

2

The Demography of Productive Aging

Charles F. Longino, Jr., and Don E. Bradley

Introduction

It is not the goal of this chapter to cram as many numbers as possible into the heads of social work students, practitioners, and allied professionals concerning the older population, although any demographer worth his or her salt would strain at the temptation. The goal, rather, is to provide an understanding of the demographic dynamics and processes underlying the growth and change of the older population. Students, thus armed, may more easily interpret the changes that are on the horizon, especially if they plan to have clients who are aging. Put another way, this chapter provides a context within which to understand the ever-changing nature of the older population.

An Aging Society

World Population Aging

Most Americans are aware that the number of persons old enough to draw social security retirement benefits is substantial and growing. Some are mildly apprehensive about this fact. Given an opportunity, they nearly always overestimate the proportion of the U.S. population that is 65 and older. In 2000, it was only 13 percent. What most Americans do not realize, however, is that the world population is aging and that our American experience is part of a much larger picture. The median age of U.S. citizens is 39 and rising, and it is rising around the world.

The Demographic Transition

One model for population change is called the *demographic transition theory*, which is not a theory, really, but an explanation of demographic processes that have become destabilized in the history of industrialized nations (Weeks, 1999). The transition has three phases.

During the first phase, population is stable. Birth rates and death rates are high. Death rates are highest among children. High birth rates are valued as necessary to replace those who die. Most human societies, from the beginning to the agricultural revolution, are thought to have remained in the first phase. This is all speculation, of course, birth and death rates were not recorded during this time.

During the second phase, death rates decline because of the "epidemiological transition" (Omran, 1977). Declining death rates in Europe occurred over a long period of time as a result of improved sanitation in cities and quarantining people with plague. More recently, in Third World countries, the decline in death rates is attributed to a combination of public health initiatives, including spraying swamps to kill disease-carrying mosquitoes and inoculating children against infectious diseases.

A few years after the epidemiological transition begins, society enters a fertility transition as well. Birth rates fall more slowly. The gap between the higher, but declining, birth rate and the more rapidly declining death rate produces population growth. The rate of growth is measured as the rate of "natural increase." The highest rates of natural increase are found today among the nations of the Middle East and sub-Saharan Africa (Weeks, 1999). Incidentally, when the reverse is true and there are fewer births than deaths, then negative natural increase occurs wherein the population declines unless migrants fill the population deficit. Today, Russia, Spain, and Italy are experiencing negative natural increase (Chesnais, 1996; Shkolnikov, Mesle, & Vallin, 1996).

The third phase of the demographic transition is entered when the birth and death rates once again balance and the population stabilizes at a much larger size. Of course, no national population ever remains perfectly stable over time. During this phase, however, growth and decline may be determined by international migration during the third phase of the demographic transition than by natural increase alone.

Furthermore, in the final phase of the demographic transition, low mortality rates mean that many more people live out their life spans; that is, their full human longevity potential and lower fertility rates mean that fewer people are being born. Under these circumstances, the median age of the population rises. Population aging, therefore, is a natural result of this demographic transition. It is not something to be feared; it occurs in all Western nations, and many others that are moving toward or through the third phase of the transition. The demographic transition has two results: population growth and population aging. Both outcomes are inevitable.

The United States does not have the oldest population in the world. In 2000, 13 percent of the U.S. population were 65 or over. The United States does not even appear in the top 10 countries with the oldest populations. According to Weeks (1999, p. 232), in 2000, nearly one-fifth of Italians were 65 and older (18.2 percent); about 17 percent of the populations of Sweden, Greece, and Belgium were 65 and over; and about 16 percent of the populations of Japan, Spain, Bulgaria, Germany, France, and the United Kingdom were 65 and older. The aging of their populations has not had an especially negative effect in these countries. Seventeen percent of Florida's population is age 65 or older, which is about the same as Sweden. America's population will approach Sweden's in relative age in 2020; however, when our baby boom cohort gets one generation older, assuming that birth and immigration rates do not change in the meanwhile.

Fluctuations in Population Growth

Historically, the United States did fit the pattern of the demographic transition (leaving aside the large infusions of population through immigration). Estimates of the birth rate in the United States in 1800 were higher than in less developed Third World countries today. By the end of the Civil War, the birth rate had declined and was comparable to the lower birth rate levels among European countries at the time (Coale & Zelnick, 1963). This decline continued until the Great Depression in the 1930s and bottomed out during World War II. Then something happened that the demographic transition theory did not predict. The birth rate rose beginning in 1946, just as the war was coming to an end, and its low level was not approached again until 1964, nearly 20 years later. Since then it has continued to shift at a very low level, similar to many European countries today (Morgan, 1996). This high bounce of the birth rate, called the *baby boom* generation, accounted for roughly one-fifth of the U.S. population in 2000.

The earliest baby boomers will not be eligible to receive full social security retirement income until 2012. Those born in the fertility rate trough during the depression and the war, just before the baby boom, however, began retiring at the turn of the century and will continue to do so until the first baby boomers join them. This means that the older population will not grow as fast as expected between 2000 and 2010, but it will continue to age. In 2010, the proportion of the 65 and older population who will be very old (85 and older) is expected to reach 15 percent for the first time, a peak that will not be reached again until 2040, when the baby boom will begin to age out of the population. As a result, the older population will *seem* older than usual during the first decade of the 21st century, and that perception will be correct. As a result, policy concerns may focus somewhat more on the plight of the very old, the frail, and vulnerable.

By 2012, however, the baby boom will begin expanding the older population whose average age, as a result, will get younger. In demographic terms, if turning 65 is like being born into the older population, the birth rates will exceed the death rates and the older population will have a "youth movement." Policy concerns will shift rapidly to those of the young-old. *Productive aging* will be on everyone's lips. This rejuvenation of the older population will last for nearly 20 years. Then, the entire older population will age rapidly between 2030 and 2050, after which the baby boom bulge will rapidly shrink until it is no longer apparent, even among the oldest old. This picture should cause students to wonder how these population age fluctuations will affect their career interests. A career that spans the first three decades of the 21st century will find the greatest range of new programs and private sector initiatives available in the history of applied gerontology. The policy focus will shift from the oldest to the youngest end of the old-age spectrum during this time, and the deaths of the last baby boomers will occur after most students reading these pages have retired. The meaning of old age may be questioned because baby boomers may behave as though they are entering a second middle age when they reach 65.

Birth Cohorts and Their Relative Status

The term demographers use to describe people born during a certain time period is a *birth cohort*. In this sense, the baby boom is a large (18 year-long) birth cohort (Morgan, 1996). Universities use an idea equivalent to "death cohorts" when they group students by the year of their graduation—that is, by their graduating class. After graduation they are expected to be alumni "angels" and nourish their alma mater with gifts from on high.

Modernization Theory

Population characteristics, in the aggregate, differ between birth cohorts because society changes over time, and these differences affect the status of persons in older (relative to younger) birth cohorts. Cowgill (1979) introduced a complex argument called *modernization theory* to explain these status differences. Societies struggling through the second phase of the demographic transition have populations swollen as a result of high levels of natural increase. It is not surprising that the policy agendas of these societies, with so many children, come to emphasize health, education, and industrial development. Consequently, young people, who are getting their education and entering the workforce, experience higher levels of good health, education, and exposure to economic technology than do their parents. Illit-

eracy levels decline during the second phase of the demographic transition, and large numbers of people move from rural villages to large cities to take advantage of these new opportunities. As a result of these opportunities for the young, however, the older birth cohorts have poorer health, higher levels of illiteracy, more rural life experience, and lower-paying jobs and, as a result, lower status.

Echoes of Modernization Theory Today

The United States is not a developing nation in the economic sense, but its society continues to change, opening more technological opportunities for the young, which result in lower relative status for older birth cohorts. The implications of modernization theory for older Americans are profound. Within the older population, the oldest birth cohort has lower levels of education, especially health education, work skills, and income and asset accumulation than the younger birth cohort. Furthermore, each birth cohort that crosses some magic old-age line will have higher levels of personal resources than the previous one. The use of the Internet is a case in point. In 2000, there were strong cohort differences in its use, which benefited the young over the old in electronic information use and communication. As baby boomers retire, however, it is good to think of them not just in terms of their numbers, but also in terms of their life experiences. They will bring many more advantages to retirement than their parents, although their skills and accomplishments may still suffer in comparison to their children. The hidden message of modernization theory is a warning not to think of an age category as unchanging, regardless of the magic age lines that delimit it. New cohorts bring new levels of characteristics, resources, and life experiences.

For example, most aging baby boom women will also have personal resources their mothers never had (Longino, 1999). Because they delayed marriage and experienced high divorce rates, many baby boom women have lived independently for years. They are accustomed to keeping their homes, managing their money, and tending to emergencies independently. Virtually all baby boom women have worked outside the home for at least part of their lives, and many will receive a pension income from work. Therefore, the trend toward living alone in old age is expected to increase in the future, assuming that gender differences in mortality rates hold constant. The strategies already in place that enable single persons to seek out friends and build friendships that are robust enough to serve as an important reservoir of social support are expected to be part of this pattern as well.

Times in Our Later Lives

An age category is fixed in time. It does not change. Its boundaries are chronological. Everyone of a certain age is in the age category. In demography, such categories as "persons age 65 and over" or "85 and over" are commonly used. People are sometimes categorized by the decade of their age—sixties, seventies, eighties, and so on—because after midlife, milestone birthday parties tend to fall on decade age markers. Although it is the stock and trade of demography,

the age category is a frustratingly oversimplified way understanding aging.

The concept of birth cohort goes beyond the static idea of age category because a birth cohort is an age category that travels through time. Cohort differences, alone, however, tend to overlook the fact individuals mature as they age; their life experiences alter their perspectives. Two people in different age categories can be in different birth cohorts, but they will also have experienced living for different lengths of time. In this sense, no two persons age exactly alike because no two "life worlds" are exactly alike.

The Life Course Perspective

A demographic context for understanding age, age differences, and the process of aging should be tempered by insights derived from the *life course perspective* as it has developed in social gerontology. Old age maintained a conceptual unity in gerontology until life course theory emerged, which emphasized that old age was part of a lifelong developmental process (Elder, 2001), not an age category. In 1974 Neugarten wrote an influential essay that distinguished between the youthful years of retirement and the older years. She referred to persons in these stages of later adult development as the "young-old" and the "old-old." The young-old, according to Neugarten, tend to have good health, and they are about as active as they want to be. The old-old, however, are more likely to be widowed and to be living dependently. The concept of old age, with its attending miseries, consequently, was only pushed later into life by this reconceptualization, which made the first decade after social security retirement benefits began seem like the second middle age (Manheimer, 1995).

The Third and Fourth Ages

A similar way of thinking has been common in Europe and is now referred to as the Third and Fourth Ages (Laslett, 1991). The *First Age* is one of schooling, and the *Second Age* is one of work. The *Third Age*, in gerontological writing, is often associated with leisure activities, and the *Fourth Age* is associated with the declines and losses of aging. Now and in the future, however, the Third Age will be seen as including a greater admixture of productive activities. The Third Age is a time of life, not chronologically but functionally. It is a period after work when one can have a great deal more control over the use of one's time. Early retirees enter the Third Age younger than later retirees. The Third Age may extend until shortly before a person's death at whatever age. These are life course distinctions, but not necessarily chronologically marked ones.

Societal changes in the United States will make the Third Age an increasingly interesting time of life and one in which opportunities for temporary or part-time work, volunteering, home maintenance, educational and spiritual growth, and political action will abound. There are some demographic reasons for this optimism.

Birth Cohorts and Values

Values are an important part of human culture. Not all members of any birth cohort will share the same values, of course, but values tend to shift with cultural and social experience.

A word of caution is in order. The tendency to reify the baby boom generation, to treat it as an undifferentiated entity, is philosophically wrong-headed and ignores that generation's rich diversity. However, the shared experience of the early baby boomers of the urban middle-class is undeniable, and these values tended to spread to many other members of the cohort.

The first half of the large 18-year birth cohort pressed against all institutional structures as it aged, like the surge of a tidal wave. On all levels, schools, the job and housing markets, and the market economy felt the pressure. Members of this birth cohort challenged tradition at every turn. Russell (1993) argued that members of this cohort give greater value to independence, the entrepreneurial spirit, and personal empowerment than their parents. Self-help books flooded the market during the 1970s and reinforced these values. Also, among early baby boomers, there is a greater distrust of authority, less company and brand loyalty, greater value for leisure over work, informality over formality, and a more relativistic understanding of ethics. The Watergate hearings, as a historical marker, separate the early and later baby boomers. That political extravaganza had a chilling effect on youthful idealism, which often transmuted into cynicism and apathy.

The second, or trailing, half of the baby boom was characterized as inward, private, self-interested; this group, called the "me" generation, greatly valued their personal leisure. One highly visible segment of this birth cohort were the *yuppies*. It may be argued that technological and organizational change, rather than population change alone, fostered these outcomes. The rise of a customized market economy that catered to rapidly changing niche markets and values convenience, quality, and flexibility makes an unbelievable range of goods and services available around the clock, through the mail, and over the Internet (Longino, 1994). Individualism is an old American value. But the baby boomers laid claim to it in a special way because of social and structural changes occurring around them.

Longino and Polivka (2001) argued that since the 1950s, a new historical era has been entered in which individuals are becoming less embedded in tradition and institutions. Changing family, political, and economic structures produce and affect, changing cultural values. Furthermore, we now live in information-based economies and communication network societies that highly value discursive, independent thought and the creative force of language and speech. In this kind of social milieu, individuals seek greater agency in their own lives, thereby increasing the value of autonomy. And there is a growing recognition of the contingency of everything once founded in traditions and institutions. Furthermore, especially during the last decade of the 20th century, there were accelerating changes in cultural perspectives and values that produced a kind of multiculturalism and the creation of new forms of culture that drew on multiple sources.

It is not clear how these values will play out in the Third Age of members of these birth cohorts, except that there will be a much more proactive stance in the use of time and resources in old age, tailored to the interests, values, and concerns of the individual. Interest groups of all kinds can find participants over the Internet. It seems safe to speculate that there will be a great diversification of activities during the Third Age of baby boomers. A kaleidoscopic, ever-changing, boutique mall of interesting activities may arise. Individualism and strong participatory tendencies would suggest more organizational efforts from the bottom up, rather than from the top down with more microentrepreneurs facilitating and marketing the activities. Institutional solutions, such as nursing home placement, may be eschewed in favor of a greater range of home care options.

Changing Population Characteristics, Resources, and Experience

New birth cohorts continuously redecorate the Third Age. The process is inevitable because each new birth cohort differs somewhat from preceding cohorts. Their values are distributed somewhat differently, but so, also, are the characteristics, resources, and experiences of the cohort members (Treas & Longino, 1997).

Health

The epidemiological transition is not over yet in America. Life expectancy continues to rise, contributing to the growth and aging of the older population. At birth, individuals can expect to live into their seventies, and if they reach 65, expectations shift upward, and they can expect, on average, 17 more years of life into their eighties. Being a woman—and a white woman, in particular—can boost those expectations by several more years. As a consequence, people age 65 and older currently include more women (100 women for every 67 men). Men, however, are expected eventually to begin closing the longevity gap.

Does a longer life expectancy mean healthier years of life? Or does it mean more years of coping with increasingly serious disabilities? The answer to these questions have important implications for the relative length of the Third and Fourth Ages. Most readers would hope for a long Third Age, when freedom and purpose can be embodied well, and a brief Fourth Age, when they cannot (Longino & Powell, 2002).

Since the late 1980s, the health status of older people appears to have improved (Crimmins & Ingegneri, 1992; Manton, Corder, & Stallard, 1993). The evidence that illness and disability are being delayed among the 65 and older group is relevant for compressing the morbidity argument espoused by Fries (1980) a generation ago. According to Fries, the onset of chronic illness would be delayed longer and longer. Fries believed that life expectancy would increase by only a small amount in the future because longevity is already pushing against the ceiling. If so, the years of life spent with a chronic health condition would be squeezed between the increasing age of the onset of illness and the less flexible age of death. Illness and disability would be compressed into a briefer period before death. Fries would vote for a long Third Age and a very brief Fourth Age, and he thinks that this goal is approached more closely with each succeeding birth cohort. This is an optimistic view, and evidence buttressing

Fries' position is gradually accumulating (Fries, Koop, Sokolov, Beadle, & Wright, 1998).

Education

The educational gap between younger and older people is narrowing over time, as modernization theory would predict for an economically developed nation. In the mid-1990s, two-thirds of Americans in the Third Age (at least those who are 65 to 74) had graduated from high school, compared with only half of those over 75. The World War II veterans, whose college enrollments were strongly boosted by the GI Bill, greatly expanded higher education in the United States. Enrollments remained high after the veterans finished college. This historical event is expected to push education levels higher in anticipated census reports.

Rising educational levels are a very desirable observation because education is a potent force that predicts positive outcomes on a number of other dimensions (Treas, 1995). Even taking into account their higher incomes, people with more education have fewer disabilities, avoid the early onset of chronic disease, and enjoy lower death rates. It is likely that better-educated Third Age Americans have greater access to information about how to promote health and prevent illness, how to recognize illness, and how to get treatment. Rising educational levels, therefore, influence falling chronic illness and death rates. For individuals, schooling shapes lifestyle preferences, too. Every year, tens of thousands of well-educated retirees attend college courses available to them across the country and take advantage of summer

Elderhostel courses taught around the world (Peterson, 2001). Ultimately, persons with more education have more human capital to put into a wide range of activities from work to volunteering; in short, they are potentially more productive citizens.

Economic Status

The economic position of the most recent cohort of Third Age Americans reflects the historical advantages of this birth cohort. Compared with those whose Second Age had spanned the Great Depression, recent retirees have led charmed lives. Their Second Age followed World War II, when employment expanded and wage growth was strong. Social security and private pensions also expanded, and Medicare was introduced. Home ownership spread, and periods of inflation swelled their home equity.

There are four sources of income in retirement: (1) social security, (2) pensions, (3) rent and investments, and (4) work. When two-career couples retire, there could be as many as eight sources of income. This ignores inherited wealth, which can be an unexpected bonus for some retirees. Whereas retirement income, on average, approaches two-thirds of income levels before retirement, relatively few 65 and older persons drop below the poverty level. The proportion of older households with incomes below poverty is about 12 percent, which is the same for all households. The same proportion (12 percent) of the 65 and older population continues to be gainfully employed. It should be remembered that older Americans cannot be characterized as affluent *or* impoverished; they

are both (Treas & Longino, 1997). An elderly poverty population exists but so, too, (subject to definition) does a larger and growing affluent population. There is even greater income inequality among people above age 65 than below that magical age marker. If all government support were removed from retirement income, however, including in-kind income (such as Medicare), half of the older households would dip below the poverty line.

Racial and Ethnic Diversity

The older population is becoming more racially and ethnically diverse. The non-Hispanic white population dropped from 80 percent to 74 percent between 1980 and 1995 and dropped still further by 2000. This decline is accounted for primarily by the rapid rise in the Hispanic population. It should be remembered that European immigrants to the United States in the early decades of the 21st century are dying out of the older population. Birth cohorts of the future will increase ethnic diversity among older Americans. Immigration has contributed greatly to ethnic diversity in the 1990s. One-tenth of the 65 and older population is foreign born. Because immigrants are usually young adults and children, their inclusion in the population tends to offset, somewhat, the population-aging effect of the epidemiological transition.

Family Roles and Living Arrangements

Births and marriages add to the kinship network, while deaths and divorces subtract from it. As the parents of the baby boomers move through their retirement years, the number of children available to help them will be large. The baby boomers had fewer children, however, and so these family ties will diminish as baby boomers enter retirement. Because women tend to outlive men and are nearly always younger than their husbands, they are more likely to live alone in old age, especially during their Fourth Age. Consequently, women outnumber men in assisted-living facilities by more than five to one. Living alone is the preferred lifestyle for older widows in the United States largely because rising economic status has made this option possible (Wolf, 1995).

Fear of the Consequence of Population Aging

The Demographic Imperative

A prevalent image of our aging society is told as a scary story. It is sometimes referred to as the "demographic imperative" in the United States and as "apocalyptic demography" in the United Kingdom (Longino, 1999). It is a story that appeals to our fears for the future and is so widely shared that it is categorized as a modern cultural myth. Indeed, in most textbooks, the treatment of population aging carries important elements of this gothic tale. The reader will recognize it immediately. It begins with the statement that America's older population is growing. It was 3.1 million strong in 1900 and doubled every 30 years throughout the century. It is expected to number 62 million in 2025. More frightening, however, it is not only growing, but it is also aging. The fastest-growing part of the 65 and older population is the oldest part. In 2000, 4.3 percent of the

older population were age 85 and older. By 2050, it will be 18.9 percent. This is highly relevant because the proportion needing assistance increases with age. Fewer than one in 10 (9.2%) people age 65 to 69 has a disability that results in the need for regular personal assistance. This proportion rises to 49.5 percent for people 85 and older. If the older population is growing and aging rapidly, then its need for assistance is also increasing rapidly. Furthermore, there were five people of working age (18 to 64) for every person over 64 in 1990, but by 2025, there will be only three working-aged people for every older person. The health care system is already too expensive, the story goes, and the older population will bankrupt Medicare and, eventually, the entire U.S. government. The final scene of the horror story is of Mother Teresa's Missionaries of Charity moving among and ministering to the hoards of old and dying citizens of the United States, much as they do in Calcutta, India.

The Counternarrative

There is a counternarrative, however, that is a good deal more hopeful. The biggest problem with the demographic imperative is that it ignores generational effects. Even if the large baby boom generation was not middle-aged, generational change would still transform the older population, the caregiving population, and society.

It is likely that several factors will work to reduce disability among elderly people, including improved health, new forms of service delivery, and improved technology. Will baby boomers, who popularized healthy lifestyles, be healthier in their old age? Some think so. Smoking has declined dramatically; the morbidity and mortality effects of this decline will show up in the future. Perhaps more older baby boomers will exercise on a regular basis than earlier generations. If so, this alone will have a dampening effect on heart disease rates. Heart disease heads the list of killer diseases nationally. These factors may mute the negative health care effect of population aging to some extent. The explosion of new pharmaceuticals that address chronic illnesses is also applicable.

In fact, the demographic imperative does not address technological developments in the future. Yet the use of assistive devices and housing modifications is rising sharply, while the long-term use of paid personal assistance is declining in the older population. Greater residential independence, combined with the development and use of personal-assistance technologies, seem to be part of a modern older person's long-term adaptive process. As the high-risk population grows, and the demographic imperative shows us that it will, a marketplace for assistive technology will grow with it.

The marketplace has targeted the baby boomers for all of their adult lives. There is no reason to believe that this will end after they retire. Therefore, businesses and industry are expected to help diffuse some of the gloom and doom attributed to the demographic imperative. Private companies that produce and distribute goods and services to enhance independence into the later years will find growing markets, and the competition they generate will make these products available at a decreasing cost over time.

The information revolution may have largely bypassed the United Staes's current citizens in their seventh and eighth decades of life; this will not be the case in the 21st century. An increasing proportion of retirees will be computer literate and accustomed to seeking out useful information electronically. It is the dawning of the age of information.

A Population Profile of Productive Persons in Their Third Age

To this point, the demography of productive aging has been approached askance, not directly, in this chapter. The reason is simple. Except for labor force participation, there is no way to define productive aging within the limitations of census data.

Digression: Our Method

Data. Therefore, we turned to another national data set to profile the characteristics of productive people in their third age: *The National Survey of Families and Households: Wave I, 1987–1988, and Wave II, 1992–1994* (Bumpass & Sweet, 1997). The data are representative of the noninstitutionalized population in the contiguous United States over 18 years of age. A national, stratified, multistage area probability sample was used. Members of ethnic minority groups and people in some smaller family types were oversampled and then weighted to their national proportions; 13,008 primary respondents were interviewed. Five years after the initial interviews, 10,008 surviving respondents were reinterviewed face to face. Data collected in the second wave serve as our primary source of information. The data extract that we created for analysis is limited to primary respondents ages 65 through 75 ($N = 1,107$).

Measures. A central advantage of the data drawn from the National Survey of Families and Households is the opportunity to measure productivity in several different ways. First, we measured hours of paid work in a typical week, the sum of hours worked on a "main job" and a "second job," if there were one.

Second, respondents were asked to estimate the hours they spent in a typical week performing the following tasks: "outdoor and other household maintenance tasks" and "automobile maintenance and repair." The sum of these activities is used here to estimate the time given by respondents to household and automobile maintenance activities.

Third, a measure of the amount of time devoted to housework and errands is constructed on the basis of the number of hours respondents report spending on the following tasks in a typical week: "preparing meals," "washing dishes and cleaning up after meals," "cleaning the house," "washing, ironing, mending," "paying the bills and keeping financial records," "shopping for groceries and other household goods," and "driving other household members to work, school or other activities." These seven activities of domestic service are collectively referred to as "housework."

The practice of using the sum of these particular items to measure hours of productive activities has been used in a number of recent studies (Coltrane & Ishii-Kuntz, 1992; Gupta, 1999;

Sanchez & Thompson, 1997). To guard against overreporting, we truncated the distribution of both measures of hours devoted to housework and household and automobile maintenance at three standard deviations above their respective weighted mean values (see Coltrane & Ishii-Kuntz, 1992). We do not discuss issues of statistical significance because we could not account for the peculiarities of the sampling design in estimating variance.

Results

Hours Worked by Types of Productive Activity. Our findings suggest that most people ages 65 through 75 are not employed. Eighty-four percent of the distribution consists of people not working for pay at all in a typical week. Only the upper one-tenth of the distribution worked more than 18 hours a week. So, on employment alone, even these Third Age people (ages 65 to 75) are not very productive. This is just the beginning of the story, however.

A higher proportion of these same people were engaged in home and automobile maintenance and outdoor activities such as garden and lawn care. Only 32 percent (the lower third of the percentile distribution) were not involved at all, and the upper third said they logged at least five hours a week in such activities. The top 10 percent reported at least 16 hours, nearly the same minimal number of hours as the top 10 percent in the employed labor distribution.

Of the three measures of productivity, however, housework was the most pervasive form of productive activity, with very few (4 percent) giving it no time at all. The first third of the distribution spent 12 hours a week or less doing housework and the upper third was engaged for more than 28 hours. People in the upper tenth of the distribution were working full time (54 hours or more per week) in these activities. The lion's share of productivity is domestic.

Selectivity Factors by Type of Productive Activity. Are the three areas of productivity equally attractive to all people in that young-old age range? Or are different kinds of people selectively filtered into one type of activity as opposed to another? One way of answering that question is to compare the characteristics of only the people who are highly and hardly productive in each type of activity. We compared

those in the upper and lower third of the percentile distribution for two types of activity—household maintenance and housework. More than one-third of the survey respondents were not employed, however. Therefore, we were forced to compare the nonemployed with the most active 10 percent who worked 18 or more hours per week.

How would those who spend more time working for pay compared with those who are not employed in this age range be categorized? They are somewhat more likely to be men, better educated, younger, more likely to say they are in good or excellent health, and upper income (Table 2-1). They are slightly more likely to be married and to be white. In summary, employment activity tends to select, or filter in, people

Table 2-1

Activities of Productive People Ages 65 to 75

Characteristic	Work for Employer Hours Worked		Household and Auto Maintenance Hours Worked		Housework Hours Worked	
	Upper 10%	Lower 85%	Upper Third	Lower Third	Upper Third	Lower Third
Male	59.1	42.7	65.9	23.0	17.7	73.0
High school graduate	79.8	68.3	72.6	66.7	71.1	67.7
Married	66.2	62.8	74.2	52.8	63.3	70.7
Less than age 70	56.5	47.0	47.3	47.6	49.8	47.3
White	89.7	84.4	85.1	83.5	84.6	85.6
Black	7.2	8.7	7.3	1.1	8.7	7.4
Hispanic	2.9	5.6	7.0	3.9	5.2	6.6
Good or excellent health	78.5	63.1	72.3	58.7	69.2	61.4
High income (upper quartile)	42.5	20.9	26.3	17.1	21.9	29.3
Unweighted N	108	930	357	397	394	349

NOTE: Figures presented in the table represent weighted percentages.
SOURCE: Bumpass, L. L., & Sweet, J. A. (1997). *The National Survey of Families and Households: Wave 1, 1987–1988 and Wave 2, 1992–1994.* Ann Arbor, MI: Inter-University Consortium for Political and Social Research.

with the following characteristics: men, better education, relative youth, good health, and higher incomes. Note, however, that these are only proportional, not absolute, differences.

Would the profile be the same for those spending the most time maintaining their house, lawn, and automobile? This type of productive activity tends to have a slightly different set of filters (Table 2-1). Age, for example, does not differentiate. Race does not matter either. However, repair and maintenance activities are much more attractive to men than to women, to the married than to the nonmarried, and to those who say their health is good or excellent. The gender and marital status differences are greater here than in the earlier comparison of the actively employed and nonemployed. To this point in our comparisons, productivity has a strong male bias.

Housework was ignored as a form of productive activity when this topic was first studied because such work was not equated with economic productivity. As it turns out, however, housework is the major form of productive activity for people in the Third Age, and it is the great gender equalizer (Herzog & Morgan, 1992). Women are more actively engaged in housework (Table 2-1). Fewer than 18 percent of the highly productive in this category are men. However, nearly three-quarters of the least productive third of the percentile distribution are men. Once again, relative age and race make very little difference. Only a slight edge is given to the better-educated, healthier, nonmarried, and people with greater income. Presumably the necessity of housework cannot be ignored by widows or by persons with moderate health problems.

Gender is the major filter—the major selectivity factor—of the three activity categories, followed in order by health, marital status, education, and income, with race and age making little difference except in employment. There are good reasons for the profile differences that will be developed in later chapters.

Combining the Three Types of Productive Activity. The comparisons found in Table 2-1 ignore the fact that a person may spend some time each week doing housework, making minor home repairs, and engaging in paid work. Types of productivity are not mutually exclusive. For this reason, it is important to combine the types of productivity to get an overall picture of how productive Third Age Americans are. In addition, this is a conservative estimate of the number of hours spent in productive activity because there are other areas of endeavor, such as volunteer work, that are not covered in the survey and are missing from our analysis.

Fewer than 2 percent of Americans between the ages of 65 and 75 say they are not engaged in any of these productive activities. The first 20 percent of the distribution is composed of people who report 13 or fewer hours of these activities in a typical week. These individuals are defined as having a low level of productive activity. By contrast, people in the top quintile reported no fewer than 51 hours a week of activities. People in this quintile are defined as being highly engaged in productive activity. To understand the population characteristics of productive aging, comparing people in the highest and lowest quintiles seems appropriate.

Productivity does tend to select the more youthful, even within a 10-year span (Table 2-2). The differences would be much greater in a broader age range. Furthermore, women are, by a very wide margin, more productive than men. The inclusion of domestic productivity as well as, perhaps, their greater numbers give women the edge here (see Table 2-1). Sixty percent of the people in the bottom quintile of productivity are men. No racial or ethnic differences are apparent. Marital status, likewise, bears little relationship to productivity.

Two measures of health are found in Table 2-2. Health does make some difference. The highly productive are more likely to say their health is good or excellent, and 90 percent have no personal care difficulties, compared with somewhat lower levels of health among respondents in the least productive quintile. Most people in their late sixties and early seventies consider themselves to be in good health, and only a small proportion of them have any personal care difficulties, such as bathing, dressing, eating, and toileting. It is worthwhile to turn this comparison around, however, and to ask how much poor health limits productive activity. It may be surprising to discover that poor health does not exclude some people from working more than 51 hours a week in productive endeavors. Nearly a third of the highly productive consider their health to be fair, poor, or very poor, and a tenth have some level of personal care limitations.

The same general comments could be made of education. Productivity

Table 2-2

A Profile of Productive Aging

Variable	% Engaged in Productive Activity	
	Upper Quintile	Lower Quintile
Age:		
65–67	32.4	25.2
68–72	49.3	46.4
73–75	18.4	28.4
Sex:		
Male	28.8	60.8
Female	71.2	39.2
Racial/ethnic status:		
White	84.5	84.1
Black	7.8	8.8
Hispanic	5.2	6.6
Marital status:		
Married	63.9	63.6
Divorced or separated	5.9	7.6
Widowed	28.5	24.1
Never married	1.7	4.7
Health status:		
Good or excellent health	66.3	54.0
Able to care for personal needs	90.4	74.3
Education:		
Less than a high school diploma	28.9	36.3
High school diploma or GED	43.0	37.6
Some college or associate degree	13.0	11.6
College degree	10.3	8.9
Graduate or professional training	4.8	5.6
Income:	19.0	37.7
Middle income (middle quartiles)	47.8	43.3
High income (upper quartile)	33.2	19.0

does tend to select people with higher levels of education. Are less educated people found among those with the highest levels of productivity? The answer, again, is yes. Over a quarter of the people in the top quintile of productive activity did not graduate from high school. Likewise, those with the highest levels of education fall nearly as frequently into the low as the high productivity category, although these small differences could be artifacts of sampling variability.

Finally, income varies with level of productivity (Table 2-2). This, perhaps, should be of no surprise since productivity also varies with education, and both education and income are markers of socioeconomic status. Furthermore, in the collective 65 and older population, the employed have higher incomes than the nonemployed, and the employed, as defined here, are productive.

Conclusion

Will people in their late sixties and early seventies later in this century seem more like middle-aged people, eagerly and actively involved in all sorts of productive endeavors? That is certainly a scenario to consider. The counternarrative to the scary demographic imperative, discussed in the section "The Demographic Imperative," would certainly illuminate that point. We are inclined to agree with this hope. However, the reader must realize that it is a hope, not yet a reality.

Are people in the Third Age highly productive? It depends on how narrowly one draws the definition of productivity. Relatively few work for pay.

The Third Age, after all, is thought of as a time after work, a time of leisure. This does not mean that the Third Age is an unproductive time of life. Housework alone provides some activity for nearly all people of that age, and for some, it may be seen as a substitute for gainful employment. When household maintenance and unidentified other types of productive activity are added, the Third Age is surely a productive time of life for many persons, even though most of them are not drawing a regular paycheck. People in the top half of the percentile distribution spent 31 hours a week working in only the three areas defined by our data set. It is clearly an error to view people in their late sixties and early seventies as unproductive, nonproductive, or as receivers rather than givers.

Furthermore, older people are not equally drawn to the various types of productivity. Some types fit more easily into the way their lives are organized, lives conditioned by decades of productive activity. For example, because baby boom women moved into the labor force early in adulthood, the male bias in late retirement may wane in the decades ahead. Certainly, the inching up of the age for receiving social security retirement benefits will delay retirement for most workers in future decades by a year or two. Because future birth cohorts entering the Third Age will have more positive education and health profiles, they may be more heavily involved in productive activity.

In any case, it is important to avoid thinking in terms of the productive, as though they are all alike in some essential way and different from the nonproductive. This kind of either/or is problematic. People heavily engaged in productive activity are no more virtuous than those who are disengaged. Furthermore, where does one draw the line on productivity? Quintiles are arbitrary, as are most boundaries and barriers that are drawn between polar concepts. In reality, after retirement, people move into and out of areas of activity depending on the meaning that the activities have in their lives, the field of experience that people bring to this time in their lives, and the human capital and resources they have accumulated. A personal assessment of productivity is likely to be different from any economic assessment. For many people, travel, recreation, education, personal and spiritual development, and political involvement do seem deeply productive to their lives and to the lives of those around them.

League bowling is declining. We doubt that the Third Age may be characterized as filled with people bowling alone. Third Age Americans balance and weave among useful, interesting, and restful activities, many of which would be considered productive by any standards, whereas some are only existentially productive. They are enriching. This chapter is offered to help social work students, practitioners, and those in allied fields to understand a segment of the older population that they are least likely to encounter in crisis. It is easy to ignore them, but they can be powerful partners in the effort to build and strengthen community.

References

Bumpass, L. L., & Sweet, J. A. (1997). *National survey of families and households: Wave I, 1987–1988, and Wave II, 1992–1994*. Ann Arbor, MI: Inter-University Consortium for Political and Social Research.

Chesnais, J. C. (1996). Fertility, family, and social policy in contemporary Western Europe. *Population and Development Review, 22*, 729–740.

Coale, A., & Zelnick, M. (1963). *Estimate of fertility and population in the United States*. Princeton, NJ: Princeton University Press.

Coltrane, S., & Ishii-Kuntz, M. (1992). Men's housework: A life course perspective. *Journal of Marriage and the Family, 54*, 43–58.

Cowgill, D. (1974). Aging and modernization: A revision of the theory. In J. F. Gubrium (Ed.), *Late life: Communities and environmental policy* (pp. 123–145). Springfield, IL: Charles C Thomas.

Crimmins, E. M., & Ingegneri, D. G. (1992). Health trends in the American population. In A. M. Rappaport & S. J. Schieber (Eds.), *Demography and retirement: The 21st century* (pp. 259–278). Westport, CT: Greenwood.

Elder, G. (2001). Life course. In G. F. Maddox (Ed.), *The encyclopedia of aging* (3rd ed., Vol.1, pp. 593–596). New York: Springer.

Fries, J. F. (1980). Aging, natural death and the compression of morbidity. *New England Journal of Medicine, 303*, 130.

Fries, J. F., Koop, C. E., Sokolov, J., Beadle, C. E., & Wright, D. (1998). Beyond health promotion: Reducing health care costs by reducing need and demand for medical care. *Health Affairs, 17*, 70–84.

Gupta, S. (1999). The effects of transitions in marital status on men's performance of housework. *Journal of Marriage and the Family, 61*, 700–711.

Herzog, A. R., & Morgan, J. N. (1992). Age and gender differences in the value of productive activities. *Research on Aging, 14,* 169–198.

Laslett, P. (1991). *A fresh map of life: The emergence of the third age.* Cambridge, MA: Harvard University Press.

Longino, C. F., Jr. (1994). Myths of an aging America. *American Demographics, 16,* 36–42.

Longino, C. F., Jr. (1999). The future population of aging in the U.S.A. and Pacific Rim countries: Implications are not always obvious. *Hallym International Journal of Aging, 1*(1), 33–43.

Longino, C. F., Jr., & Polivka, L. (2001). The effects of changing values on the provision of long-term care. *Generations 25*(1), 64–68.

Longino, C. F., Jr., & J. L. Powell. (2002). Embodiment and aging. In V. Berdayes, L. Esposito, & J. Murphy (Eds.), *The body in human inquiry: Interdisciplinary explorations of embodiment.* Cresskill, NJ: Hampton Press.

Manheimer, R. J. (1995). *The second middle age.* Washington, DC: Invisible Ink Press.

Manton, K. G., Corder, L. S., & Stallard, E. (1993). Estimates of change in chronic disability and institutional incidence and prevalence rates in the U.S. elderly population from the 1982, 1984, and 1986 national long term care surveys. *Journal of Gerontology: Social Sciences, 48,* S153–S166.

Morgan, S. P. (1996). Characteristic feature of modern American fertility. In J. B. Casterline, R. D. Lee, & K. A. Foote (Eds.), *Fertility in the United States: New patterns, new theories.* New York: Population Council.

Neugarten, B. L. (1974). Age groups in America and the rise of the young-old. *Annals of the American Academy of Political and Social Sciences, 415,* 187–198.

Omran, A. (1977). Epidemiological transition in the United States. *Population Bulletin 32*(2), 3–42.

Peterson, D. A. (2001). Adult education. In G. F. Maddox (Ed.), *The encyclopedia of aging* (3rd ed., Vol. 1, pp. 22–24). New York: Springer.

Russell, C. (1993). *The master trend: How the baby boom generation is remaking America.* New York: Plenum Press.

Sanchez, L., & Thompson, E. (1997). Becoming mothers and fathers: Parenthood, gender, and the division of labor. *Gender and Society, 11,* 747–775.

Shkolnikov, V., Mesle, F., & Vallin, J. (1996). Health crisis in Russia, Pt. I: recent trends in life expectancy and causes of death from 1970 to 1993. *Population: An English Selection, 8,* 123–154.

Treas, J. (1995). Older Americans in the 1990s and beyond. *Population Bulletin, 50*(2), 1–45.

Treas, J., & Longino, C. F., Jr. (1997). Demography of aging in the United States. In K. Ferraro (Ed.), *Gerontology: perspectives and issues* (pp. 19–50). New York: Springer.

Weeks, J. R. (1999). *Population.* Belmont, CA: Wadsworth.

Wolf, D. A. (1995). Changes in the living arrangements of older women: An international study. *Gerontologist, 35,* 724–731.

Conceptualizing Productive Aging

Nancy R. Hooyman

Conceptualizing Productive Aging

Rapid societal, demographic, and global changes are altering the meaning and purpose of growing old, and dominant social, economic, and political institutions are reshaping aging. In turn, old age has transformed institutions in our society, particularly employment–retirement and health and long-term care systems. From a social policy perspective, the key issues facing the older population are not solely finances, retirement, the welfare state, or the provision of health services, but also how to maximize older adults' contributions to society through new roles and opportunities (Phillipson, 1998). As average life expectancy has increased, and corporate and public policies have encouraged early exits from the workforce, American workers have been retiring from full-time jobs at earlier ages, producing an expanding Third Age of personal fulfillment in life (Laslett, 1991). In effect, a new stage of life has been added that is as long in duration as childhood or the middle years (Freedman, 1999, 2001).

The Third Age is a collective circumstance and one of personal achievement. It can only be experienced in the company of a nationwide society of those with the inclination, freedom, and means to act in the appropriate manner. The emergence of the Third Age requires demographic and economic requisites, appropriate cultural and educational conditions, along with the health, vigor, and attitudes that enable people to conduct their lives with a longer future in view (Laslett, 1991). From the perspective of productivity, a critical question is, What will be the options and opportunities available to older adults in the larger social environment for them to experience productive engagement in the Third Age?

Many policy analysts overstate the changing demographics as a crisis and thereby overlook the opportunity presented: how to match older adults' untapped resources—their time, talent and life experiences—with some urgent needs of American communities. One major resource is time. Retirement frees up 25 hours a week for men, 18 for women; this time is largely used, however, for leisure activities, watching TV, and housework, not in the civic life of communities. In fact, after sleep (35 percent), recreation is the biggest single late-life activity (Freedman, 1999). Another resource is practical knowledge and wisdom gained from life experience, which is often lost to younger adults. Time left to live may give older adults a special reason to become involved in ways that both provide personal meaning and make a significant difference to others, as captured in Erikson's (1981, 1982) concept of "generativity" and the legacy we want to leave. In identifying the Third Age, Laslett (1991, p. *x*) argues that older adults need a "fresh map of life that balances personal fulfillment with responsibilities to others." The concept of the Third Age does not embrace imitating earlier periods, but rather it embraces building on the strengths and perspective of those stages and finding new meaning and purpose in the later life stages (Bass, Caro, & Chen, 1993; Fahey, 1996).

Baby boomers are presumed to have the energy and the interest to continue in productive roles, to maintain competence and skills through extensive practice, and to find new means of overcoming declining abilities. To maximize these remarkable gains, however, our society lacks a compelling vision for how to spend the third stage of life, "a season in search of a purpose" (Cole, 1992; Moody, 1998). In fact, more resources go into denying aging than in planning for productive aging, as evidenced by the antiaging lotions, cosmetic surgery, and the antiaging movement that seeks to extend the life span.

A new vision and practice of later life is needed not only for continued learning and growth, but also for contributions to community and care for the future. The challenge is how to invent new roles or refashion old ones that accommodate the reality of this third stage of life—beyond grandparenting, neighboring, socializing, and pursuing hobbies. Such roles need to be integrative in providing culturally sanctioned ways of participating in the broader community. As Betty Friedan (1993) noted in *The Fountain of Age*, if we are to leave a legacy to younger generations, we must not be solely focused on personal fulfillment, but we must also be willing to work on the problems confronting our society with whatever wisdom and generativity we have attained. It is critical to move away from defining aging as a problem to focusing on older adults' positive contributions to society and the potential of collective value. This shift is even more urgent given uncertainties facing our society after September 11, 2001, combined with human resources shortages in areas vital to our society's future, such as teaching and nursing.

Definitions of Productivity

Definitions of productivity vary in the range of activities included. Some focus only on paid work and volunteer services, "activities that produce goods and services that otherwise would have to be paid for and that will reduce the demand for goods and services produced by others" (Morgan, 1986). Others expand the production of goods and services to include housework, child care, and help to family and friends (Herzog, 1989). The broadest definitions encompass nearly all activities of older adults, including leisure and recreation that are defined as personally productive (Bond, Cutler, & Grams, 1995; Moody, 2001; Sherraden, Morrow-Howell, Hinterlong, & Rozario, 2001).

In this chapter, productivity is defined as any activity that produces goods and services such as housework, child care, volunteer work, help to family and friends, along with training and skills to enhance the capacity to perform such tasks. If there is a good fit between societal and individual expectations about roles in old age, then the activity—formal or informal, paid or unpaid—can have a positive influence on older adults' mental and physical well-being (McIntosh & Danigelis, 1995). Consistent with the person–environment theoretical perspective discussed later, productive older adults choose and adjust their behavior and aspirations to maintain a sense of competence in a changing environment, with many contributing to their families, communities, and larger society.

Productive aging and *successful* aging hold different perspectives about older adults. Productive aging emphasizes the contributory roles that older adults can play in society and how to expand such opportunities. However, the concept of productive aging is not intended to mandate such activities or place an obligation on those who choose not to be engaged in this way. In contrast, the concept of successful aging emphasizes individual physiological and psychological capacity and performance. Given this difference, productive aging may not encompass all that is positive about aging (for example, leisure time, personal enrichment) nor is it to be

prescribed for all older adults. Morrow-Howell and Sherraden (2001) extended these distinctions by differentiating productive aging and the concept of productivity in later life. The latter term suggests that productivity is among many possible pursuits in later life, including leisure and spirituality, and is less inclined to imply that productivity is the highest attainment of later life.

Theoretical Models

Work related to productive aging reflects Bengtson and Schaie's (1989) observation that gerontology is data rich and theory poor. Survey data exist about select productive activities, such as volunteering, but efforts to use theory to explain processes and outcomes of productive engagement are few. Until the 1960s, most research examined aging as a problem arising from individual concerns. Key concepts were individual adjustment, activity, and life satisfaction (Cavan, Burgess, Goldhamer, & Havighurst, 1949; Cottrell, 1942; Havighurst, 1954). Some theories of adjustment focused on personal characteristics (health, personality, needs), while others emphasized society's demands on and expectations of the aging individual. Growing old was conceptualized as the individual encountering problems of adjustment due to role changes in later life.

These concepts were to be understood as a working language describing the central processes of growing old. They were not part of a formal theoretical system whose major problems were whether or not it provided an adequate explanation of aging. Rather, the concepts were treated as the "facts" of growing old. . . . (Ageing) was seen as a process whereby individuals, not social systems, structures of domination of ideologies—hope to alter themselves in some way to deal satisfactorily with their experiences. The problem was not retirement or poverty, ill health and/or social isolation per se; these conditions were seemingly "natural ones." Being natural, they were accepted by researchers as the way things were, the facts of elderly life. (Lynott & Lynott, 1996, p. 750)

One of the earliest attempts to explain how individuals adjust to aging involved an application of *role theory* and typical age-related role changes (Cottrell, 1942). Age norms serve to open up or close off the roles that people of a given chronological age can play. They are assumptions of age-related capacities and limitations—beliefs that a person of a given age can and ought to do certain things. Individuals also hold norms about the appropriateness of their own behavior at any particular age, so that social clocks become internalized and age norms operate to keep people on the "typical" time track (Hagestad & Neugarten, 1985). In the past, most people have held age-normative expectations about when to graduate from school, start working, marry, have a family, reach the peak of their career, and retire. With increased life expectancy, however, these expectations are shifting.

Every society conveys age norms through socialization, a lifelong process by which individuals learn to perform new roles, adjust to changing roles, relinquish old ones, learn a "social clock"

of what is age appropriate, and thereby become integrated into society. In addition, older adults must learn to deal with role losses believed to lead to an erosion of social identity and self-esteem. Older people were also assumed to experience *role discontinuity*, whereby what is learned at one age may be useless or conflicting with a subsequent period in one's life. With age, roles have also become more ambiguous. In the past, older adults have lacked positive models of role gains and alternative roles. Later research identified that it is not only the roles older adults hold, but also the congruity between those role sets and individualized preferences that affect their well-being (Herzog & House, 1991).

Activity theory also attempted to answer how individuals adjust to age-related changes. On the basis of Robert Havighurst's (1963, 1968) analyses of the Kansas City Studies of Adult Life, the well-adjusted older person was perceived as assuming a larger number and variety of productive roles and age-appropriate replacements through activities in voluntary associations, churches, and leisure organizations. It was presumed that being active, being productive, and maintaining or creating new social networks enhanced life satisfaction, self-concept, and adjustment (Bengtson, 1969; Gubrium, 1973, 1993; Herzog & House, 1991). Activity theory, however, fails to account for how personality, socioeconomic status, and lifestyle variables may be more important than maturational ones in the association between activity and life satisfaction, health, and well-being (Covey, 1981). Activity theory defined aging as an individual social problem to be addressed by trying to retain status, roles, and activities similar to those of earlier life stages, not as a societal or collective concern.

Disengagement theory challenged this perspective by shifting attention away from solely the individual to the social system as an explanation for successful aging. Cumming and Henry (1961) argued that aging cannot be understood separate from the characteristics of the social system in which it is experienced. All societies need orderly ways to transfer power from older to younger generations. Therefore, the social system deals with the problem of "slowing down" with age by institutionalizing mechanisms of disengagement or separation from society. Accordingly, older people decrease their activity levels, seek more passive roles, interact less frequently with others, and become more preoccupied with their inner lives. Disengagement theory thus related the changing needs of individuals to those of social system, with older adults viewed as "naturally" withdrawing from social roles in order to maintain a sense of self-worth (Cumming and Henry, 1961).

> Aging is an inevitable mutual withdrawal or disengagement resulting in decreased interaction between the aging person and others in the social systems he belongs to. The individual or others may initiate the process in the situation. . . . When the aging process is complete, the equilibrium which existed in middle life between the individual and his society has given way to a new equilibrium characterized by a greater distance and an altered type of relationship. (p. 14)

The core assumptions of disengagement theory, debated and often discounted by other researchers, have generally not been supported by empirical research (Achenbaum & Bengtson, 1994). Blau (1973), for example, critiqued disengagement theory for legitimating a form of social redundancy among the old:

> The disengagement theory deserves to be publicly attacked because it can so easily be used as a rationale by the non-old, who constitute the 'normals' in society, to avoid confronting and dealing with the issue of old people's marginality and rolelessness in American society. (p. 152)

It is also criticized for not acknowledging variability in individual preferences, personality, and sociocultural and environmental opportunities within the older population (Achenbaum & Bengtson, 1994; Estes & Associates, 2001; Marshall, 1994).

Nevertheless, disengagement theory was significant in fostering theoretical debates regarding the individual and social aspects of aging. It thus served to stimulate a range of complementary and alternative theoretical approaches: modernization (Cowgill & Holmes, 1972), social exchange (Dowd, 1975), life course perspectives (Neugarten & Hagestad, 1976), and age stratification (Riley, Johnson, & Foner, 1972; Riley, Kahn, & Foner, 1994), some of which are briefly addressed in the following section.

Social exchange theory also challenged activity and disengagement. Drawing on economic cost–benefit models of social participation, Dowd

(1975) attempted to answer why social interaction and activity often decrease with age. He maintained that older people are most likely to benefit when social exchanges are balanced, and they are able to reciprocate when others do things for them. Withdrawal and social isolation are not the result of system needs or individual choice, but rather of an unequal exchange process of "investment and returns" between older people and others. Because of the shift in opportunity structures, roles, and skills that accompanies advancing age, older people typically have fewer resources with which to exert power in their social relationships and their status declines accordingly (Hendricks, 1995). With fewer opportunity structures and little to exchange in value, some older people feel forced to accept the retirement role and to turn to deference and withdrawal to balance the exchange equation (Lynott & Lynott, 1996). Yet exchange theory discounts the nonmaterial resources that older people often can bring to exchanges—respect, approval, love, wisdom, and time for voluntary activities.

According to the continuity or life course perspective, individuals tend to maintain a consistent pattern of behavior as they age, substituting similar types of roles for lost ones and maintaining typical ways of adapting to the environment. It highlighted the environmental context along with processes of development and change over the life span, including the life history of role involvement and relationships throughout adulthood. It also articulated how older people are embedded in a changing social, cultural, and economic environment as well as products

of a life history of events, relationships, and behavior (Moen, 1995). However, it is difficult to test empirically because an individual's reaction to aging is explained through the interrelationships among the biological and psychological changes and the continuation of lifelong patterns.

The concept of "structural lag" articulated how institutional roles and opportunities have not kept pace with the older population's growth, capabilities, and interests. For example, senior centers and retirement communities are largely focused on leisure in the postretirement years, not older adults' potential to be engaged in productive activities (Freedman, 1999). In addition, most social policies focus on older adults' needs, and aging advocates defend existing policies—a process that has fueled the intergenerational conflict debates. Although the basic needs of older adults must be met through social policies and programs, new institutions with creative roles and opportunities at the community level are also needed to reconceptualize aging. Estes and Associates (2001) argued that an age-integrated society would compensate for structural lag by developing policies, such as extended time off for education or family across the life span and new work roles for older adults, to bring social structures into balance with individuals' needs. Similarly, Riley and colleagues (1994) offered a vision of an age-integrated society where education, work, and leisure are allocated more equally across the life span (Riley & Loscocco, 1994; Riley & Riley, 1994).

In general, traditional social gerontological theory avoided questioning the social problems and conditions facing older adults. From the late 1970s on, however, the "naturalness" of such concerns came under question. Critical gerontology emerged from the need for a different kind of gerontology that identifies both the structural causes of older adults' problems along with their potential and positive contributions.

Critical Gerontology

Challenging traditional gerontological perspectives, critical gerontology developed in the late 1980s and 1990s as an alternative approach to understanding the process of growing old (Cole, Achenbaum, Jakobi, & Kastenbaum, 1993; Phillipson & Walker, 1987). It is concerned with

> a collection of questions, problems and analyses that have been excluded by mainstream gerontology. These vary from questions about the role of the state in the management of old age to issues about the purpose of growing old within the context of a postmodern life course. (Cole, 1992)

The concept of lives as socially constructed is a central theme in critical gerontology. The tacit contract between generations—that older people leave the workforce to provide employment options to younger adults—illustrates the principle that becoming old is a socially created condition, related in a seemingly arbitrary way to the individual's physiological status (Lynott & Lynott, 1996).

Within this context, greater awareness emerged of the structural pressures and constraints affecting older people. In particular, greater attention was given to how the state and the econ-

omy influence the aging experience and further divisions associated with age, class, gender, and ethnicity (Danigelis & McIntosh, 1993). Among these conceptualizations, *political economy* critiqued how age segregated policies ("the aging enterprise") singles out, stigmatize, and isolate older adults. Age was viewed as a social rather than biologically constructed status (Estes, 1979). This perspective challenged a view of growing old as an individualized and medicalized process, dominated by physical and mental decline (for example, the biomedical or disease model of aging where older adults are responsible for their problems; Estes & Binney, 1989). Accordingly, the barriers facing older adults are less biological, but more in the images and practices that society maintains about them. Changing and transforming these is a central social policy issue.

From this critical approach, gerontological research should enhance our understanding of the relationship between aging and economic life; the differential experience of aging by age, social class, gender, and ethnicity; and the role played by social policy in contributing to elders' dependency (Estes, Gerard, & Swan, 1984; Estes, Linkins, & Binney, 1996; Minkler & Estes, 1998; Myles, 1984). Many of older adults' experiences are products of a particular division of labor and structural inequality, rather than a natural part of the aging process. Accordingly, the *social creation of dependency* was defined as resulting from the forced exclusion of older people from work and other productive roles, leading to poverty, institutionalization, and restricted domestic and community roles (Walker, 1981).

The political economy perspective still serves to challenge the "alarmist" or "apocalyptic" demography of the late 20th and early 21st centuries, whereby the increase in older adults is viewed largely as a crisis. The basic questions—Can we afford an aging society? Can we afford to grow old in the 21st century?—are articulated in debates around the financing of pensions, reductions in public funding, privatization, greater personal responsibility, and intergenerational competition for limited resources (Bengtson, 1993; Robertson, 1998). In contrast to the perceptions of the 1960s and 1970s of older adults as deserving of public benefits, a "politics of resentment" has surfaced (Turner, 1989).

As an example, retirement in the 1950s and 1960s was viewed as a period of relative stability; government policies focused on promoting a healthy and financially secure retirement to make way for younger workers in the workforce, and early retirement was a valued social and economic objective. In contrast, more adults now choosing early retirement and facing 20 to 30 years of nonwork time, larger global changes, and the growing instability in the 21st century have spawned a growing population attempting to construct a secure identity for later life. Therefore, these changes require that our society rethink the obligations and guarantees of the past. At the same time, the stock market's poor performance and the sagging economy of the early 21st century may mean that more older adults, who counted on investments for economic security, may be forced to return to temporary, part-time, and often low-paying jobs. This may well pose new economic challenges for our society, making it less feasible to focus on nonwork productive roles in the near future.

The critical gerontology perspective also maintains that responsibilities for an aging population should not be offloaded to particular generations or cohorts. Aging is an issue for generations, but it is one to be solved with generations. Integrating older adults across and within different social groups and institutions must rest on a framework of generational cooperation and support (Phillipson, 1998). The exchange theory perspective of older adults having strengths and resources that flow across generations is inherent within the conceptualization of productive aging.

Feminist and empowerment perspectives emerged from the critical gerontological context. In fact, empowerment is a concept central to feminism but is also widely adapted by social change theorists and social work advocates. Empowerment is both an outcome of practice and a process of working. Five central themes are (1) control, (2) confidence, (3) power, (4) choices, and (5) autonomy (Gutierrez, Parsons, & Cox, 1998). Similar to the political economy perspective, institutions, not only individuals, must change. With regard to productive engagement in later life, institutions need to provide older people with opportunities to develop adequate knowledge and skill to elect and then support the potential for autonomy and control that lives within each older person (Meredith & Wells, 1994). This is also defined as institutions' eliciting "personhood"—those attributes and strengths that make each individual unique as a human being (Buzell, Meredith, Monna, Ritchie, & Sergeant, 1993). Although personal control is emphasized, empowerment-based practice is not limited to the individual level. More important, it is a way to change the larger social structure (for example, ageism and age discrimination; lack of resources for older people to contribute). As noted in the section on interventions, efforts to increase older adults' self-efficacy must be coupled with institutional responsiveness to them.

Many of the critical gerontological perspectives, however, can be criticized for their focus on the social structure and corresponding inadequate attention to broader issues of meaning and purpose in lives of the old and the moral and existential issues faced by older people (Bury, 1995; Giddens, 1991). Later refinements of the political economy perspective—the "moral economy of aging"—raised concerns about both societal attitudes and cultural assumptions regarding older people (Minkler & Cole, 1998; Moody, 2001). It is within this context that questions of meaning in old age became salient.

Meaning and Purpose in Later Life

Instrumental gerontology is often criticized for seeking to be too objective about what is essentially a subjective, human-lived experience. Theorists who focus on the subjective meaning of aging maintain that critical gerontology must move beyond a negative critique to offer a vision of a different approach to aging: "a positive idea of human development. That is, aging as move-ment toward freedom beyond domination (autonomy, wisdom, transcendence") (Moody, 1988, pp. 32–33).

Identifying a "crisis of meaning," Cole (1992) argued that our society has shifted from viewing aging as an existential problem to one focused on scientific and technical management. In doing so, we have lost sight of the fact that aging is "biographical as well as biological," that "old age is an experience to be lived meaningfully and not only a problem of health and disease." (Cole, 1992, pp. 192–194)

> We must acknowledge that our great progress in the material and physical conditions of life has been achieved at a high spiritual and ethical price. Social security has not enhanced economic security or dignity in old age. The elderly continue to occupy an inferior status in the moral community marginalized by an economy and culture committed to the scientific management of growth without limit. (p. 237)

This position was further developed by Moody (1988, 1992, 1993, 2001) who acknowledged the central place of meaning and interrelationships in the construction of social life. There are no straightforward "facts" about social aging. Moody (1988) illustrated this by taking what seems to be the deceptively simple question: What is it that constitutes retirement?

> The uncritical acceptance of retirement rates as an unambiguous "fact" about the social world becomes a kind of mystification of the lived experiences of unemployment and chronic

illness, and this mystification has political as well as ideological consequences. (Moody, 1988, p. 32)

Questions about the meaning of old age coincided with concern about the new circumstances and conditions brought about by the characteristics of postmodern societies (Conrad, 1992). These include industrial changes, with flexible forms of work organization increasingly displacing mass production; the globalization of social life; and a weakening in the institutions and practices of the nation state (Kumar, 1995). It is argued that a crisis of meaning around issues of identity and social relationships is a fundamental condition of living in a postmodern world (Taylor, 1989). This crisis occurs in situations in which individuals are uncertain about their position in the world and lack a framework within which daily living assumes a stable significance. Accordingly, the available options seem to lack meaning and substance and appear unfixed and undetermined. The postmodern self is characterized by insecurity, especially in old age. Modern living is viewed as undercutting the construction of a viable identity for living in old age because consensus no longer exists regarding retirement and the welfare state. As a result, older adults experience marginality in a new and somewhat distinctive way (Phillipson, 1996, 1998).

Increasingly, the theoretical and practical issue is how to make sense of human life wherein survival into old age is combined with release from the need for productive employment and the creation of significant space for personal development. In contrast to an earlier view of retirement as an impediment to good health, the positive notion (for example, the Third Age) of (re)constructing an identity within active retirement has emerged. From this perspective, older people face new possibilities absent in traditional approaches to aging—to reposition their own identities and to redefine the scope of aging as a personal and social event.

The late modernity perspective posits that old age can be reconstructed as a period of potential choice, but also of risk and dangers, a time of fears and anxieties about greater personal financial responsibility, poor health, and disability and dying. According to Phillipson (1998), we ride a "juggernaut" in old age—the threat of poverty, severe illness, loss of loved ones—but old age also brings with it the possibility of freedom from restrictive work and domestic roles, new relationships, and a greater feeling of security. The concept of reconstructing identity differs markedly from past stereotypes of "identity work" as largely complete in old age. For example, Giddens (1991) rejected the view of self as a stable entity persisting unchanged over time. "Self identity is something that is routinely created and sustained in the reflexive activities of the individual" (p. 52). Yet, if people constantly have to recreate and reconstruct their identity and worldview and to maintain a narrative about themselves, what lies ahead for older people? What is there beyond retirement and the welfare state? What are the moral resources that older adults can draw on if these institutional changes place in doubt the implicit intergenerational contract? Concerned by the absence of meaning in older people's lives, Moody (1992) turned to the humanities, especially the use of biographical approaches to emphasize the interplay between the self and society (Kenyon, 1996). Others have articulated the concept of empowerment to encompass both the transformation of society and the development of new rituals and symbols to facilitate changes through the life course (Kaminsky, 1993). We turn now to theoretical concepts within the broad framework of person in environment.

A Person–Environment Theoretical Perspective

The broad person–environment perspective is useful for conceptualizing interventions to increase institutional opportunities for older people to experience productivity and meaning. This view considers the physiological, psychological, and social–environmental changes that affect how older people approach the Third Age. It posits that the environment (for example, the larger society, the community, the neighborhood, or the home) changes continually as the older adult takes from it what he or she needs, controls what can be manipulated, and adjusts to conditions that cannot be changed. Adaptation thus implies a dual process in which the individual adjusts to some characteristics of the social and physical environment (for example, downsizing of his or her company) and brings about changes in other environmental aspects (for example, lobbying the legislature to mandate benefits for early retirees).

Competence is a key concept within the dynamic interactions between the person's physical and psychological characteristics and the social and physical environment. The model whereby individual competence interacts with "environmental press" was first developed by Lawton and Nahemow (1973) and examined further by Lawton (1975, 1989) and by Parmelee and Lawton (1990). *Environmental press* refers to the demands that environments make on the individual to adapt, to respond, or to change; it can range from minimal to quite high. For example, less environmental press is present in an institutional setting than in a multigenerational family sharing a home. As the environmental demands change over time, the individual must adapt to changes to maintain his or her sense of competence.

Individual competence is the theoretical upper limit of an individual's abilities to function in the areas of health, social behavior, and cognition (Lawton & Nahemow, 1973). A lack of fit exists when a person's skills decline as a function of advancing age or a person's skills are maintained, but the environmental or contextual demands increased substantially. Dixon (1995) further defined competence as how well one uses one's abilities and skills to perform activities required by new or demanding situations—the higher a person's competence, the better that person can tolerate higher levels of environmental press. Individuals perform at their maximum capacity when the environmental press slightly exceeds the level at which they adapt. In other words, the environment challenges them to test their limits but does not overwhelm them.

Maintaining competence also involves using compensation to improve the match between environmental demands and the individual's resources (Krause, 1995). Despite demands in cognitive and psychomotor skills with age, performance in specific domains can be maintained and enhanced. For example, through training or practice, an individual whose employer encouraged him or her to retire early recovers enough skill to meet demands in select areas, such as volunteering or part-time work. Alternatively, substitution can be an effective way to maintain competence, for example, by establishing alternative goals to change the demands or by relaxing the criteria for success. Within this framework, competence can be conceptualized as the capacity to engage in productive roles and opportunities.

If the level of environmental press becomes too high, an older adult experiences excessive stress or overload. When the environmental press is far below an individual's adaptation level, sensory deprivation, boredom, and dependence may result. In contrast, a situation of mild to moderate stress, just below the person's adaptation level, results in maximum comfort and is probably most conducive to engagement in productive activities. In either situation—too much or too little environmental press—the person or the environment must change if the individual's adaptive capacity is to be restored.

This model has implications for identifying interventions to enhance older adults' contributions to their families, their communities, and their society. Most social and health services for older adults are oriented toward minimizing environmental demands and increasing supports. A fine line exists, however, between minimizing excessive environmental press and creating an environment that is not conducive to developing new roles, skills, and purpose in one's life. For example, well-meaning families who take over household tasks or insist that their older relative move to a nursing home minimize opportunities for the older adult to contribute to their families, their neighborhoods, or their communities.

Implications for Interventions

The remainder of this chapter illustrates ways to enhance productive engagement in old age by modifying the environment or increasing older adults' level of competence. Where relevant, the application of empowerment theory is articulated.

Individual Competence

The person–environment model posits that enhancing individual competence allows older adults to realize more fully their potential for continued growth and development. Competence, in effect, refers to how well an individual uses his or her level of abilities to adapt to new or demanding situations. Developing competence can maintain and, in some instances, enhance older adults' feelings of worth, value, integrity, and dignity, which are all components of self-esteem (Dixon, 1995). Competence involves the use of varied abilities through a process of compensation that balances one's strengths and weaknesses at different times and circumstances (Bond et al., 1995). Compensating for losses involves basic biological functioning and positive aspects of personal agency, such as cognitive efficacy, productivity, and personal control and life satisfaction. Older adults learn to compensate for or accept the limitations that they cannot change (for example, chronic illness) while trying to maintain and even improve performance in areas where change remains possible (for example, communication skills).

As an illustration, consider the aging chess master who has developed compensatory techniques related to cognitive declines or who may exchange participating in national chess tournaments for teaching chess to children in an inner-city school. Compensation thus fosters the sense that one is contributing something of significance to the world by using talents and resources to benefit others. Interventions that focus on individual compensation can encourage the continued use of older adults' abilities in appropriate contexts; continued productivity in old or alternative domains of competence; and emergence of new domains of competence. This process whereby an aging individual selectively optimizes his or her functioning to be congruent with the environment is identified as "selective optimization" with compensation (Baltes & Baltes, 1990; Dixon, 1995). This is also a process of empowerment, when the person's self-efficacy increases, a group consciousness begins to form, self-blame declines, and older adults become more proactive rather than reactive (Gutierrez, 1990).

Most theorists agree that competence and positive self-esteem involve feelings of control over one's life. Primary control (for example, "I'm in charge"; "I directly control what is happening") probably peaks between 50 and 60 years of age. It shifts to compensatory secondary control (for example, "I retain a sense of power because I have made necessary arrangements to say that things are under control"; Dixon, 1995). For example, a retired former executive may shift from running a large corporation to managing his own investment portfolio to ensure his family's economic security. Having a sense of control is inherent within empowerment processes.

Control is differentiated from autonomy (Zautra, Reich, & Newsom, 1995). *Autonomy* refers to a person's capacity to perform functions of everyday life (for example, to dress oneself, prepare one's meals, maintain one's home). Loss of autonomy often results from activity limitations, typically measured by activities of daily living or instrumental activities of daily living. Autonomy has been mistakenly equated with independence of the influence of others. Instead, as lifespan and continuity theories posit, no one is completely independent of the influence of others. Instead, people tend to be interdependent throughout life, with the nature of the interdependency shifting with age. Thus, constraints on autonomy can come from within as well as outside. The older person who breaks a hip and simply gives up rather than participating in rehabilitation to gain mobility is constraining his or her own options. Sometimes loss of control is often felt by elderly people who experience loss of autonomy, but this is not always the case. For example, some older adults who face severely diminished capacity in their daily activities can still experience feelings of control—their perceptions of their ability to shape the course of life events remains, especially if they can shift from past life circumstances to focus on how current circumstances. For example, a homebound older person shifts from visiting friends or volunteering at church to calling friends to provide emotional support or checking on children's safety. This older adult can experience feelings of control because control is vested in ongoing interrelationships between the person and the environment, rather than solely as a property of individuals or of the environment.

Autonomy and control beliefs do not take shape in a vacuum; they depend on the context of responses from the social and physical environment. For example, whether a wheelchair-bound person can travel into the city depends on not only his or her own physical capacities or personal resolve, but also on the availability of social and physical supports, such as a driver, accessible transportation, sidewalks, and building ramps. Wheelchair-bound older adults may have inner strengths of optimism, hardiness, and self-esteem, but without environmental supports, their options are constrained. In fact, beliefs of control may not necessarily be beneficial for older adults with physical disabilities if the environment is not congruent with their beliefs. Professionals and family members need to be cautious not to encourage self-reliant forms of control for those with new impairments without also ensuring environmental changes (for example, modifying the home and accessing transportation and necessary buildings). These examples suggest that the timing of interventions to modify individual competence or the environment is crucial.

Models of control also differentiate between those that seek to identify a person's beliefs about control compared with control perceptions that arise out of a person's specific transactions with his or her social and physical environment. *Transaction control* involves researchers' rating perceived control and efficacy over specific events or actual experiences, aggregated across occasions. Control over positive versus negative outcomes also differs. Someone may be able to control aversive conditions (for example, they maintain their economic security in their retirement years) but feel unable to make positive events happen with any confidence (for example, financially secure, they withdraw from social interactions and opportunities to learn new productive roles). Others may believe that they are able to find sources of pleasure in their lives but cannot predict or control the experience of negative effects (for example, the volatile stock market reduces their economic security in retirement). To enhance one's sense of competence and ability to engage in new productive roles, the meaning and value of control beliefs depend on whether those beliefs are congruent with the needs of the person at the time (Zautra et al., 1995).

Environmental Changes

As noted in Lawton's (1975, 1989) model, the environment, a central component of the empowerment process, can exacerbate or compensate for losses associated with aging. Drawing on the concept of empowerment, Maluccio (1981) emphasized the importance of identifying, understanding, and manipulating environmental obstacles and supports affecting a person's competence. Institutions and structural factors, not individuals, need to change. Programs and policies are needed to provide opportunities for older adults to engage in activities that they choose and define as positive (Morrow-Howell & Sherraden, 2001). Environmental factors that can be changed to enhance productivity range from the most basic—adequate housing, economic security, health care, nutrition, and safety—to developing educational and culturally sensitive interventions to reduce institutional ageism. Without attending to older adults' basic needs, the concepts of productivity and purpose in life have little meaning; for example, an older women who is poor, living alone, socially isolated, and in poor health may consider concepts of meaning and productivity to be irrelevant to her daily survival. In fact, low-income women of color are the most vulnerable to environmental stresses (Belle, 1990; Holstein, 1999; Krause & Shaw, 2000). Interventions to provide greater economic security may be necessary to increase such individuals' sense of competence and capability to pursue new productive roles (Bond et al., 1995).

Economic security, however, is not always an environmental condition required for achieving meaning and purpose in later life. Instead, despite their poverty, many low-income older adults, typically women and people of color, have extensive social networks and a strong sense of religiosity that enhance their self-esteem and positive identity. For example, African American older women tend to have large and diverse social networks. They are more likely to live with extended family and to have a broader range of informal instrumental and emotional supports than white older adults. Intergenerational households, in which older women often play major caregiving roles, illustrate the resourcefulness of African American families whose domestic networks expand and contract according to economic resources. Norms of reciprocity are strong and have evolved from a cooperative lifestyle that served as a survival mechanism in earlier times and continues to be a source of support (Johnson, 1999).

Spiritual orientation and religious participation, important in many African American elderly peoples' lives for adaptation and support, are related to feelings of well-being, self-esteem, and personal control. Older low-income African American women often turn to faith in God to cope with their economic hardships and to enhance their feelings of self esteem, well-being, and personal control (Black, 1999). Their religion provides a support network of spiritual help, companionship, advice, financial aid, and opportunities to contribute to the church and community.

In sum, economic security and education are environmental conditions likely to enhance one's sense of competence, control, empowerment, and involvement in productive activities such as volunteering. This occurs because these contextual factors tend to be associated with enhanced communication, social skills, and problem-solving skills. However, economic security and education are not necessary conditions. Race, ethnicity, gender, living arrangements, and the social supports of family, neighborhood, and community, which are not necessarily correlated with socioeconomic class, are also associated with self-esteem, competence, and involvement in productive roles, often through informal helping of others. For example, families that recognize their mutual need for assistance or social exchange across generations—a balance of resources and needs—can enhance feelings of competence and productivity within the family (Krause & Shaw, 2000).

Institutionalized ageism is a major barrier to older adults' learning new productive roles. A significant stressor for many older adults is inadequate knowledge about what is likely to happen in old age along with fears of dependence and decline (Laslett, 1991). Their anticipation is shaped by the age-related negative changes that are often most visible in the media, advertisements, and the general public. Educational programs to plan for a productive Third Age can provide a more realistic portrayal of old age, promote ways to anticipate and deal with age-related physiological and psychological changes, and strengthen older adults' capacity to adapt to stressful events (Bond et al., 1995). Under such conditions, people are more likely to define themselves as empowered active agents of their aging, not passive recipients of negative life events.

Programmatic interventions often seek to increase formal and informal social supports. For example, many volunteer opportunities geared to older adults, such as Foster Grandparents and the Retired and Senior Volunteer Program, build on reciprocity of exchange, often across intergenerational support systems. Other interventions foster an environment in which older people build their own social support networks through mutual help organizations and natural helpers in neighborhoods. Congruent with empowerment practice, older adults may experience feelings of competence, self-esteem, and empowerment through such system-level interventions. The benefits of programs that provide opportunities for elders to become involved in their own communities are well documented, although some gains in self-esteem may decline over time for those who are low income (Bond, et al., 1995; Krause & Shaw, 2000). However, social support tends to be ineffective if it is prescriptive rather than voluntary (Chappell, 1995). Programs that seek to increase social support must attend to its meaning in old age and whether it is, in fact, efficacy enhancing. For example, community-based family care may place too large a burden on social support systems, resulting in caregiver burnout or neglect. With the growing emphasis on social supports and family care, the optimal combination of formal and informal services for community-dwelling older adults needs to be assessed.

System-level interventions encompass creating more opportunities for older people to experience competence—to have goals, some control over their environment, and a feeling of empowerment and ability to contribute productively to their environments. The concept of cultural or structural lag points to how institutions are slow to adjust in response to changing social conditions, such as the growing number of retirees. As a result, voluntary associations, educational programs and volunteer programs have not always acknowledged older adults' growing need to experience competence and productivity. Some societal institutions actually create barriers to older adults' participation, rather than create attractive opportunities (Bass et al., 1993) Programs are needed to stimulate and challenge abilities that older adults elect to sharpen and interests they wish to pursue. Fortunately, lifelong learning for productive roles, Elderhostel, corporate-based training for new work roles, and volunteer programs that match older people's talents with specific tasks are positive environmental interventions.

Conclusion

This chapter has reviewed several theoretical perspectives for conceptualizing productive aging and interpreting it in different life contexts. Our discussion focused on individual competence within a changing environment for older adults and the interrelationship of this approach with empowerment theory. Emphasis was placed on structural and institutional strategies to enhance competence compensation and to create productive opportunities conducive to purpose, meaning, and self-esteem. These strategies along with the conceptualization of productive aging vary by culture, race, ethnicity, health, economic security, gender, and age. What is common to all of them, however, is to alter institutions to value and build on older adults' capacity to engage in productive activities in the Third Age of life.

References

Achenbaum, W. A., & Bengtson, V. C. (1994). Re-engaging the disengagement theory of aging: Or the history and assessment of theory development in gerontology. *Gerontologist, 34,* 756–763.

Baars, J. (1991). The challenge of critical studies. *Journal of Aging Studies, 5*(3), 219–243.

Baltes, P. B., & Baltes, M. M. (1990). Psychological perspectives on successful aging: The model with selective optimization and compensation. In P. B. Baltes & M. M. Baltes (Eds.), *Successful aging: Perspectives from the social sciences* (pp. 1–34). Cambridge, England: Cambridge University Press.

Bass, S. A., Caro, F. G., & Chen, Y. P. (1993). Introduction: Achieving a productive aging society. In S. A. Bass, F. G. Caro, & Y. P. Chen (Eds.), *Achieving a productive aging society* (pp. 3–26) Westport, CT: Auburn House.

Belle, D. (1990). Poverty and women's mental health. *American Psychologist, 4,* 385–389.

Bengtson, V. (1993). Is the "contract across generations" changing? Effects of population aging on obligations and expectations across age groups. In V. Bengtson & V. W. Achenbaum (Eds.), *The changing contract across generations* (pp. 3–24). New York: Aldine de Gruyter.

Bengtson, V. L. (1969). Occupational differences in retirement. In R. J. Havighurst, M. A. Munnicks, B. C. Neugarten, & H. Thomas (Eds.), *Adjustments to retirement: A cross national study* (pp. 53–70) Assen, The Netherlands: Van Gorkum.

Bengtson, V. L., & Achenbaum, W.A. (1993). *The changing contract across generations.* New York: Aldine de Gruyter.

Bengtson, V. L., & Schaie, W. H. (1989). *The course of later life: Research and reflections.* New York: Springer.

Black, H. K. (1999). Poverty and prayer: Spiritual narratives of elder African American women. *Review of Religious Research, 40,* 359–374.

Blau, Z. (1973). *Old age in a changing society.* New York: New Viewpoints.

Bond, A., Cutler, S. J., & Grams, A. (Eds.). (1995). *Promoting successful and productive aging.* Thousand Oaks, CA: Sage Publications.

Bury, M. (1995). Ageing, gender and sociological theory. In S. Arber & J. Ginn (Eds.), *Connecting gender and aging: A sociological approach* (pp. 15–29). Buckingham, England: Open University Press.

Buzzell, M., Meredith, S., Monna, K., Ritchie, L., & Sergeant, D. (1993). *Personhood–A teaching package.* Hamilton, Ontario: McMaster University Press.

Cavan, R. S., Burgess, E. W., Goldhamer, H., & Havighurst, R. J. (1949). *Personal adjustment in old age.* Chicago: Science Research Associates.

Chappell, N. (1995). Informal social support. In L. A. Bond, S. J. Cutler, & A. Grams (Eds.), *Promoting successful and productive aging* (pp. 171–185). Thousand Oaks, CA: Sage Publications.

Cole, T. R. (1992). *The journey of life: A cultural history of aging in America.* Cambridge, England: Cambridge University Press.

Cole, T. R., Achenbaum, W. A., Jakobi, P. L., & Kastenbaum, R. (Eds.). (1993). *Voices and visions of aging: Toward a critical gerontology.* New York: Springer.

Conrad, C. (1992). Old age in the modern and postmodern world. In T. Cole, D. V. Tassell, & R. Kastenbaum (Eds.), *Handbook of the humanities and aging* (pp. 62-95). New York: Springer.

Cottrell, L. (1942). The adjustment of the individual to his age and sex roles. *American Sociological Review 7,* 617–620.

Covey, H. A. (1981). A reconceptualization of continuity theory: Some preliminary thoughts. *Gerontologist, 2,* 628–633.

Cowgill, D., & Holmes, L. D. (1972). *Aging and modernization.* New York: Appleton-Century Crofts.

Cumming, E., & Henry, W. E. (1961). *Growing old.* New York: Basic Books.

Danigelis, N. C., & McIntosh, B. R. (1993). Resources and the productive activity of elders: Race and gender as contexts. *Journal of Gerontology, 48*B, S192–S203.

Dixon, R. A. (1995). Promoting competence through compensation. In L. A. Bond, S. J. Cutler, & A. Grams (Eds.), *Promoting successful and productive aging* (pp. 220–239). Thousand Oaks, CA: Sage Publications.

Dowd, J. J. (1975). Aging as exchange: a preface to theory. *Journal of Gerontology 30,* 584–594.

Erikson, E. H. (1982). *The life cycle completed: A review.* New York: W. W. Norton.

Erikson, E. H., & Erikson, J. M. (1981). On generativity and identity: From a conversation with Erik and Joan Erikson. *Harvard Educational Review, 51,* 249–69.

Estes, C. L. (1979). *The aging enterprise.* San Francisco: Jossey-Bass.

Estes, C. L., Gerard, L. E., & Swan, J. S. (1984). *Political economy, health, and aging.* Boston: Little, Brown.

Estes, C. L., & Binney, E. A. (1989). The biomedicalization of aging: Dangers and dilemmas. *Gerontologist, 29,* 587–598.

Estes, C. L., Linkins, K. W., & Binney, E. A. (1996). The political economy of aging. In R. H. Binstock & L. K. George (Eds.), *Handbook of aging and the social sciences* (4th ed.). San Diego, Academic Press.

Estes, C. L., & Associates. (2001). *Social policy and aging: A critical perspective*. Thousand Oaks, CA: Sage Publications.

Fahey, M. C. (1996). Social work education and the field of aging. *Gerontologist, 36*, 36–41.

Freedman, M. (1999). *Prime time: How baby boomers will revolutionize retirement and transform America*. New York: Public Affairs.

Freedman, M. (2001) Structural lead: Building new institutions for an aging America. In N. Morrow-Howell, J. Hinterlong, & M. Sherraden (Eds.), *Productive aging: Concepts and Challenges* (pp. 245-259). Baltimore: Johns Hopkins University Press.

Friedan, B. (1993). *The fountain of age*. New York: Simon & Schuster.

Giddens, A. (1991). *Modernity and self-identity*. Cambridge, England: Polity Press.

Gubrium, J. F. (1973). *The myth of the golden years*. Springfield, IL: Charles C. Thomas.

Gubrium, J. F. (1993). *Speaking of life: Horizons of meaning for nursing home residents*. New York: Aldine de Gruyter.

Gutierrez, L. M. (1990). Working with women of color: An empowerment perspective. *Social Work, 35*, 149–163.

Guttierez, L. M., Parsons, R. J., & Cox, E. G. (Eds.) (1998). Empowerment in social work practice. Pacific Grove, CA: Brooks/ Cole.

Hagestad, G., & Neugarten, B. (1985). Age and the life course. In R. Binstock & E. Shanas (Eds.), *Handbook of aging and the social sciences* (pp. 35–61). New York: Van Nostrand Reinhold.

Havighurst, R. J. (1954). Flexibility and the social roles of the retired. *American Journal of Gerontology, 59*(1/2), 309–311.

Havighurst, R. J. (1963). Successful aging. In R. H. Williams, C. Tibbitts, W. Donahue, & J. Birren (Eds.), *Processes of aging: social and psychological perspectives* (pp. 299–320). New York: Atherton Press.

Havighurst, R. J. (1968). Personality and patterns of aging. *Gerontologist, 38*, 20–23.

Hendricks, J. (1995). Exchange theory in aging. In G. Maddox (Ed.), *The encyclopedia of aging* (pp. 000–000). New York: Springer.

Herzog, A. R. (1989). Age differences in productive activity. *Journals of Gerontology, 44*, S129–S138.

Herzog, A. R., & House, J. S. (1991). Productive activities and ageing well. *Generations, 1991*, 49–54.

Holstein, M. (1999). Women and productive aging: Troubling implications. In M. Minkler & C. Estes (Eds.) *Critical gerontology: Perspectives from political and moral economy* (pp. 359–373). Amityville, NY: Baywood.

Johnson, C. L. (1999). Fictive kin among oldest old African Americans in the San Francisco Bay area. *Journals of Gerontology, 54*B, S386–S375.

Kaminsky, M. (1993). Definitional ceremonies: Depoliticizing and reenchanting the culture of age. In T. R. Cole, W. A. Achenbaum, P. Jakobi, & R. Kastenbaum (Eds.), *Voices and visions of aging: Toward a critical gerontology*. New York: Springer.

Kenyon, G. (1996). Ethical issues in ageing and biography. *Ageing and Society, 16*(6), 659–676.

Krause, N. (1995). Promoting competence through compensation. In L. A. Bond, S. J. Cutler, & A. Grams (Eds.), *Promoting successful and productive aging* (pp. 171–185). Thousand Oaks, CA: Sage Publications.

Krause, N., & Shaw, B. A. (2000). Giving social support to others: Socioeconomic status, and changes in self-esteem in late life. *Journals of Gerontology 55*B(6), S323–S333.

Kumar, K. (1995). *From post-industrial to post-modern society*. Oxford, England: Basil Blackwell.

Laslett, P. (1991). *A fresh map of life: The emergence of the third age*. Cambridge, MA: Harvard University Press.

Lawton, M. P. (1975). Competence, environmental press, and the adaptation of older people. In P. G. Windley & G. Ernst (Eds.), *Theory development in environment and aging*. Washington, DC: Gerontological Society of America.

Lawton, M. P. (1989). Behavior-relevant ecological factors. In K. W. Schaie & C. Scholar (Eds.), *Social structure and aging: Psychological processes*. Hillsdale, NJ: Lawrence Erlbaum.

Lawton, M. P., & Nahemow, L. (1973). Ecology and the aging process. In C. Eisdorfer & M. P. Lawton (Eds.), *Psychology of adult development and aging* (pp. 619–674). Washington, DC: American Psychological Association.

Lynott, R. J., & Lynott, P. P. (1996). Tracing the course of theoretical development in the sociology of aging. *Gerontologist, 36*, 749–760.

Maluccio, A. N. (1981). *Promoting competence in clients*. New York: Free Press.

Marshall, V. W. (1994). Sociology and psychology in the theoretical legacy of the Kansas City studies. *The Gerontologist, 34*, 768–774.

McIntosh, B. R., & Danigelis, N. C. (1995). Race, gender and the relevance of productive activity for elders' affect. *Journals of Gerontology, 50*B, S44–S54.

Meredith, S. D., & Wells, L. (1994). An empowerment perspective: A key factor in meeting the challenge of gerontological social work. In L. Gutierrez & P. Nurius (Eds.), *Education and research for empowerment practice* (pp. 137–148). Seattle: University of Washington School of Social Work Center for Policy and Practice Research.

Minkler, M., & Cole, T. R. (1998). Political and moral economy: getting to know one another. In M. Minkler & C. Estes (Eds.), *Critical gerontology: Perspectives from political and moral economy* (pp. 37–50). Amityville, NY: Baywood Press.

Minkler, M., & Estes, C. (Eds.). (1998). *Critical gerontology: Perspectives from political and moral economy*. Amityville, NY: Baywood Press.

Moen, P. (1995). A life-course approach to postretirement roles and well-being. In L. A. Bond, S. J. Cutler, & A. Grams (Eds.), *Promoting successful and productive aging* (pp. 171–185). Thousand Oaks, CA: Sage Publications.

Moody, H. R. (1988). Toward a critical gerontology: The contribution of the humanities to theories of aging. In J. E. Birren & V. L. Bengston (Eds.), *Emergent theories of aging* (pp. 19–40). New York: Springer.

Moody, H. R. (1992). Gerontology and critical theory. *Gerontologist, 32*, 294–295.

Moody, H. R. (1993). Overview: What is critical gerontology and why is it important? In T. R. Cole, W. A. Achenbaum, P. Jakobi, & R. Kastenbaum (Eds.), *Voices and visions of aging: Toward a critical gerontology* (pp. xi–xii). New York: Springer.

Moody, H. R. (2001). Productive aging and the ideology of old age. In N. Morrow-Howell, J. Hinterlong, & M. Sherraden, (Eds.), *Productive aging: Concepts and challenges* (pp. 175–196). Baltimore: Johns Hopkins Press.

Morgan, J. (1986). Unpaid productive activity over the life course. In Committee on an Aging Society, National Research Council (Ed.), *Productive roles in an older society*. Washington, DC: National Academy Press.

Morrow-Howell, N., & Sherraden, M. (2001). Advancing research on productivity in later life. In N. Morrow-Howell, J. E. Hinterlong, & M. W. Sherraden (Eds.). *Productive aging: Concepts and challenges* (pp. 285–311). Baltimore: Johns Hopkins University Press.

Myles, J. (1984). *Old age in the welfare state: The political economy of public pensions.* Lawrence: University of Kansas Press.

Neugarten, B. L., & Hagestad, G. O. (1976). Age and the life course. In R. Binstock & E. Shanas (Eds.), *Handbook of aging and the social sciences* (pp. 35–55). New York: Van Nostrand Reinhold.

Parmelee, P. A., & Lawton, M. P. (1990). The design of special environments for the aged. In J. E. Birren & K. W. Schaie (Eds.), *Handbook of the psychology of aging.* San Diego, Academic Press.

Phillipson, C. (1996). Interpretations of aging: Perspectives from humanistic gerontology. *Ageing and Society, 16,* 359–369.

Phillipson, C. (1998). *Reconstructing old age: New agendas in social theory and practice.* Thousand Oaks, CA: Sage Publications.

Phillipson, C., & Walker, A. (1987). The case for critical gerontology. In S. DiGregorio (Ed.), *Social gerontology: New directions.* London: Croom Helm.

Riley, M. W., Johnson, M., & Foner, A. (Eds.). (1972). *Aging and society: Vol. 3. A sociology of age stratification.* New York: Russell Sage Foundation.

Riley, M. W., Kahn, R. L., & Foner, A. (Eds.). (1994). *Age and structural lag: Society's failure to provide meaningful opportunities in work, family and leisure.* New York: John Wiley & Sons.

Riley, M. W., & Loscocco, K. A. (1994). The changing structure of work opportunities: Toward an age-integrated society. In R. P. Abeles, H. C. Gift, & M. G. Ory (Eds.), *Aging and quality of life.* New York: Springer.

Riley, M. W., & Riley, J. W. (1994). Age integration and the lives of older people. *Gerontologist, 34,* 110–115.

Robertson, A. (1998). Beyond apocalyptic demography: Toward a moral economy of interdependence. In M. Minkler & C. Estes (Eds.), *Critical gerontology: Perspectives from political and moral economy* (pp. 55–74). Amityville, NY: Baywood Press.

Rosow, J. (1985). Status and role change through the life cycle. In R. Binstock & E. Shanas (Eds.), *Handbook of aging and the social sciences.* New York: Van Nostrand Reinhold.

Sherraden, M., Morrow-Howell, N., Hinterlong, J., & Rozario, P. (2001). Productive aging: Theoretical choices and directions. In N. Morrow-Howell, J. Hinterlong, & M. Sherraden (Eds.), *Productive aging: Concepts and challenges* (pp. 260–284). Baltimore: Johns Hopkins University Press.

Taylor, C. (1989). *Sources of the self.* Cambridge, England: Cambridge University Press.

Turner, B. (1989). Ageing, status politics and sociological theory. *British Journal of Gerontology, 40,* 588–606.

Walker, A. (1981). Towards a political economy of old age. *Ageing and Society, 1,* 73–94.

Zautra, A. J., Reich, J. W., & Newsom, J. T. (1995). Autonomy and sense of control among older adults: An examination of their effects on mental health. In L. A. Bond, S. J. Cutler, & A. Grams (Eds.), *Promoting successful and productive aging* (pp. 153–171). Thousand Oaks, CA: Sage Publications.

Part 2

Dimensions of Productive Aging

4

Labor Force Participation of Older Adults: Benefits, Barriers, and Social Work Interactions

Michàl E. Mor-Barak and Steve Wilson

ocial work is faced with a unique challenge in the 21st century: Americans are getting older, and the workplace has done little to prepare for the growth of the aging workforce. By the year 2020, people age 55 and older are projected to exceed 20 percent of the population, compared with 12.5 percent in 1990 (Social Security Administration [SSA], 1999). With improved health, increased life expectancy, and a general desire to continue working, the number of individuals age 55 and over in the workforce will continue to grow over the next few decades. However, although there are increasing numbers of older workers on the job and available for work, the work environment is changing in ways that are detrimental for this population. Most problematic are the systemic barriers that send conflicting and often negative messages to the older worker, clearly indicating a lack of enthusiasm to develop and fully use this human capital. In an examination of the current problems of older workers, multiple contradictions emerge:

- Although demographic trends indicate a shrinking workforce because of diminishing cohorts of younger workers, there is still an expectation that older workers retire at the normative age or even earlier.
- Despite laws aimed at preventing age discrimination, overt and covert practices against hiring and retaining older adults are still prevalent in many organizations.
- Although our social and economic well-being could benefit from the inclusion of older workers, legislation and public policies to enhance the employment opportunities of mature workers have been limited.

These contradictions, coupled with young managers' myths and stereotypes of older workers, have led to the inevitable disenfranchisement of older workers. Clearly, there is a growing social problem that calls for innovative social work interventions. Social workers can play an important role on multisystemic levels: by helping organizations prepare for the changing workforce, by helping older adults better prepare for a 21st century workplace, and by helping shape public policy for greater advocacy for this underrepresented group.

Workforce Demographic Trends

The demographics of the U.S. workforce have changed dramatically over the last several decades. Since 1950 the proportion of the U.S. population age 65 or older has increased from 8 percent to 12 percent. As members of the baby boom generation—people born between 1946 and 1964—approach retirement age, the demographic profile of the U.S. population will undergo a profound change. By 2050, when the last of the baby boomers will have entered older adulthood, it is estimated that more than 30 percent of the population will be over 55 (U.S. Census Bureau, 2000b; Figure 4-1). These demographic trends are a result of the decline in fertility rates and the steady increase in life expectancy. In 1960, the baby boom generation averaged 3.61 children per woman; by 2020, the fertility rate is projected to be down to 1.9 children per woman (SSA, 1999).

The impact of these demographic changes on the U.S. workforce will continue to be dramatic. The number of young people entering the workforce after the baby boom generation will decline. Over the next 10 years, the number of people ages 25 to 54—the ages when labor force participation rates are at their highest—is projected

Figure 4-1

Number of People 55 Years of Age or Older: 2000–2050

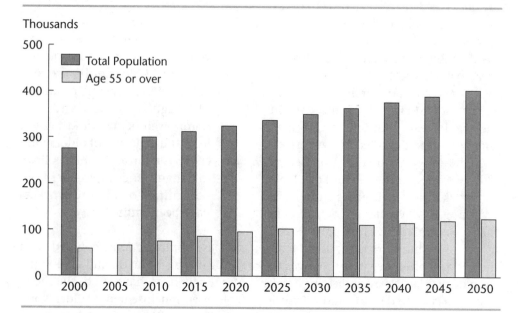

SOURCE: U.S. Census Bureau Population Projections. Available online at http://www.census.gov/ipc/www/usinterimproj/

to increase by only 2.5 percent. At the same time, the number of people ages 55 to 64 is expected to increase by more than 47 percent (U.S. Census Bureau, 2000b). Oddly, a marked decrease in labor force participation among older adults is accompanying this population shift. Although there are more older adults in society now and they are healthier than ever before, they are less involved in work than they have ever been. For example, in 1900, two-thirds of U.S. men who were 65 or older were working; in 1950, the number was down to 45 percent, and the most recent figures show less than 30 percent involvement (Federal Interagency Forum on Aging-Related Statistics, 2000).

Until the past decade or so, this pattern did not apply to women. Women's employment was influenced by family caregiving roles, including elder and child care, which often interrupted the life cycle of women's paid employment. As a result, women's retirement received little attention as a distinctive phenomenon until recently. More recently, women's work patterns have become similar to those of men, including the pattern of decline in labor force participation of women as they age (Figure 4-2). This trend toward earlier retirement for both men and women, despite the current and projected shortage in younger workers, raises some questions about the impact of public and private policies on the match between demographic trends and workforce participation.

The increase in the number of older adults who retire early is partly a result of rising living standards in the United

Figure 4-2

Labor Force Participation of Adults Ages 55 and Older by Gender: 1991–2000

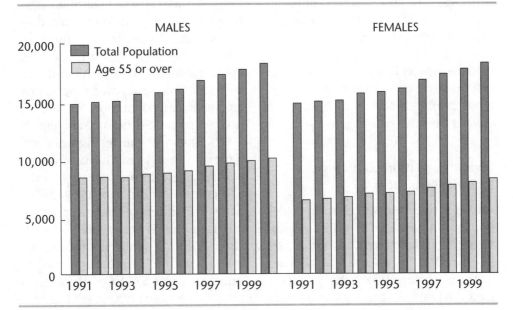

Source: U.S. Census Bureau. (2000). *Current population survey: Design and methodology* (Technical Paper No. 63). Washington, DC: U.S. Department of Commerce.

States and indicates a desirable improvement in economic well-being. However, it also reflects the inflexibility of the workplace. Most work organizations do not actively recruit older people, nor do they make special efforts to accommodate their needs, such as by offering part-time employment and flexible hours. There are strong indications that many retirees would welcome the opportunity to go back to work. Such continued activity corresponds to a wish to remain contributing members of society, as well as to supplement incomes. A recent survey of baby boomers (American Association of Retired People [AARP], 1998) showed that more than 70 percent expect to work at least part-time post-retirement, which reflects a strong interest in continuing their involvement with the work world. This also indicates that large numbers of older workers will move from long-tenure or career jobs to "bridge" or "transitional" employment before entering full-time retirement (AARP). To facilitate this development, society in general and the workplace in particular must overcome the institutional barriers to employment of older adults that have been created over the years.

Diversity and Its Implications for Older Employees

Although the poverty rates for the older population have declined in both absolute and relative terms over the past two decades, the poverty rates of older women, African Americans, and Hispanics remain well above the average for their age group. The economic security package that emerged in the

post-World War II United States was intended to give older people a secure position in the economy. The ideal package included full employment, social security and private pensions, job-based health insurance, and seniority protection. Data confirm that the majority of today's older workers have secured the benefits of career employment, stable earnings, and adequate pensions. These relative advantages, however, are not evenly distributed throughout the older population (Sum & Fogg, 1990). Specifically, four groups have experienced the most severe difficulties: (1) ethnic minority groups, (2) women living alone, (3) working poor people, and (4) displaced workers. These vulnerable groups are the most rapidly growing segments of the older population (Doeringer, 1990).

In 1986, for example, the poverty rate among older black families was four times as high as that of white families, and older Hispanic families experienced a poverty rate more than three times higher than that of white, non-Hispanic families. Currently, 21.9 percent of African Americans and 21.8 percent of Hispanics are living in poverty (Current Population Survey, Annual Social and Economic Supplement, 2002). The most glaring disparity of financial status is in the median net worth (assets minus debts) of older adults age 65 or older. In 1999 median net worth among older African American households was estimated to be about $13,000, while the median net worth of older income for white Americans was $181,000 (Federal Interagency Forum on Aging Related Statistics, 2000). Older women, especially those living alone, have continued to live in poverty approximately 60 percent more frequently than men (Sum & Fogg, 1990).

These groups—women and ethnic minorities—are more likely to face discrimination in the workplace because of their race-ethnicity, gender, and age. They are also more likely to be excluded from important information networks and the decision-making process, and they are less likely to obtain and retain jobs (Mor-Barak, 2000). The changing demography of the nation's older population, including the growing numbers of those who are members of racial and ethnic minorities, will complicate the task of combating future poverty problems among elderly people.

How Old Is Old? Legislation and Social Policy Relevant to Retirement Age

One of the most common questions with respect to older workers is, when is an employee considered old? Retirement at a specific age is an artifact of the social security laws. The United States first introduced the standard retirement age in 1935 when the Social Security Act established 65 as the minimum age at which people can obtain retirement benefits (with a few exceptions). Congress selected age 65 as a compromise between age 60, which appeared too low from a cost standpoint, and age 70, which appeared too high—given that life expectancy at the time was 59 years for men and 63 years for women (AARP, 1998). Since 1956 women have had the option to take reduced benefits at age 62, and since 1961 this option has also been available to men. As a result, age 62 has been defined as the early eligibility age (EEA),

and 65 is considered the normal retirement age (NRA).

Although there is no agreement on any given number, there seems to be a consensus forming around the age of 55 as the defining point between "middle-aged" and "older" employees. Age 55 is useful, because many individuals consider turning 50 an important crossroads in their lives. Furthermore, organizations begin offering early retirement options at this age, which also demonstrates their disinclination to make future investments in these workers. But most important, it is at approximately age 50 that certain types of age discrimination have traditionally become operable (Shea, 1991). Therefore, we define the older labor force in this chapter as workers 55 years of age or older.

Historically, humane considerations were claimed to be the main reason for a set retirement age. Because much of the labor in the early and middle stages of the Industrial Revolution consisted of heavy, physical effort over a long work day and work week, relief through retirement was a desirable goal. In 1889, under the leadership of its chancellor, Otto von Bismarck, Germany (at the time, the Prussian Empire) became the first nation in the world to adopt an old age social insurance program and to introduce a standard retirement age (www.ssa.gov, the official Web site of the Social Security Administration). The desire to keep the German economy operating at maximum efficiency and to stave off calls for more radical socialist alternatives motivated Bismarck to introduce social insurance in Germany. Bismarck is said to have offered the benefit of retirement pensions at age 70 first to his soldiers as a reward for prolonged and loyal service in his army. At the time, this was not a costly proposition, given that many of the soldiers died in battle and those who survived rarely reached age 70 (the average life expectancy was 45).

Federal law has now abolished any mandatory retirement age except for some special categories of employees (for example, airline pilots). Over the years, retirement at age 65 has acquired certain conveniences, leading to its perception and de facto adoption as normative. First, it enables employers to dispense with the services of older workers gracefully, avoiding the administrative difficulties of selectively firing often "faithful" workers. Second, it enables older workers to salvage more self-respect when they are members of a class that employers are required to release from the workforce than they would if they were individually removed. Third, it enables younger workers to look forward both to advancement and to the benefits of seniority.

These conveniences do not mean that the current retirement system is beneficial for everyone. Although many people still perceive retirement as a great achievement for the worker, those who feel that they can and want to continue participating in the workforce now view retirement as an obstacle. Improved health and increased life expectancy prolong the period in which older adults can be productive in society. In addition, the larger variety of jobs that do not demand physical strength enables more older people to continue working. These changes call for policy alterations

to provide older adults with options and real choices with respect to work and retirement.

A Matrix Model for Labor Force Participation of Older Adults

A two-dimensional (3 × 3) model can provide a deeper understanding of the converging and conflicting issues faced by older adults who wish to continue their employment or who are returning to work after retirement (Table 4-1). By using a systems perspective (Anderson, Carter, & Lowe, 1999), the benefits for the continued employment of older adults, the barriers that they face, and the social work interventions that could help them achieve their goals can each be examined from three distinct system levels: the personal, the organizational, and the social/cultural.

Benefits of Continued Employment for Older Adults

Personal Benefits. From a personal perspective, work not only helps meet retirees' economic needs, but also contributes to an increased sense of accomplishment and responsibility, and provides an important emotional/social outlet (Alexander & Kaye, 1997). The large percentage of baby boomers planning for post-retirement employment contrasts with the actual work participation rates of current or past retirees. Older adults' motivations to continue active employment include economic need, health care coverage, and emotional/social fulfillment.

Although the majority of older people and their families do not experience poverty, older workers are more likely to lose their jobs and to experience

Table 4-1

Benefits, Barriers, and Social Work Interventions with Older Workers

	Benefits	Barriers	Social Work Intervention
Personal	Financial necessity	Discouragement resulting from age discrimination	Counseling and supporting older workers and their families
	Health care coverage		
	Social/emotional fulfillment	Lack of education and high technology skills	Elder care programs
		Physical limitations	Retirement planning and job counseling
Organizational	Fewer younger workers available	Forced or "encouraged" retirement	Job modifications
	Desirable work qualities of older worker	Myths and prejudices about older workers	Flexible options and benefit packages
		Financial barriers	Improved training programs
	Age discrimination legal costs		
Social/cultural	Economic imperatives	Youth orientation	Ending age discrimination in the workplace
	Diminishing work force	Limited enforcement of existing laws	Providing programs that link older workers with employers
	Social and cultural contributions of older workers	Lack of political advocacy for older workers	Making the workplace more inclusive

greater financial difficulties than younger workers. The economic security package that emerged in the United States after World War II was intended to give older people a secure position in the economy. Data confirm that the majority of today's older workers have secured the benefits of career employment, stable earnings, and adequate pensions. As indicated earlier, however, these relative advantages are not evenly spread throughout the older population. Poverty rates tend to be higher among those who did not secure a complete retirement package, primarily women living alone, and among members of ethnic and racial minority groups (Doeringer, 1990). Economic necessity is often the main motivation for older adults to seek employment or continue their employment beyond the retirement age.

In recent years, employers have become less likely to pay the entire cost of retirees' health insurance. Many are shifting costs to their current retirees or eliminating benefits to future retirees (Herz, 1995). Employer decisions on medical benefits and the increase of health costs with age play an important role in the work and retirement decisions for those over age 50. Continuing to work after retirement or postponing retirement enables workers to share the costs of their medical insurance with their employers.

If the primary reason cited for continuing to work in later years is financial necessity, the second most common reason is emotional–social fulfillment (Fontana, 1990; Rock, 1989). This suggests that older workers are looking not only for sufficient compensation in their work (both pre- and post-retirement), but also for a feeling of usefulness and an opportunity to share their knowledge and experience with the following generations (Mor-Barak, 1995). According to a 1998 study by the AARP, more than one-third of retiring baby boomers say that they will continue to work primarily for the sake of interest and personal enjoyment (AARP, 1998).

Organizational Benefits. There are several incentives for organizations to employ older workers, including the anticipated shortage of qualified younger workers, the desirable work qualities of older workers (for example, loyalty, punctuality, commitment), and the legal costs involved in discriminating against older workers.

As indicated earlier, the demographic projections show increasing labor force shortages in the coming decades. As members of the baby boomer generation gradually retire, there are fewer young people in the next cohorts to replace them in the workplace. Labor force projections through 2008 indicate that the number of workers ages 16 to 24 will increase 15 percent through 2008, and the number of workers ages 25 to 54 will increase only 5.5 percent (Figure 4-3). These data contrast with a 48 percent increase in the number of older workers through this same time period (Fullerton, 1999). Although younger workers are traditionally more educated, there will inevitably be a numerical differential in the workforce as a declining number of younger workers gradually replace the human capital of older workers. Work organizations, therefore, need to encourage older workers to stay longer at their jobs or to come back to modified positions.

An AARP study (2000) found that older employees possess many of the qualities that companies consider most desirable in any employee. Older workers are mature; their judgment tends to be sound, and they are less inclined toward impulsive risk. Older people are not inherently more conservative than younger people, but they base their decisions on lifelong experiences or wisdom. They have a greater ability for synthesis: As people approach older adulthood, they begin to synthesize a lifetime of observations, facts, and data into "elaborate and often elegant systems of thought that allow them to extrapolate and draw new conclusions about their experiences and learning" (Shea, 1991, p. 68). This synthesized or "distilled" knowledge can help to solve organizational problems. Most important, older

Figure 4-3

Labor Force Projections to 2008

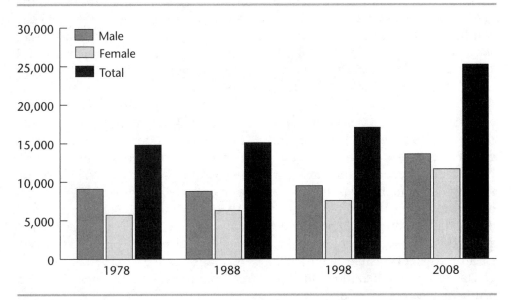

Source: U.S. Bureau of the Census. (1999). *Current population survey*. Washington, DC: U.S. Department of Commerce.

workers are universally recognized as loyal and committed to the work organization, and they have excellent work ethics (AARP, 2000).

The Age Discrimination in Employment Act (ADEA, P.L. 90-202), enacted in 1967, protects older adults in hiring, firing, and other employment practices. Still, many employers engage in subtle discriminatory practices in an attempt to replace older workers with younger ones or eliminate their jobs altogether. The number of cases in which investigators found "reasonable cause" to suspect age discrimination has risen dramatically, from 2.2 percent in 1992 to 8.3 percent in 1999. The monetary judgments to plaintiffs who win their cases in court have also sharply increased. In 1996, for example, the U.S. Equal Employment Opportu-

nity Commission (EEOC) settled an age bias case brought on behalf of 2,000 former employees of the Martin Marietta Corporation for $13 million (http://www.eeoc.gov/press/11-21-96.html). It is often difficult to prove age discrimination, but the damages awarded in a successful lawsuit can be significant. Eliminating or reducing such potential costs is a strong incentive for employers to create a more hospitable environment for older workers.

Social/Cultural Benefits. From a social/cultural perspective, the incentives for the continued employment of older adults include economic imperatives, broad workforce issues, and the social and cultural contributions of this group, through their continued employment, to the broader society.

The ratio of working age adults (ages 16 to 64) to retirees (age 65 or over) is projected to fall from 5.1:1 in 2000 to 2.9:1 in 2050 (Table 4-2).This decrease will have a detrimental effect on the social security system (SSA, 2002). In 1935, when social security was conceived, there were roughly 16 workers for every beneficiary—more than enough to support a "pay-as-you-go" program. Over time, however, program expansions and behavioral changes have steadily reduced this ratio, and shifting demographics will further reduce the worker-to-beneficiary ratio during the next 30 years. If no changes are made to the social security system, trust funds will be exhausted in 2032, and tax revenues at that time will cover only three-quarters of benefit payments. Many older adults are dependent on social security as their sole or main source of income and as a means to offset increasing health care expenditures. In 1998, annual out-of-pocket expenditures on health care—which included health insurance premiums, medical services, supplies, and prescription drugs—ranged from 9 percent to 16 percent of total expenditures among households headed by older people (Federal Interagency Forum on Aging-Related Statistics, 2000). Baby boomers'

decisions about work and retirement will play an important part in alleviating or exacerbating the strains on the social security system. Extending the work lives of older workers will serve the national interest as much as it will the employers' and workers' interests (see Table 4-2).

Given the impending labor force crunch that will result from the shrinking younger cohorts, corporate efforts to encourage workers to continue working as long as possible would serve the economy well (Reynolds, 1994). A survey by the International Foundation of Employee Benefit Plans reported that only 24 percent of Fortune 2,000 corporations made efforts to retain employees after they reach retirement age, and only 13 percent of these companies claimed to hire older workers who have already retired from another job. According to recent estimates, some 70 percent of firms that offer defined benefit pension plans are subsidizing their employees' early retirement. Reversing the trend toward early retirement cannot be left to corporate America alone; it requires public policies that will promote work opportunities for those older adults who wish to stay in the workforce, thereby providing some relief to the projected labor force shortages.

Table 4-2

Ratio of Younger Workers to Older Retirees, 2000–2050

Age	2000	2010	2020	2030	2040	2050
16–64	177,974	196,586	202,498	206,903	221,276	236,602
65+	34,835	39,715	53,733	70,319	77,177	81,999
Ratio	5.1:1	5.0:1	3.8:1	3.0:1	2.9:1	2.9:1

NOTE: Numbers in 000s.
SOURCE: U.S. Census Bureau (2000).

Older adults are the repositories of any culture's traditions and history, and they possess important experiences that can be beneficial to the following generations. Staying involved, particularly in jobs that provide opportunities for contact with younger people, allows for the intergenerational transfer of knowledge and experience. This transfer is important not only to the people involved in the interaction, but also to the larger society.

Barriers to Employment of Older Adults

Older workers face multiple obstacles to their continued employment. These barriers exist on several levels from the personal (for example, health and esteem barriers), through the organizational (for example, age discrimination in the workplace), to the social/cultural (for example, the absence of organized advocacy groups). Many employers simply see no benefit in encouraging longer work lives. Many high-technology firms prefer to hire someone who is young and willing to work long hours for less than the cost of an older, more experienced worker. This intolerance or pragmatism hits older workers hardest. Further, there are few immediate consequences to not hiring or eliminating older employees from the workforce. The loss of their experience and wisdom is often not felt immediately, and the short-term economic impact of discriminatory practices is very limited.

Personal Barriers. Faced with overt and covert age discrimination, limited opportunities for professional development, and an obvious emphasis on hiring and promoting younger employees, many older workers choose to retire early despite a desire to continue working. This semivoluntary job loss, although shrouded in the positive light of retirement with the stereotypical travel and leisure, can have powerful negative effects on psychological and physical health. Major career transitions, especially those that are sudden and unexpected, are times of stress, discouragement, and self-doubt (London, 1996). Retirement can also have a devastating financial impact on those who do not have the means to retire comfortably.

The ADEA was enacted to support employment of older people based on their ability rather than their age and to prohibit arbitrary age discrimination in employment and promotion opportunities. Many older individuals who have experienced age discrimination choose not to fight it because suing for age bias is expensive, emotionally exhausting, and rarely successful. The employer is favored, partly because of the 1993 Supreme Court decision in *Hazen Paper Co. v. Biggins.* The Supreme Court's ruling in this case suggested, in part, that a company's action does not necessarily constitute age discrimination if the consequences of that action are more harmful to older workers than to younger workers. This judgment has been interpreted broadly such that employers now justify the reduction of an older workforce on the basis of cost rather than age (Silbergeld & Tuvim, 1993).

Technological skills have taken on a greater importance in today's workforce. Many older workers lack the technical education and computer skills that younger people learn in college and even in high school. Older workers often feel that they cannot compete along side their younger counterparts. Although some may possess appropriate skills, there is an ongoing need for people who can understand, operate, and ultimately repair highly sophisticated computer systems. Just as they are reluctant to battle the age discrimination dragon, many older workers take themselves out of competition instead of facing the humiliation of rejection and failure.

Physical limitations also play a role in retirement decisions for many older workers. The incidence of physical impairments and health problems does increase with age. Physical declines are often gradual, however, and older individuals still at work tend to adapt by acquiring skills or switching to positions that are less physically demanding (Sterns & Sterns, 1995). Again, the perceptions of limited work capability because of physical demands tend to be self-imposed or the result of employer stereotypes rather than the inherent reality.

Organizational Barriers. Organizations in the United States have been concerned with eliminating sexism and racism in the workplace as the public consciousness has risen about the prejudices toward women and minorities. Unfortunately, these attitudes have not translated to attitudes toward older workers, who are still considered disposable (London, 1996; Thornburg, 1995).

The private sector has encouraged the early retirement of older workers in recent decades for a number of reasons. First, the cost of health benefits tends to increase substantially as workers age. Second, most organizations have wanted to make room at the top for younger workers who are rising up the career ladder. Third, many employers feel it is not economically prudent to retain older workers at their compensation levels, which generally relate to their years of seniority. Finally, the number of employers who are downsizing, participating in mergers, and closing plants has increased, and older workers are often the first to be let go in an economic downturn.

Many human resource managers still hold outdated and untrue cultural stereotypes that older workers are inflexible, averse to change, and resistant to learning new technology. Today's older worker tends to have a much longer life expectancy, is more health conscious, and is employed in work that is less physically demanding than was the case several generations ago. However, the stereotypes persist, particularly among younger managers. Despite the fact that there are as many advantages to hiring older workers as younger ones, the recent study by the AARP (2000) clearly demonstrated that companies are more likely to hire younger workers than older workers. Although managers report positive attitudes toward older workers, their corporate practices contradict their words.

Although strictly prohibited by the ADEA, older workers also experience organizational barriers associated with long-term seniority. The later career worker becomes particularly vulnerable to "opportunistic downsizing" or reduction-in-workforce strategies. In such cases, older workers have multiple factors working against them, such as job-specific training that may not be transferable, employment and pension benefits linked to seniority, and larger salaries (Minda, 1997). Given the prevailing judicial attitudes about age discrimination laws that prevent the legal system from effectively intervening in customary economic downsizing (for example, *Hazen Paper Co. v. Biggins)*, these organizational factors can contribute to older workers' acquiescence in their employers' desires to replace them with younger workers.

Social/Cultural Barriers. The older worker population does not have enough influence or clout to protect themselves in the workplace. Despite the strength of the AARP, older workers have not organized effectively to advocate for systemic changes in the work environment. In order for employers to recognize the abilities of older workers and fully use them, older workers need a stronger arm than the ADEA. On a broader level, the youth orientation that prevails in our society, the limited enforcement of existing laws, and the lack of political action in advocating for work-related changes serve as barriers for continued employment of older adults in our society.

At the same time that the number of older people available for and willing to work is increasing, the workplace is changing as businesses seek to become more cost-efficient (doing more for less) and more competitive. The most noticeable changes are the increased use of information technology and a less hierarchical work structure that focuses on team rather than individual accomplishments. The high-technology industry has traditionally been considered a young person's field, with older age being equated to dated

skills. Employers perceive young workers as having the newest, cutting-edge skills and as being willing to put in longer hours for less money. Conversely, they perceive older workers as 'dinosaurs' with inadequate technological skills. These perceptions work against older workers in managers' decisions on hiring and retaining employees (Weinberg, 1998).

With much of the "bite" of the ADEA being side-stepped (the aforementioned *Hazen Paper Co. v. Biggins* ruling), the likelihood of older employees filing a complaint with the EEOC and ultimately prevailing against the employer is slim. The process is cumbersome, time-consuming, and emotionally draining. In age discrimination cases, the courts have developed a somewhat convoluted procedure. First, the worker bringing a complaint must establish a prima facie case, which raises the presumption that unlawful discrimination occurred. In a discharge case, for example, the employee must show that he or she was discharged; he or she was a member of a protected class (40 or over) at the time of the discharge; he or she was qualified for the job in question; and he or she was replaced by someone outside the protected class (under 40), replaced by someone within the protected class but younger than the plaintiff, or otherwise discharged because of his or her age. Once the employer has presented the reason for the discharge, the plaintiff must then prove by a preponderance of the evidence that the legitimate reason offered by the employer is not the true reason, but is merely a pretext for discrimination. Few older employees have the energy and fervor to pursue this in the interest of justice. It is no wonder that fewer complaints of age discrimination are filed each year with the EEOC than any other type of employment discrimination complaints (Powers, 1999).

Currently, there are few social or political organizations that advocate strongly for the rights and opportunities of the older worker. The percentage of older workers and older new hires represented by unions is much lower than that of younger workers, even in highly unionized occupations, perhaps indicating employer reluctance to hire older workers in union jobs with generous health and pension benefits. Today's leaders of the American Federation of Labor–Congress of Industrial Organizations (AFL–CIO) have vowed to reverse the long-time negative drift by putting much more emphasis on organizing among specialized groups not previously organized, such as temporary workers. Could a union dedicated to older workers be sustainable? As a group, mature employees have some age-specific and often unaddressed concerns that lend themselves to the political advocacy of unions. The AARP might be considered the model for a union organization (Foegen, 2000). Perhaps a replication of this organization's activity within specific unions might help address the plight of older workers and their need for strong advocacy.

Social Work Interventions

The social work profession can offer its skills and ethics to help older workers and businesses to meet their own, as well as each other's, needs. Despite the interest in continued employment for older adults, both companies and in-

dividuals are often at a loss when faced with the obstacles that have been described. Social workers who are trained in occupational social work and gerontology are in a unique position to respond to these challenges. Their responses, like the incentives and barriers, should deal with all system levels from the individual, through the organizational to the social and cultural.

Personal Interventions: Counseling and Services to Individuals and Families. Social work interventions focused on coping with family and personal problems can enhance older adults' emotional and physiological well-being and facilitate their continued participation in the labor force. The primary areas for intervention are counseling and supporting older workers and their families, providing the much needed relief in eldercare, and facilitating sound and systematic retirement planning.

Many older adults experience major life events such as widowhood, loss of friends and relatives, and forced relocation. Crisis intervention and bereavement counseling are, therefore, important areas for social work intervention with older adults who are already in the workforce or who are preparing to return to work. Another concern is health deterioration, and social workers can help to alleviate this concern by setting up wellness programs in the workplace. Offering workshops, educational lectures, and support groups that focus on reducing health risks such as obesity, alcoholism, and tobacco use not only can enhance older workers' health and well-being, but also can improve their ability to continue their productive participation in the labor force.

Counseling programs offered through employee assistance programs have expanded in the past several decades to include helping employees manage their personal problems, emotional problems, drug and alcohol abuse, difficulties finding care for a child or elderly parent, physical ailments, financial problems, and even job stress (Mor-Barak & Bargal, 2000). Although these are not corporate problems per se, they do affect productivity, efficiency and job loyalty—in other words, the "bottom line." Both internal and external employee assistance programs can help by providing counseling services or referrals to outside resources without enmeshing the employer in the workers' personal affairs (Segal, 1995).

Many older adults have spouses or parents who are disabled by Alzheimer's disease, stroke, and heart disease. Today, an estimated 22.4 million U.S. households, nearly one in four, provide eldercare to a family member. The process of providing eldercare can be both exhausting and emotionally draining, forcing many caregivers to reduce their work hours or to quit their jobs altogether (Scharlach, Lowe, & Schneider, 1991). Social work programs can provide support, counseling, and brokerage services to the individual and the family, but more important, they can also bring the severity of the problem to the attention of corporate America.

A few corporations are responding to the growing needs of their caregiving employees, many of whom are older workers, by altering benefit packages to include assistance with eldercare. According to *HR Magazine*, a 1999 survey of 1,020 major U.S. employers conducted by Hewitt Associates showed that the percentage of employers offering elder care assistance has grown significantly from 24 percent in 1994 to 47 percent in 1999 (Wells, 2000). The most common approaches to eldercare assistance were resource and referral programs, offered by 79 percent of the employers with eldercare programs. Long-term care insurance was offered by 25 percent of employers surveyed, up from just 5 percent in 1991. Corporations with innovative programs include Coopers and Lybrand, a Big Six accounting firm with 19,000 employees nationwide, which offers employees and their families a nationwide resource, referral, and consulting service; Citibank and GE Capital Services offer on-site caregiver fairs with creative promotional activities by eldercare service vendors (U.S. Department of Labor, 1998). Even though the few existing eldercare programs appear to have positive outcomes for both the worker and the corporation, one corporate survey indicates that only 7 percent of these organizations plan to develop future policies and programs to address the problems of eldercare. The reason for such a low percentage may be the fact that caregivers tend not to inform their employers of their problems (Kola & Dunkle, 1988).

As baby boomers approach retirement age, financial and employment/leisure planning become an important area for social work intervention with older adults in the workplace. Studies on retirement indicate that economic status and health problems are major concerns for older adults (Beehr, 1986). Retirement planning aimed at reducing transitional stress should focus on economic and health challenges, and it should be available to those employees expressing the need for assistance (Rappaport, 2001).

In the 21st century, older workers need to be better prepared for later-life economic realities by becoming retirement planners instead of merely retirement savers. Learning to make good financial decisions and to monitor those decisions has become critical because the longer expected retirement time span requires retirees to make more financial decisions, both in preparation for retirement and during retirement itself. Moreover, as longevity increases, so does the need for asset management, tax and estate planning, expanded insurance policies, and other financial strategies (National Endowment for Financial Education, 1999). One reason people have been savers, not planners, is that many workers are unaware of how much they need to accumulate for a comfortable retirement. Although 63 percent of individuals have begun saving for retirement, only 45 percent have even tried to determine how much they will actually need (Employee Benefit Research Institute, 1998).

In the past, social workers have been reluctant to assist individuals in financial planning, but they can no longer afford to overlook this important part of planning for the long retirement years. Creating collaborations with financial planners has become essential. Social workers need to work closely with financial planners to actively counsel older adults on preparing for retirement and creating the right balance of work and leisure to provide for an affordable retirement.

Organizational Interventions. Companies have several strategies that they can use to keep their older workers in their jobs, bring back retired employees, or hire new employees who are older. These strategies include alterations in the job, flexible options and benefits, and on-the-job training.

Research in industrial gerontology has pointed to six job arrangements that can be used effectively to accommodate the work needs and preferences of older workers. These arrangements fall within two broad categories: part-time work schedules and job modification for full-time older employees (Paul, 1988). The part-time category includes job sharing (employing two part-time workers to perform one full-time job), phased retirement (gradually reducing the number of hours until full retirement), and rehiring retirees part-time. The job modification category includes job redesign (restructuring the work to be performed or reshaping the physical environment surrounding the worker), job transfer (transferring the older worker to a less physically or mentally demanding job), and job retraining (updating the employee's job skills to keep pace with the changing technology).

The passage of the Family Medical Leave Act of 1993 (P.L. 103-3) at the federal level and modifications to jobs such as flex-time and job sharing have helped older workers with their evolving concerns and needs relative to work, family, and personal challenges. In some cases, job demands may be difficult for the older worker to meet. Employers may find it useful to offer older workers a choice of alternatives to the jobs that they have held for years.

Currently, 21 percent of older workers can be found in what the Bureau of Labor Statistics refers to as "alternative work arrangements," a category that includes independent contractors, on-call workers, temporary workers, temporary help agency workers, and contract firm workers (Cohany, 1998). It is interesting that nontraditional work arrangements are more common among older men, particularly those over age 65, than among older women.

A choice of work arrangements for older workers may permit those experiencing health problems or skill obsolescence to work more productively (Paul, 1988). Older employees and management can mutually benefit from flexible options and benefit packages, because these programs encourage the extension of the older worker's tenure with the company. Conversely, the presence or absence of traditional benefits may influence an older employee's decision to continue working or to leave the company through retirement. For instance, Medicare coverage begins at age 65, but does not include additional medical services, such as prescription drugs, routine dental care, or vision care. With prescription drug costs rising at a rate second only to that of inpatient hospitalization, the availability of an employer-provided health care plan that covers these ancillary medical services and supplies may provide an incentive for older adults to keep working (Kramer, 1995).

Some companies offer unique retirement plans for older workers, such as gradual or incremental retirement plans. For example, Varian Medical Systems has developed a Retirement Transitions program that offers a reduced workweek and the option of changing to a less stressful position (Committee for Economic Development, 1999). The Polaroid Corporation has implemented several unique pre-retirement programs, such as a "rehearsal retirement" that allows workers to try out retirement through an unpaid leave of absence and a tapering schedule that allows workers to have a gradual transition to "full-time" retirement (Committee for Economic Development, 1999).

As the 21st century begins, the tired cliché about teaching "old dogs new tricks" is not only untrue, but ageist. Employers need to adapt cookie-cutter programs to take into account the fundamental learning differences between older workers and younger ones. Older employees learn best by working at their own individual pace, need hands-on relevance to experiences rather than abstract principles, and prefer participative learning to individual study (Shea, 1991).

Several organizations have developed programs consistent with these principles. The nonprofit group Green Thumb received a $250,000 U.S. Department of Labor grant to institute a training program aimed at lower income older workers (Lodge, 2001). Their mission is to prepare disadvantaged older U.S. residents for work in computers and health care. Microsoft has also contributed $350,000 to this effort in order to draw new workers into its information technology labor pool (Berry, 1998). Another step in the direction of improving access to training for older adults is the Workforce Investment Act of 1998 (P.L. 105-220) signed by President Bill Clinton. This act consolidates all the more than 100 federally sponsored job-retraining programs into simpler categories, which will then be administered at the state and local level. Under this act, students will be trained for jobs that they select from lists provided by local employers. In this way, employers are assured that the training meets the needs of the local market.

Social–Cultural Interventions. Taking into consideration social and cultural elements, social work interventions should focus on ending overt and covert age discrimination in the workplace, providing programs that link older job seekers and employers, and promoting programs that will make the workplace more inclusive.

Not only may ending age discrimination in the workplace bring retirees back to the workforce, but also it may slow the trend toward early retirements. Practices such as mandatory retirement, refusal to hire middle-aged people, and preference for younger workers in promotions create barriers to the employment of older adults and constitute age discrimination. As stated by Congress, the purposes of the ADEA are to promote the employment of older people based on their ability rather than their age, to prohibit arbitrary age discrimination in employment, and to help employers and workers find ways to meet problems arising from the impact of age on employment.

Social workers can help management identify practices of covert age discrimination by conducting an organizational assessment via questionnaires, focus groups, and personal interviews. They can train employees to deal with myths and misconceptions about older adults, and they can help companies establish in-house policies that discourage any and all types of discrimination. It should be made clear to employers, and to society as a whole, that they cannot afford to waste the talent and experience of men and women who have many active, productive years ahead of them.

Many older adults who are interested in obtaining a job do not actively seek employment, and although some companies may be aware of their need to hire older workers, they rarely seek out those workers. Social workers can help bridge this gap by working with older job seekers on the one hand and with corporate management on the other. The job-seeking process can be discouraging for a person who has not actively looked for a job for several years, and social workers can help older adults cope successfully with the process by organizing support and instruction groups. These groups can help individuals prepare a resume, rehearse for interviews, and become assertive in combating age discrimination in job interviews. Social workers can also work with companies to set recruitment policies that are sensitive to older adults' needs. Activities that may be helpful include job fairs aimed at older workers, advertisements that emphasize job flexibility and job options that may be attractive to older workers, and programs to train managers on the desirable qualities of older employees and in nondiscriminatory job interview practices.

To encourage the continued employment of older adults and to successfully recruit those who have already left the workforce, employers need to initiate changes in their organizational culture that will create a more inclusive workplace environment. Employers must change their attitudes to develop a more effective strategy to manage a maturing workforce. Social workers trained in gerontology and occupational social work can provide management with information about demographic trends and their implications for an aging society, and they can help management evaluate how current programs and practices affect older workers and their families.

The social work profession has the value system, the knowledge, and the skills needed to implement programs to increase workplace inclusion (Mor-Barak, 2000). With appropriate training, managers at all levels can prevent and resolve work-related problems by using a variety of services within the organization or in the broader community. When services such as retraining, wellness programs, and pre-retirement counseling are available in-house, the company should bring them to the attention of managers at all levels. In addition, managers should become familiar with services in the community, such as older worker coordinating councils, job referral programs for older adults, retraining programs, career counseling services, retirement planning programs, rehabilitation agencies, and age discrimination information, and they should use these services to benefit older workers.

Conclusion

We are fortunate to live at a time when people can enjoy a relatively prolonged, healthy, and productive older adulthood. Research on older employees in recent years clearly indicates that our aging population can rise to the challenge if we manage our critical human resources more effectively. This is a matter that involves our national health and wealth, as well as our individual well-being. Much has been written about the increase in the number of older experienced workers; however, most human resource managers hold on to cultural stereotypes of older workers and are not yet implementing recruitment strategies or programs to promote greater use of older employees. Human resource managers do not yet regard the aging of the workforce as a compelling business issue. This is evident by the small number of companies that have actually implemented programs or policies that could help employers fully use older employees. The social work profession is well positioned to provide the necessary interventions that will allow everyone to reap the rewards of older workers' continued involvement in the workforce. The success of existing and emerging older worker programs will help dispel the stereotypes and myths about this population and alter the corporate culture that generates policies adverse to the older worker. Corporations, businesses, and society as a whole should be challenged to make the necessary changes in the workplace to accommodate the needs of older workers. The social work profession can enhance awareness and facilitate change through interventions at all levels.

References

Age Discrimination in Employment Act of 1967 (ADEA), 29 U.S.C. §§ 621-634 (1994 & Supp. IV 1998).

Alexander, L., & Kaye, L. (1997). *Part-time employment for the low-income elderly.* New York: Garland Publishing.

American Association of Retired Persons (AARP). (1998). *Boomers approaching midlife: How secure a future?* (Publication No. D16687). Washington, DC: Author.

American Association of Retired Persons (AARP). (2000). *American business and older employees: A summary of findings* (Publication No. D17107). Washington, DC: Author.

Anderson, R. E., Carter, I., & Lowe, G. (1999). *Human behavior in the social environment: A social systems approach* (5th ed.). New York: Aldine de Gruyter.

Beehr, T. A. (1986). The process of retirement: A review and recommendations for future investigation. *Personnel Psychology, 39*, 31–35.

Berry, J. (1998). Older workers go for the green. *Internetweek, 720,* 39–41.

Cohany, S. R. (1998). Workers in alternative employment arrangements: A second look. *Monthly Labor Review, 121*(11): 3–21.

Committee for Economic Development. (1999). *New opportunities for older workers.* Washington, DC: Author.

Doeringer, P. B. (1990). Economic security, labor market flexibility, and bridges to retirement. In P. B. Doeringer (Ed.), *Bridges to retirement* (pp. 3–22). Ithaca, NY: ILR Press.

Employee Benefit Research Institute. (1998). *What is your savings personality? The 1998 Retirement Confidence Survey* (EBRI Issue Brief No. 200). Washington, DC: Author.

Family Medical Leave Act of 1993. P.L.103-3, 107 Stat. 6..

Federal Interagency Forum on Aging-Related Statistics. (2000). *Older Americans 2000: Key indicators of well-being.* Washington, DC: U.S. Government Printing Office.

Foegen, J. (2000). "Temp" workers: Ready for unions? *Business and Economic Review, 46*(4), 28–30.

Fontana, A. (1990). Post-retirement workers in the labor force. *Work and Occupations, 17*(3), 355–362.

Fullerton, H. (1999). Labor force projections to 2008: Steady growth and changing composition. *Monthly Labor Review, 122*(11), 19–33.

Hazen Paper Co. v. Biggins, 507 U.S. 604 (1993).

Herz, D. (1995). Work after early retirement: An increasing trend among men. *Monthly Labor Review, 118*(4), 13–21.

Kola, L. A., & Dunkle, R. E. (1988). Eldercare in the workplace. *Social Casework, 69,* 569–574.

Kramer, N. (1995). Employee benefits for older workers. *Monthly Labor Review, 118*(4), 21–28.

Lodge, M. (2001). IT's golden oldies keep businesses in tune. *Information Week, 824,* 116–120.

London, M. (1996). Redeployment and continuous learning in the 21st century: Hard lessons and positive examples from the downsizing era. *Academy of Management Executive, 10,* 67–80.

Minda, G. (1997). Opportunistic downsizing of aging workers: The 1990s version of age and pensions discrimination in employment. *Hastings Law Journal, 48,* 511–576.

Mor-Barak, M. E. (1995). The meaning of work for older adults. *International Journal of Aging and Human Development, 41*(4), 325–344.

Mor-Barak, M. E. (2000). The inclusive workplace: An ecosystems approach to diversity management. *Social Work, 45,* 339–353.

Mor-Barak, M. E., & Bargal, D. (2000). Human services in the context of work: Evolving and innovative roles for occupational social work. In M. E. Mor-Barak & D. Bargal (Eds.), *Social services in the workplace.* New York: Haworth Press.

National Endowment for Financial Education. (1999). *Retirement planning in the 21st century: A think tank sponsored by the National Endowment for Financial Education.* Englewood, CO: Author.

Paul, C. E. (1988). Implementing alternative work arrangements for older workers. In H. Dennis (Ed.), *Fourteen steps in managing an aging workforce* (pp. 113–122). Lexington, MA: Lexington Books.

Powers, D. (1999). Consensual workplace relationships: The stereotypes, policies, and challenges. *Compensation & Benefits Management, 15*(3), 20–32.

Rappaport, A. M. (2001). Postemployment benefits: Retiree health challenges and trends—2001 and beyond. *Compensation & Benefits Management, 17*(4), 52–58.

Reynolds, L. (1994). Corporate practices and federal policies headed for expensive collision. *HR Focus, 71*(9), 1–3.

Rock, A. (1989). Retirement planning: The truth about post-job jobs. *Money, 18*(12), 73–77.

Scarlach, A., Lowe, B., & Schneider, E. (1991). *Elder care and the workforce.* Lexington, MA: Lexington Books.

Segal, J. (1995). Ignorance is bliss. Employee assistance programs legal trends. *HR Magazine, 40,* 33–38.

Shea, G. (1991). *Managing older employees.* San Francisco: Jossey-Bass.

Silbergeld, A., & Tuvim, M. (1993). Supreme Court decisions favor employers, reaffirm employee's trial burden of proving unlawful discrimination. *Employment Relations Today, 20,* 337–346.

Social Security Administration. (1999). *The 1999 annual report of the board of trustees of the Federal Old-Age and Survivors Insurance and Disability Insurance Trust Funds.* Washington, DC: U.S. Government Printing Office.

Social Security Administration. (2002, March 26).. *The 2002 Annual Report of the Board of Trustees of the Old-Age and Survivors and Disability Insurance Trust Funds.* Washington, DC: U.S. Government Printing Office.

Sterns, H. L., & Sterns, A. A. (1995). Health and employment capability of older Americans. In S. Bass (Ed.), *Older and active: How Americans over 55 are contributing to society.* New Haven, CT: Yale University Press.

Sum, A. M., & Fogg, W. N. (1990). Profile of the labor market for older workers. In P. B. Doeringer (Ed.), *Bridges to retirement* (pp. 23–32). Ithaca, NY: ILR Press.

Thornburg, L. (1995). The age wave hits: What older workers want and need. *HR Magazine, 40,* 40–46.

U.S. Census Bureau. (1995). *Population profile of the United States* (CPR P23-189). Washington, DC: U.S. Department of Commerce.

U.S. Census Bureau. (2000a). *The Current Population Survey: Design and Methodology* (Technical Paper No. 63). Washington, DC: U.S. Department of Commerce.

U.S. Census Bureau. (2000b). *Population projections of the United States by age, sex, race, Hispanic origin, and nativity: 1999 to 2100* (NP-T3). Washington, DC: U.S Department of Commerce.

U.S. Department of Labor. (1998). *Work and elder care: Facts on Working Women Report* (Publication No. 98–1). Washington, DC: Author.

U.S. Department of Labor, Women's Bureau. (1998). *Work and elder care* (Bulletin 98–1). Washington, DC: Author.

Weinberg, N. (1998). Help wanted: Older workers need not apply. Retrieved September 14, 1998, from *http://www.cnn.com/*

Wells, S. (2000). The elder care gap. *HR Magazine, 45*(5), *38–43*.

Workforce Investment Partnership Act of 1998. P.L.105-220, 112 Stat. 936.

Productive Engagement of Older Adults: Volunteerism and Service

Nancy Morrow-Howell, Melinda Carden, and Michael Sherraden

Volunteerism and service in later life are growing rapidly and are likely to grow more in the future. Three trends are particularly noteworthy (Morrow-Howell, Hinterlong, & Sherraden, 2001). First, volunteerism among adults is at an all-time high. A Gallup survey in 1999 found that 56 percent of the adult population had volunteered during the previous year (Independent Sector, 1999), a 13.7 percent increase from earlier years. This marks the highest level of participation ever recorded. In 1999, U.S. adults donated a remarkable total of 19.9 billion hours of labor (Independent Sector, 1999). This is the equivalent of 10 million full-time, year-round jobs, which is about 7.4 percent of total U.S. employment.

Second, human and environmental problems in the United States remain challenging, but the government-as-problem-solver ideology that emerged in the 20th century is on the wane as the 21st century begins. Support for public expenditures does not keep up with work that needs to be done in schools and libraries, along streams and waterways, in family service agencies, and in hospitals and nursing homes. Volunteers can partly fill these gaps (Abraham, Arrington, & Wasserbauer, 1996; Bass & Caro, 2001; Cnaan & Cwikel, 1992). Volunteers cannot do everything in human and environmental services—professional skills are essential—but in certain areas, they can do a great deal. Indeed, volunteers can bring unique commitment and involvement in critical areas, such as tutoring young children, monitoring air and water quality, and caring for the chronically ill.

Third, the longevity revolution means that more people are living longer, healthier lives. Currently, there are 34 million people over age 65, and more than 70 percent of these older Americans are fit and functioning. At 65 years of age, the typical American can look forward to another 18 years of life, and about 12 of these will be active years (Centers for Disease Control and Prevention [CDC], 1999). These numbers will continue to rise. The elderly population is larger, healthier, better educated, and better off financially than it has ever been. And older adults have the precious commodity of time, sometimes 20 or 30 years beyond the years that they spent in the formal labor market. In sum, the resources embodied in the older population are enormous and growing. Will these resources be put to use in volunteerism and service? Quite likely they will. A large proportion of the elderly population is motivated to make significant contributions to their families and communities (Caro & Bass, 1992).

Taken together, these three trends call for a new perspective on later-life productivity. This new perspective views the older population as a fount of growth in volunteerism and service, and older adults become the "new trustees of civic life" (Freedman, 2001). The engagement and contribution of older adults in all spheres—economic, environmental, cultural, social, civic, political, and spiritual—fall under the broad term "productive aging." From this perspective, current and future generations of older Americans become a valuable resource, as yet largely untapped. Volunteerism and service are the most likely pathways through which this great resource will be put to use in day care centers, schools, churches, courts, parks, and cultural centers around the United States.

In this chapter, we assess the current status of volunteerism in later life, including current levels of participation, associative factors, and effects of volunteering. We also assess service programs available to older adults, distinguishing service as a subset of volunteering and reflecting on the potential of older adults in service to society. We offer a theoretical perspective that highlights the central place of institutions in creating volunteer and service opportunities. And we offer some thoughts on social work roles and responsibilities in developing a society in which productive aging plays an important role for individuals and communities.

Extent of Involvement: Current and Future

As it always has been, volunteerism is alive and well in the United States. In 1996, 47 percent of people age 55 to 64, 43 percent of people age 65 to 74, and 37 percent of people over age 75 participated in volunteer work (U.S. Census Bureau, 1996). In the last few years, volunteering has increased among those over 75, with up to 43 percent of these older Americans doing some volunteer work. Although notable and growing, these participation rates remain lower than those of younger adults. In 1998, 67 percent of 35-to-44-year-olds volunteered, and 63 percent of 45-to-54-year-olds (Independent Sector, 1999). However, several studies have provided evidence that although older volunteers are fewer in number than younger adults, they invest more hours in the volunteer work that they provide (Gallagher, 1994; Van Willigen, 2000). Caro and Bass (1995) noted that the amount of time spent in volunteer activity varies widely from survey to survey, and they documented that 10 percent of older volunteers contribute 20 or more hours per week, with 60 percent contributing 1 to 4 hours a week. These figures are similar to the findings of Herzog and colleagues (1989), indicating that the average amount of volunteer time for older adults is 6 hours per month.

In assessing the social contribution of older adults, it is also important to note that older adults also provide assistance informally, such as caregiving and helping their adult children and grandchildren (Cnaan & Cwikel, 1992). These other productive activities most likely limit the time available for formal volunteering and service.

The Independent Sector survey in 1999 revealed that older adults are asked to volunteer less often than younger adults, but when they are asked, they volunteer at equivalent rates. In fact, survey researchers showed that more older adults are available and interested in volunteering than are currently involved. In terms of availability and capability, Caro and Bass (1995) estimated that 12 percent of people over 55 years of age are in good health and are not engaged in any work, volunteer, or caregiving activities; 20 percent of those in good health are engaged in these activities less than five hours a week. Other studies suggest that desire and motivation to serve are also present. The Administration on Aging found that 37.4 percent of older adults are or may be willing to serve if asked (Marriott Seniors Volunteerism Study, 1991); the Commonwealth Fund survey reported that 15 percent of people over the age of 55 who are not volunteering are willing to do so (Caro & Bass, 1995). Caro and Bass (1992) concluded that for every two older volunteers, another older person is willing and able to volunteer.

Other research reinforces the potential of later-life volunteerism, especially among future generations. A survey conducted by the AARP Public Policy Institute (1998) suggested that 80 percent of baby boomers plan to keeping working in some manner after retirement age, highlighting the sociocultural trend that older people may be less inclined to "retire" into near-total leisure in later life (Sherraden, Morrow-Howell, Hinterlong, & Rozario, 2001). In a survey by Peter D. Hart Research Associates (1999), 50 percent of 50-to-75-year-olds reported that volunteering and community service are important parts of their retirement plans, while only 12 percent reported being interested only in leisure activities. Data from the MacArthur Foundation Study of Aging suggested that older adults want both "well-deserved leisure" and "to continue to be productive" (Rowe & Kahn, 1998).

Using data from the Commonwealth Fund survey, Caro and Bass (1995) determined that almost 50 percent of the volunteering done by older adults is associated with religious-based organizations. Health service organizations (hospitals, nursing homes, hospices) make up the second largest group of organizations in which older volunteers serve. Other service organizations (for example, Rotary, Lions), senior centers, political organizations, libraries, museums, and child-care programs engage smaller percentages of older volunteers.

It has been shown (Sundeen, 1990; Wilson & Musick, 1997) that older adults spend their volunteer time in different organizations than younger volunteers and that younger adults are more likely to engage in volunteer roles that are extensions of their work or family roles (for example, volunteering at their children's schools). The Commonwealth Fund survey (Caro & Bass, 1995) further revealed that 29 percent of older volunteers provide direct service to other people (for example, as tutors, advisors, companions), while another 22 percent do manual work indoors or outdoors, and another 16 percent do fundraising. Other activities on the diverse list of older volunteers' responsibilities include participating on boards and committees, doing office work, providing transportation, preparing/distributing food, serving as receptionists, and providing skilled/technical work.

Factors Associated with Volunteering

Researchers have identified several factors associated with later-life volunteering. Compared with older adults who do not volunteer, older volunteers are more likely to be the younger old (under age 75), be female, have a high level of education, be in good health, be secure financially, own a home, be married, and be religious (Chambre, 1993; Fischer & Schaffer, 1993; Okun, 1994; Soo & Gong-Soog, 1998). Prior experience with volunteering, regular church attendance, and involvement in education or "personal growth" pursuits have also been associated with volunteering (Bradley, 2000). Among those older adults who still work, flexible work schedules are also related to volunteering (Soo & Gong-Soog, 1998).

Kuehne and Sears (1993) noted that some of these same characteristics also may differentiate short- and long-term volunteers. In a study of longevity in the Family First program, volunteers who stayed beyond the minimum time of commitment were more educated, had higher incomes, were more often involved in other volunteer activities, and had higher levels of life satisfaction than did short-term volunteers. However, these researchers joined others (for example, Fischer, Mueller, & Cooper, 1991) in expressing concern that recruitment focusing on volunteers with these attributes reinforces patterns of unequal opportunity and fails to take into account the evidence that the older adults who benefit most from volunteering often come into the role with the greatest apparent challenges and needs. Furthermore, many important volunteer roles in the human and environmental arenas do not require knowledge gained through formal education. Future recruitment and training efforts should encourage volunteerism among older adults who may have been reluctant to come forth previously because they lack formal education in the areas where volunteers are needed (Soo & Gong-Soog, 1998).

One of the most important findings is that age is not the most salient factor in determining who volunteers. In fact, data suggest that volunteering is rather stable throughout middle age into later life. Caro and Bass (1992), as well as Herzog and colleagues (1989), noted that there are no major age differences in volunteer hours across the adult life span until very late in life. In a study using data from 12 nationally representative surveys, Cutler and Hendricks (2000) demonstrated that when the effects of male mortality and educational attainment are controlled, and different age groups with similar human capital and sociodemographic characteristics are compared, age is not associated with formal volunteer membership. Chambre (1993) predicted that the link between volunteerism and age will continue to weaken with the demographic revolution and trends toward productive engagement.

Effects of Volunteering on Older Adults[1]

Many researchers have documented a positive relationship between volunteering and a positive effect on well-being and life satisfaction, suggesting that volunteering can play an important role in maintaining good health and a positive outlook in later life (Havighurst, Neugarten, & Tobin, 1968; Herzog et al., 1989; Maddox, 1968; Ward, 1979). Most studies on the effects of volunteering on well-being are limited to associative factors rather than causal relationships, but several well-designed studies offer compelling evidence of the positive impact of volunteering.

Moen, Dempster-McClain, and Williams (1992) studied a sample of 300 women over a 30-year period. When they controlled for baseline health status, they found that involvement in clubs and organizations at the first observation was related to the duration of health over the observation period. Volunteering was also related to subsequent functional ability. These researchers concluded that occupying multiple roles, including volunteer

roles, is associated with ongoing social integration and has subsequent positive health outcomes, even after other background and health variables are considered. Furthermore, Musick, Herzog, and House (1999) found in an eight-year prospective study of more than 1,200 adults over the age of 65 that the mortality risk is lower in volunteers than in non-volunteers. The positive effect of volunteering occurred even after researchers control for several aspects of health, socioeconomic status, and social integration, suggesting that volunteering has a positive effect over and above these factors.

Older adults serving in the Senior Companion Program (a federally sponsored program in which older adults are paired with and provide support to frail or isolated elderly people) showed improved mental health after volunteering, compared to a waitlist control group who showed no significant changes (SRA Technologies, 1985). Similarly, a large study of the Foster Grandparents Program compared participants to those on the waitlist. Over a three-year observation period, mental health and social resources improved for the volunteers, while they declined for those who did not gain access to the program. Also, 71 percent of Foster Grandparents volunteers reported "never feeling lonely" while only 45 percent of the waitlist group reported "never feeling lonely." Over 80 percent of the Foster Grandparents volunteers reported being more satisfied with their lives since beginning to volunteer (Litigation Support Services, 1984).

Research has yet to reveal the complex causal links between volunteering and improved health outcomes. Given

---

[1]This section was prepared by Dr. Morrow-Howell as part of a White Paper commissioned by the Longer Life Foundation. The Longer Life Foundation has given permission for this section to be reproduced in this book.

the reciprocal relationships among health, social resources, and volunteering, this will be a challenging area of study. It is possible that older volunteers benefit from the experience because of increased feelings of usefulness and boosted self-esteem (Hunter & Linn, 1980-81). Volunteer roles may replace work roles and prevent elderly people from the negative effects of role loss (Chambre, 1987) and social isolation (Moen et al., 1992). Freedman (1994, p. 40) observed that the desire of older adults to volunteer may be driven as much by a "strong and straightforward desire for structure, purpose, affiliation, growth, and meaning" as by altruism. Or perhaps volunteering provides an "inoculation" from the hazards of retirement, physical decline, and inactivity (Fischer & Schaffer, 1993).

In an early study of 1,400 elderly people in New England (Fengler, 1984), volunteering was related to life satisfaction when health, education, and work status were controlled. Fengler found an especially strong relationship between service-oriented volunteering (like through the federally sponsored RSVP program) and life satisfaction. Most notable in this study is that Fengler looked at subgroups of the older population and found a stronger relationship between volunteering and life satisfaction within what he called "disadvantaged" subgroups—elderly people living alone, in urban areas, and in poor health. Building on the work of Larson (1978), Fengler suggested that when personal and social resources are scarce, productive activities have greater significance for the volunteer.

Musick and colleagues (1999) also demonstrated the importance of conditions leading to positive outcomes by documenting the fact that volunteers are not affected equally by their participation. This study revealed a curvilinear relationship between level of involvement and mortality, with moderate involvement offering the most benefit. That is, the positive effects of volunteering were strongest among those volunteering for only one organization and volunteering for modest amounts of time. These authors concluded that an older adult does not have to volunteer to a great extent to benefit. Their findings also suggest that, in terms of personal well-being, extensive volunteering may be no better than none at all. This result should receive greater scrutiny in future research. Although not conclusive, their work also suggests that volunteering has the most positive effect on older adults with lower levels of informal social interaction.

In sum, several sophisticated studies demonstrate that volunteering contributes to improved health and well-being outcomes for the older volunteer. However, social work needs a more refined research agenda that seeks to understand subpopulations and specific conditions that lead to the most positive outcomes. It would also be helpful to expand inquiry regarding benefits of volunteering to outcomes at multiple levels, including the older adult, the service recipients, families, and communities.

Theoretical Perspectives on Later-Life Volunteerism

Continuity theory, which postulates that motivations, preferences, and behaviors are consistent over the life course (Atchley, 1995), has been used to explain later-life volunteerism, and researchers have provided evidence that older adults who volunteer tend to have been volunteers in earlier years (Chambre, 1987; Fischer & Schaffer, 1993). People who volunteered in their youth and middle age, who have developed skills as volunteers, and who have experienced the satisfaction of making a positive contribution are more likely to be volunteers as older adults than are those who consider volunteering as an option for the first time late in life (Bass & Caro, 2001). Continuity theory suggests that it is necessary to instill the value of volunteering early in the life course if the older population is to choose volunteer roles. Continuity theory focuses on the individual and the individual's life course to explain later-life volunteering, and most existing empirical research on volunteering maintains this focus on the individual.

Not everyone views this focus positively. Critics of the productive aging perspective warn that individual older adults may be held responsible for their productive value and that social structures and policies will not be transformed to enable older adults to assume these productive roles (Estes & Mahakian, 2001; Holstein, 1992). These critics express the concern that ethnic minorities and women will continue to face discrimination in their efforts to engage in productive activities, especially given their increased levels of morbidity and disability, and thus will experience further marginalization in later life.

Indeed, there has been more focus on the individual characteristics than on the social structures that promote volunteerism, and Riley (1998) challenged the "successful aging" work by Rowe and Kahn (1998) for lack of attention to the social structures that strongly influence the later-life experience. Clearly, weak institutional arrangements to recruit and support older people may inhibit elder volunteering (Caro & Bass, 1997). The conceptual framework that may be the most useful in achieving the volunteer potential of the elder population is the aging and society paradigm (Riley, Foner, & Riley, 1999). This paradigm, which grew from the age stratification framework, considers the interplay between individual lives and social structures, and seeks to explain how they affect each other as each changes to accommodate the phenomena of an aging society. Building on this perspective, Sherraden and colleagues (2001) specified a theoretical model of productivity in later life (Figure 5-1). The model highlights the dynamic relationship between individuals and social structures regarding later-life productivity. Individual and institutional capacities together lead to productive behavior, and outcomes from this engagement, in turn, change individuals and institutions.

As a result of the longevity revolution, the individual capacity for later-life productive engagement is greater than ever before in human history. Exogenous factors, including sociodemographic characteristics such as gender, race, cultural background, age, education, and residence, are life course determinants of an individual's capacity in later life. Current capacity is physical and cognitive health, as well as resources such as financial assets,

Figure 5-1

Productive Engagement in Later Life: Individual and Institutional Capacity

Sociodemographic

Education
Race/ethnicity
Gender
Urban/rural
Age

Individual capacity

Physical functioning
Cognitive functioning
Time
Income/assets
Knowledge and skills
Social support
Transportation

Public policy

Programs
Regulation
Taxation

Institutional capacity

Number, types and quality of roles
Linkages to roles:
Information
Incentives
Access
Facilitation

Productive behavior:
Volunteer and service activities

Effects on:
Individuals
Families
Society

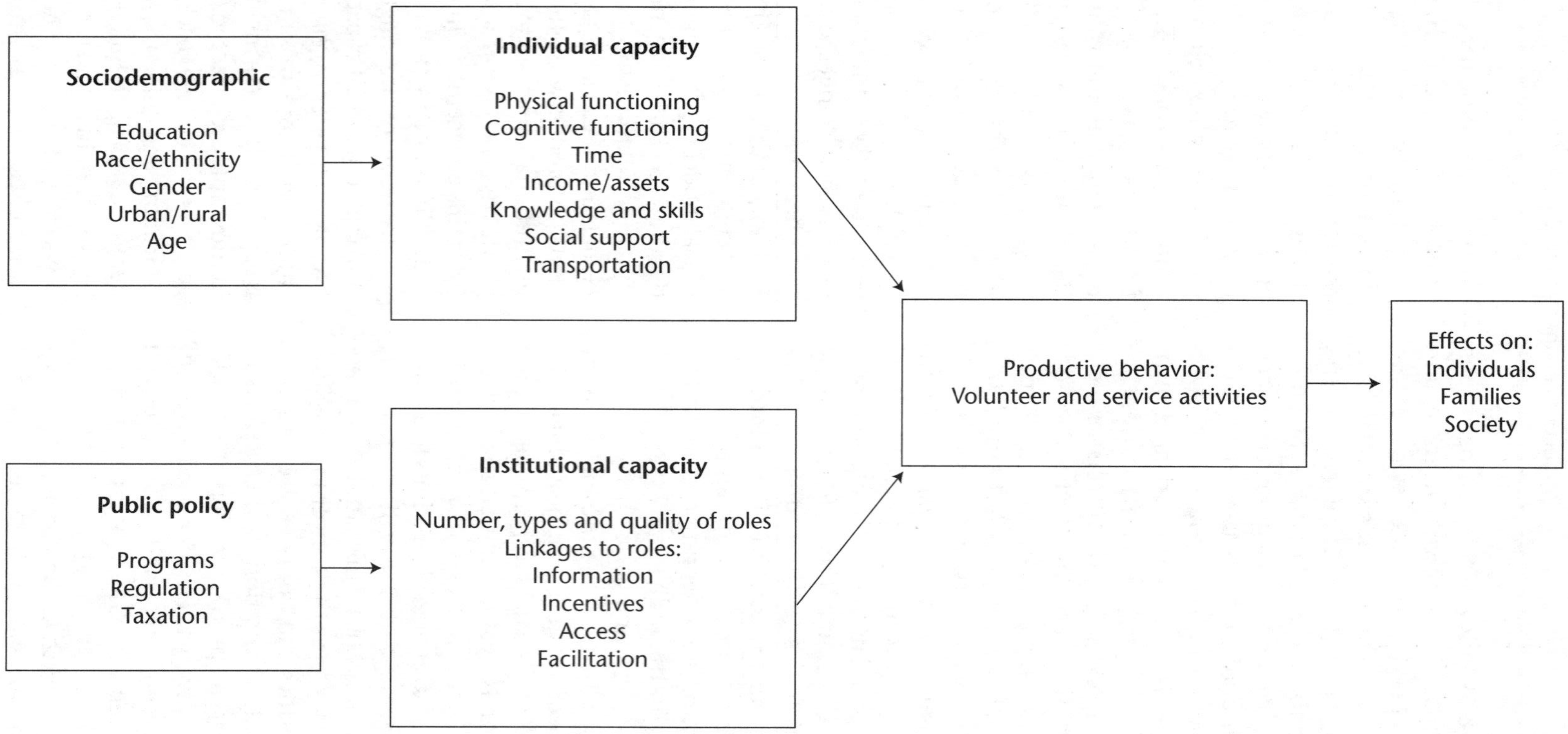

social support, and time. These individual factors have been the focus of research to explain volunteering and other productive behavior in later life. To increase productive engagement, society's institutional capacity must be developed to engage the growing individual capacity.

Institutional capacity refers to the ability of social institutions, such as businesses, public and private agencies, churches, legal institutions, and social/civic clubs, to offer, create, and promote productive roles for older adults (Sherraden et al., 2001). Institutions vary in the number and types of roles that they create for older volunteers and the extent to which they enable older adults to link to these roles. Linkage to roles varies in terms of the amount of information offered, the incentives provided for engagement, the accessibility of the role, and the degree to which the institution facilitates sustained involvement. For example, an organization can provide more or less information to individuals and the public about the opportunities, benefits, and costs of volunteer roles. Volunteer assignments can vary in terms of stipends (for transportation, meals, etc.) or other incentives. Volunteer opportunities may be limited in a certain geographic area or by a physical environment that precludes access by older adults. Also, volunteer roles may be facilitated through such factors as transportation, training programs, the availability of supervision, attitudes of paid personnel, and/or supportive services.

Freedman (2001) described the institutional attributes that he believed to be important for the success of "Experience Corps," a service program in which older adults work with public schools in urban areas: the right name for the program, critical mass or presence of older volunteers, flexibility, leadership possibilities, and opportunities to learn and to work on a team. Thus, institutional capacity has many variables, which may explain a large part of the variance in the productive engagement of older adults, including volunteerism. This is also the fundamental viewpoint in the "structural lag" theory (Riley, Kahn, & Foner, 1994), wherein structures to facilitate volunteerism are portrayed as lagging behind the potential for volunteerism.

As Riley and colleagues (1994) noted, people create and change institutions. Public policy is a means to transform institutional capacity to engage the full potential of the older population in volunteer roles. For example, the power of social policy is clear in an individual's decision to "retire." What kinds of programs, regulations, and tax laws would influence older adults' decision to engage in volunteer roles? What social structures would such policies create, especially in terms of number and types of roles and linkages to these roles through information, incentives, access, and facilitation (Sherraden et al., 2001)?

As mentioned previously, most research has focused on individual characteristics as predictors of later-life volunteering. Little research has focused on institutional characteristics and volunteerism, although several scholars have discussed structural concerns, such as insufficient attention paid by organizations to the specific concerns of older volunteers, the undemanding or unfulfilling nature of many volunteer tasks, and the lack of training and supervision (Gerson, 1997; Glickman & Caro, 1992; Morris & Caro, 1996). Issues regarding the nature of volunteer assignments are quite important, given the increasing educational levels of older volunteers and the likelihood that unskilled and clerical tasks will not be fulfilling for them (Chambre, 1993). Morris and Caro (1996) urged community service organizations to assign more challenging responsibilities to older volunteers and pointed out the need to understand the impact of different volunteer roles for older adults. How much challenge do older volunteers want? How can current services be restructured to give more responsibility to older volunteers? To what extent will worker–volunteer relationships be strained if volunteers assume more challenging roles?

Service: An Emerging Institution

In light of the increased capacity of the older population and the increased urgency of certain issues (for example, illiteracy, incarceration, environmental degradation, need for grandparents to raise grandchildren), there is a movement toward organized and substantial volunteer programs that can be classified as service. As a subset of volunteer activities, these volunteer roles have certain features that qualify them as a service:

- Formal organization and structure
- Identification as a service program (for example, Senior Volunteer Corps, Experience Corps)
- Defined role for service, comparable to a job description
- Training and supervision

- Required level of commitment
- Required duration of commitment
- Acknowledgment and recognition of the service contribution

In sum, service occurs through highly structured volunteer roles that are formalized and widely acknowledged in both public and private sectors. A service role is part of a larger organized effort, with the goal of improving a specific area of human or environmental affairs.

Senior service programs are becoming more common, emerging as part of the intergenerational movement of the last two decades. Table 5-1 summarizes some exemplary senior service programs, although the listing is by no means exhaustive. These programs actively seek older volunteers for their talents and experience; they engage older adults in tasks aimed at improving social conditions; and they have conducted program evaluations to demonstrate outcomes.

These senior service programs go beyond traditional volunteer activities and take advantage of seniors' skills and experience to tackle some of the nation's most troubling problems, such as failing schools, environmental degradation, drug abuse, and child maltreatment. They ask that seniors contribute their career skills, personal commitment, and advocacy talents to make significant inroads in addressing these challenges. In exchange for giving seniors tough assignments, most of these service programs offer incentives that surpass token reimbursement; these incentives may include stipends, extensive training, supplemental insurance, college credit, health screenings,

Table 5-1

Selected Senior Service Programs

Programs	Program Description	Target Populations or Conditions	Recruitment Strategy	Program Process	Program Evaluation
Programs Across Ages, Temple University Center for Intergenerational Learning (CIL) [a, b, c, d]	Provides intergenerational mentoring for at-risk youths in poor urban communities; focuses on drug abuse prevention, school success, and future planning.	Sixth-grade students (ages 10–13) who have experienced school failure and/or behavioral problems. Most students are at least one year behind in school and have multiple family problems.	Older adults are recruited from the community; most are low-income and from a minority. Churches, community groups, and informal networks are used. Participants are given a stipend and ongoing training.	Older adults spend at least four hours per week with their student match, mentoring them during and after school. Mentors are encouraged to participate in family and school activities as well.	Students were randomly assigned to various conditions and compared on school records and psychological and social measures. Outcomes include reduced absenteeism, improved attitudes about substance abuse and school prevention and school success, and decreases in substance abuse and suspensions from school. Outcomes vary by the quality of the mentoring relationship.
Family Friends, National Council on Aging, and Robert Wood Johnson Foundation [e, f, g]	Matches older adults with families experiencing stress and at risk for dysfunction because of strains of the child's disability.	Families with children with a disability or chronic illness; also homeless families and grandparents raising grandchildren.	Volunteers are recruited through newspaper advertisements, neighborhood and community organizations, Internet, outreach from local participating agencies.	Volunteers provide respite care, encouragement, service linkage, and compassionate listening. Volunteers receive extensive training.	A three-year evaluation with a control group was conducted. Outcomes include reduced hospitalization for children, increased well-being for adults, and reduced loneliness and isolation for families.

(Table continues on the following page.)

Table 5-1

Selected Senior Service Programs (continued)

Programs	Program Description	Target Populations or Conditions	Recruitment Strategy	Program Process	Program Evaluation
HomeFriends, Temple University CIL[h]	Provides older volunteers to work as mentors and advocates for families at risk or reported for child abuse and/or neglect.	Families that have risk factors for violence or that are involved in the child protective system.	Older adults are recruited through neighborhoods where families live, including senior centers, door-to-door canvases, and churches.	Volunteers provide support to parents, attend school events, mentor children, and assist parents in caregiving.	An evaluation with an experimental design is under way. Preliminary results indicate reduced parental distress and increased knowledge and use of community resources.
Generations of Hope[i]	Creates an intergenerational community to support children and families in the foster care system. The goal is to promote stability, adoption, and family support.	Difficult-to-place children and their new foster families. A total of 35 children in 12 families are currently involved.	Ads are placed in newspapers and outreach efforts made to current foster parents. Each applicant (family and seniors) undergoes five interviews and ongoing training.	Senior housing is intermingled with housing for foster families. Seniors receive reduced rent in exchange for tutoring, providing child care, and supporting families.	Program saves approximately $45,000 annually per child over residential care.
Seniors for Schools, Corporation for National Service programs in FL, MA, MN, MO, NY, OH, OR, PA, and TX[j]	Provides literacy instruction to low-performing students in K–3 grades. Currently, approximately 430 senior volunteers are serving 2,800 students in 39 schools.	Children, ages 5–8, at risk of reading failure.	Seniors are recruited through newspapers, radio, senior and community centers, Internet, and other Corporation for National Service programs. Volunteers receive reimbursement and supplemental insurance.	Volunteers receive extensive literacy training and work with children intensively to enhance their reading skills. Volunteers target parent involvement and help with school projects.	Pre- and post-tests are used to assess attitudes about the program and changes in reading scores. It was found that 92% of students increased their reading skills. Teachers report positive changes in reading and self-esteem.

Program	Description	Target population	Recruitment/involvement	Activities	Evaluation
Experience Corps, Corporation for National Service, Johns Hopkins University, Civic Ventures[k,l]	Provides intensive tutoring and mentoring to low-income students in schools and youth centers. The model varies considerably across sites.	Poor children at risk for school failure and negative outcomes.	Involvement may be long-term or very short-term. Program provides stipends and recruits through senior information channels, public advertisements, face-to-face contact, and direct mailings.	Volunteers develop after-school programs, parent involvement campaigns, fundraisers, education campaigns about the needs of poor schools, and tutoring programs.	Evaluation has shown improved literacy and basic math skills, enhanced student concentration and comprehension, improved study habits and attitudes about school, and augmented language development.
Foster Grandparents, Corporation for National Service—programs nationwide[m,n,o]	Provides tutoring and supportive relationships for at-risk children.	Children at risk for poor educational outcomes and/or behavioral problems because of environmental constraints.	Volunteers receive tax-free stipends, paid training, meals, health screenings, transportation, and other supportive services. People age 60 and over are eligible.	Volunteers serve in poor schools, hospitals, shelters, Head Start sites, juvenile detention centers, and community centers. They provide tutoring 20 hours per week.	More than 80,000 children are served currently. Service provided last year is valued at $286 million, a 400% return on cost. Volunteers demonstrate improved mental health and social resource outcomes, compared to waitlist controls.
Environmental Alliance for Senior Involvement[p] (Senior Environmental Corps, which started in PA)	Works on environmental projects designed to meet local community needs. The program is operated in 16 states with over 12,000 local organizations participating.	Environmental needs specific to local community.	Minorities are targeted for recruitment. Most recruitment is done by current volunteers.	Seniors work on radon testing, well-head protection, education on global climate change, animal protection, brown field redevelopment, and testing of solar energy installations. Training is provided for all participants. Members support each other via the Internet.	Organizations are evaluated on successful completion of their initial chosen project within the first 18 months of program operation. Outcome evaluation is under way.

(Table continues on the following page.)

Table 5-1

Selected Senior Service Programs *(continued)*

Programs	Program Description	Target Populations or Conditions	Recruitment Strategy	Program Process	Program Evaluation
Seniors for Childhood Immunization, Denton and Dallas, TX,[q] Center for Public Service	Works in hospitals, clinics, and community centers to increase immunization rates, especially within at-risk population groups; also educates policymakers about immunization needs.	Populations at risk for underimmunization of children against preventable diseases.	Volunteers are accessed through formal institutions such as RSVP, university extension centers, or other community service agencies.	Volunteers educate new mothers about immunization and places to get children vaccinated, enroll mothers in immunization reminder programs, encourage immunization, and mark files when children are behind.	Evaluation of age-appropriate immunization rates for babies born at four Denton County hospitals in 1996 showed that 53% of babies born during the study period were contacted. Of these, 54% completed all four required immunizations. No comparison data are provided.
OASIS Intergenerational Tutoring Program[r, s]	Provides volunteers to work one-on-one with children at schools to increase reading skills and self-esteem. The program currently operates in 19 cities, serving 13,000–15,000 children a year, with 5,000–6,000 tutors.	Children who are reading below grade level, but who do not qualify for special services; grades K–4.	Volunteers are recruited through community agencies, RSVP, local media, word-of-mouth, school districts, and the OASIS Web site.	Volunteers receive 12 hours of training on teaching reading, communicating, and motivating children. Tutors meet with children one hour a week throughout school year. Tutors have monthly support meetings.	Tutors, teachers, and principals are surveyed annually; teachers and principals report positive impact on children and school. Eighty-eight percent of tutored students increase academic performance. Telephone survey in 1996 showed that 83% of tutors reported increased socialization; 86% reported increased generativity; 93% reported increased well-being.

a. LoSciuto, L., Townsend, T., Rajala, A., & Taylor, A. (1996). An outcome evaluation of Across Ages: An intergenerational mentoring approach to drug prevention. *Journal of Adolescent Research, 11*(1), 116–129.

b. Rogers, A., & Taylor, A. (1997). Intergenerational mentoring: A viable strategy for meeting the needs of vulnerable youth. *Journal of Gerontological Social Work. 28* (1&2), 125–140.

c. Taylor, A., LoSciuto, L., Fox, M., & Hilbert, S. (1999). The mentoring factor: An evaluation of Across Ages. In *Intergenerational program research: Understanding what we have created.* New York: Haworth Press.

d. Temple University Center for Intergenerational Learning. (2000). *Across Ages Program.* Available from http://www.temple.edu/cil/Acrossageshome.htm.

e. Temple University Center for Intergenerational Learning. (2000). *Family Friends Program.* Available from http://www.temple.edu/cil/Moreaboutfamilyfriends.htm.

f. National Council on Aging. (2000). *Family Friends Program.* Available from http://www.ncoa.org/friends/family_friends.htm.

g. Rinck, C., & Naragon, P. (1995). *Family Friends Evaluation.* Kansas City, MO: UMKC Institute for Human Development.

h. Temple University Center for Intergenerational Learning. (2000). *HomeFriends Program.* Available from http://www.temple.edu/cil/Homefriendshome.htm.

i. Generations of Hope. (2000). *Program Overview.* Available from http://www.hope4children.org/.

j. Corporation for National and Community Service. *Seniors for Schools Program.* Available from http://seniorcorps.org/pdf/research/seniors4schools00.pdf.

k. Blake, A. R. (2000, September). *Senior volunteers in literacy programs.* Report prepared for Corporation for National Service Fellowship Program. Retrieved from http://www.cns.gov/research/fellows_reports/2000/blake.pdf.

l. Civic Ventures. (2000). *Experience Corps Program: Frequently asked questions.* Available from http://www.experiencecorps.org/site/about/faq.html.

m. Corporation for National Service. (2000). *Finding the right program for you.* Available from http://www.cns.gov/senior/joining/finding_nssc.html.

n. Corporation for National Service. (2000). *Fiscal 1999 performance report: Activities authorized by the National and Community Service Act and the Domestic Volunteer Service Act.* Washington, DC: ACTION.

o. Litigation Support Services. (1984, September). *Impact evaluation of the Foster Grandparent Program on the foster grandparents.* Washington, DC: ACTION.

p. Environmental Alliance for Senior Involvement. (2000). *Program overview.* Available from http://www.easi.org/about.html.

q. Center for Public Service. (2001). *Senior Volunteers for Childhood Immunization.* Available from http://www.cps.unt.edu/svci/.

r. OASIS Intergenerational Tutoring Program. *OASIS Institute 2003 annual report.* Available from http://www.oasisnet.org.

s. Kinney, S., & Morrow-Howell, N. (1999). Perceived benefits of intergenerational tutoring. *Journal of Gerontological Social Work, 20,* 3–17.

and/or meals. Financial support for most of these senior service programs comes from foundations and private/corporate contributions, with some partnerships with state or local governments. Few programs receive substantial federal support, with Experience Corps and Foster Grandparents being notable exceptions.

Evaluations of senior service programs vary in rigor and completeness, but results overall are encouraging (Table 5-1). Initially, the evaluation of intergenerational programs focused on process outcomes and the benefits to senior volunteers of their participation (Ward, 1979). The programs listed in Table 5-1 demonstrate that current evaluation efforts surpass process analyses to demonstrate tangible impacts on the targeted issues. Evaluations document benefits to service recipients and their families. The trends toward increased rigor and assessment of the impacts of senior service should continue.

Table 5-2 summarizes intergenerational senior service programs that have innovative programs or apply to a unique population or issue. Unlike the programs in Table 5-1, we are not aware of any outcome evaluations conducted on these programs, so only very limited conclusions can be drawn about their efficacy.

Some of the programs in Table 5-2 engage seniors in working with marginalized groups, such as incarcerated juvenile offenders, youths placed in residential treatment, and non–English-speaking students. Other programs involve seniors and youths working together to address mutual concerns, such as community crime. Still other programs address issues that have

emerged more recently, such as the need for grandparents to care for their grandchildren and the destabilization of the post–high school job market. These programs indicate that senior service can go far beyond "feel-good" interactions with school children. However, because of the challenging nature of these assignments, volunteers need substantial training, ongoing support, and encouragement. Furthermore, older adults may not think of themselves as able to undertake these tasks, so well designed outreach and recruitment procedures may be necessary.

Public policy can play a large role in creating and expanding service opportunities for older adults. The Foster Grandparents and Senior Companion programs, in which the government provides the infrastructure to sustain service provision by older adults, demonstrate the success of public policy in creating service roles. Public and private programs alike may offer small monetary compensations to offset the cost of volunteering and to provide minimum payment for services provided. To date, publicly stipended service programs solicit elderly people at lower income levels. (In fact, they were initially designed as employment programs.) Privately supported programs involve a broader range of elderly people, with different levels of financial resources. The programs overviewed in Tables 5-1 and 5-2 show that older adults from diverse backgrounds are filling important volunteer roles. Our society should continue to create programs and structures that are not elitist, but rather build on the competence of a diverse group of seniors, including those living in poverty or with disabilities.

Research is essential to increase knowledge for policy and program development. Many important questions remain to be answered (Morrow-Howell et al., 2001). Does the type of service activity and the organizational environment affect recruitment, retention, and benefits obtained? What attributes of the volunteer, of the role, and of the organization lead to more successful outcomes for the target population? What training and facilitation efforts are optimal, according to program goals? What type of rewards and recognitions are most effective? How can volunteer and service programs attract elderly people from diverse backgrounds? What are the costs and benefits of different types of compensation, including tax credits, service credits, education credits, and long-term care credits (Peter D. Hart Research Associates, 1999)? What balance of professional staff and volunteers is most cost-effective in service programs?

Social Work Roles

The productive aging perspective began as an advocacy effort aimed at confronting stereotypes of old age and reversing the devaluation of elderly people in society (Hinterlong, Morrow-Howell, & Sherraden, 2001). Researchers have accumulated convincing evidence that older adults make great contributions to their families and communities through work, caregiving, and volunteer roles, and they would likely do much more if given the opportunity. This is not a fantasy of what aging might be or could be. It is a realistic picture of aging today. But this realistic picture of productive aging has

not yet been widely accepted. Beliefs and attitudes about late life in the general population have not changed very much. The image of the greedy geezer or dependent elder prevails over that of an older volunteer vitally engaged in an important social or environmental program. Gerontological social workers have a responsibility to educate other social workers and the public at large about the realities of older age in the United States today. They must make it clear that older adults have both the motivation to continue making meaningful contributions to their communities and the abilities to assume challenging roles.

Social workers have traditionally been involved in recruiting, training, and supporting volunteers. To date, however, most leaders in senior service programs have not been social workers; they have been gerontologists, sociologists, and social entrepreneurs working in universities and nonprofit organizations to create and implement senior service initiatives. Yet social workers are in key positions to carry this agenda forward, to assume leadership in providing older volunteers with opportunities that differ from those available in the past. Social workers can recognize and assess the social problems and client populations, and determine where senior volunteer and service programs may be the most feasible and have the most benefit. They have the knowledge and experience in developing and influencing social policies to support this program development, and they can take leadership roles in program evaluation and research projects. Overall, the social work profession can lead the way in developing

Table 5-2

Selected Innovations in Senior Service

Programs	Program Description	Target Populations or Conditions	Program Process	Innovation or Potential Contributions
Surrogate Parents, Illinois Intergenerational Initiative[a]	Older adults serve as educational advocates for incarcerated youth.	Incarcerated juvenile delinquents and their families.	Seniors attend meetings, observe students in alternative classrooms, review educational files, and work with parents and youth.	Demonstrates that older adults can work with youth already involved in criminal behavior.
Howe-to-Industries, Clemson University[b]	Elders and students collaboratively run a public market.	At-risk adolescents, especially those in residential treatment settings.	Together, they work on product development, marketing, bookkeeping, and business management.	Engages seniors with youth in out-of-home placements, working collaboratively on a project that enhances income while teaching job skills.
HomeFriends	Senior volunteers work with grandparents who are raising their grandchildren.	Grandparents raising their grandchildren, and the children themselves.	Volunteers provide respite care, mentoring, education, and companionship to both grandparents and children.	Uses older adult peers to work with a nontraditional, but growing, family type.
Intergenerational Bridges, MD[c]	Volunteers help non–English-speaking immigrant children learn English and catch up in school.	Immigrant children with limited English proficiency.	In addition to teaching English, mentors help students adjust to the U.S. and to their new school, help families access services, and serve as a companion.	Helps meet challenges associated with increasing numbers of immigrant students in schools across the U.S.

100

Program				
Vocational Education Mentors, Illinois Intergenerational Initiative[a]	Seniors speak in high school vocational education classes about their jobs and support youth through internships and jobs.	Youth in vocational education tracks in junior high and high school.	Retired factory workers, administrative personnel, and other people retired from occupations that did not require college speak about career options and mentor newly employed youth.	Reaches out to high school students who usually fall between the cracks and helps to smooth transitions into the work world.
Generations United,[d] Washington, DC (national coalition)	Volunteers promote an intergenerational legislative agenda to advance the needs of children and elders.	Health and well-being of people of all ages.	Volunteers perform research and lobbying on caregiving supports, health care reform, increased services for low-income families, and expanded funding for intergenerational programs.	Has the potential to reduce divisions in public policy and alter political discourse about young and old.

a. Illinois Intergenerational Initiative. (1999). *Model program initiatives*. Available from http://www.siu.edu/offices/iii/
b. Strom Thurmond Institute. (2000). *Intergenerational Entrepreneurship Demonstration Project*. Available from http://www.strom.clemson.edu/teams/risl/howe-to.html
c. Montgomery County Public Schools. (1997, September). Intergenerational program receives state award. *Bulletin, 40*(3), 1.
d. Generations United. (2000). Web site. Available from http://www.gu.org/

institutional capacity, recruiting and training participants, and managing programs that engage the tremendous potential of older adults in volunteer and service roles.

Given the profession's experience with volunteerism (indeed, its roots in volunteerism), social workers can also lead the way in defining the relationship between professional staff and volunteers engaged in meaningful service roles. Moving forward with volunteer service program development is likely to increase tensions among professional staff, and social workers need to articulate and defend the complementary volunteer roles that are possible, indeed necessary, for successful programming. Their experience with professionalization and their understanding of what it takes to provide quality service over time places social workers in key positions to address, through practice and research, the difficult questions that have already been raised about restructuring services to give more responsibility to older volunteers and about promoting successful worker–volunteer relationships in the face of more challenging volunteer assignments.

Social workers understand the power of social roles in improving the lives of older individuals and their families. They are aware of the ample evidence that links social involvement to positive physical and mental health outcomes. Thus, social workers may view volunteer involvement as an intervention for older adults who may be adapting to role loss in later life or seeking ways to increase generativity or find new purpose. Indeed, social workers may view volunteerism as an interven-

tion with multiple benefits—to the older adults themselves, to the other people they serve through the volunteer role, and to communities.

The creation of programs and policies to engage the volunteer capacity of our aging society is consistent with the objectives and values of the social work profession. Social workers are committed to the creation of options for people and the self-determination of individuals in pursuing those options. Older adults are currently limited in the options available to them in retirement. They may feel coerced into leisure roles by the lack of employment and volunteering opportunities in their communities. The volunteer movement among older adults represents the creation of opportunity and choice, both highly valued by gerontological social workers. Furthermore, the extension of volunteer opportunities must go past the affluent elderly to older adults of all socioeconomic and ethnic backgrounds. Indeed, social workers should assume responsibility for ensuring that the fears of productive aging critics are not realized—fears that these new visions of later life will contribute to the further marginalization and disadvantage of frail or poor elderly people.

Conclusion

The United States, indeed the world, is in the midst of a longevity revolution. How individuals will spend their time and talents in these extended years is not yet fully determined and is open to inquiry and innovation. It is hoped that society will be purposeful in the roles and expectations created for this new stage of human life. Opportunities should evolve from knowledge of what improves the physical health, mental health, and life satisfaction of the older population and what improves society. Out of necessity, U.S. society in the 21st century may seek the involvement of its older citizenry in work, volunteer, and caregiving roles. Simultaneously, baby boomers and subsequent generations may seek increased involvement. How volunteer and service roles are shaped and how older adults are matched and supported in those roles will determine the impact of volunteering and service by older adults in the decades ahead. Butler (1997) cogently argued that retirement should be transformed by extending work life and expanding volunteer roles for the benefit of society as well as the individual. The bottom line is that society cannot afford to waste the tremendous resource of elderly people, and the older years are likely to be significantly redefined from retirement to productive engagement.

References

AARP Public Policy Institute. (1998). *Boomers approaching midlife: How secure a future?* Washington, DC: Author.

Abraham, I. L., Arrington, D. T., & Wasserbauer, L. I. (1996). Using elderly volunteers to care for the elderly: Opportunities for nursing. *Nursing Economics, 14,* 232–238.

Atchley, R. (1995). Continuity theory. In G. Maddox (Ed.-in-Chief), *The encyclopedia of aging* (pp. 227–230). New York: Springer.

Bass, S. A., & Caro, F. G. (2001). Productive aging: A conceptual framework. In N.

Morrow-Howell, J. E. Hinterlong, & M. N. Sherraden (Eds.), *Productive aging: Concepts and challenges* (pp. 37–78). Baltimore: Johns Hopkins University Press.

Bradley, D. B. (2000). A reason to rise each morning: The meaning of volunteering in the lives of older adults. *Generations, 23*(4), 45–50.

Butler, R. N. (1997). Living longer, contributing longer. *JAMA, 278,* 1372–1373.

Caro, F. G., & Bass, S. A. (1992). *Patterns of productivity among older Americans.* Boston: University of Massachusetts, Gerontology Institute.

Caro, F. G., & Bass, S. A. (1995). Increasing volunteering among older people. In S. A. Bass (Ed.), *Older and active: How Americans over 55 are contributing to society* (pp. 71–96). New Haven, CT: Yale University Press.

Caro, F. G., & Bass, S. A. (1997). Receptivity to volunteering in the immediate postretirement period. *Journal of Applied Gerontology, 16,* 427–442.

Centers for Disease Control and Prevention. (1999). United States life tables. *National Vital Statistics Report, 47*(28).

Chambre, S. M. (1987). *Good deeds in old age: Volunteering by the new leisure class.* Lexington, MA: Lexington Books.

Chambre, S. M. (1993). Volunteerism by elders: Past trends and future prospects. *Gerontologist, 33,* 221–228.

Cnaan, R., & Cwikel, J. (1992). Elderly volunteers: Assessing their potential as an untapped resource. *Journal of Aging and Social Policy, 4,* 125–144.

Cutler, S. J., & Hendricks, J. (2000). Age differences in voluntary association memberships: Fact or artifact? *Journals of Gerontology: Social Sciences, 55B*(2), S98–S107.

Estes, C. L., & Mahakian, J. (2001). The political economy of productive aging.

In N. Morrow-Howell, J. E. Hinterlong, & M. N. Sherraden (Eds.), *Productive aging: Concepts and challenges*. Baltimore: Johns Hopkins University Press.

Fengler, A. P. (1984). Life satisfaction of sub-populations of elderly. *Research on Aging, 6,* 189–212.

Fischer, L. R., Mueller, D. P., & Cooper, P. W. (1991). Older volunteers: A discussion of the Minnesota senior study. *Gerontologist, 31,* 183–194.

Fischer, L. R., & Schaffer, K. B. (1993). *Older volunteers: Enlisting the talent.* Newbury Park, CA: Sage Publications.

Freedman, M. (1994). *Seniors in national and community service: A report card prepared for the Commonwealth Fund's Americans Over 55 at Work Program.* Philadelphia: Public/Private Ventures.

Freedman, M. (2001). Structural lead: Building new institutions for an aging America. In N. Morrow-Howell, J. E. Hinterlong, & M. N. Sherraden (Eds.), *Productive aging: Concepts and challenges* (245–250). Baltimore: Johns Hopkins University Press.

Gallagher, S. K. (1994). Doing their share: Comparing patterns of help given by older and younger adults. *Journal of Marriage and the Family, 56,* 567–580.

Gerson, D. (1997, April 28). Do do gooders do as much good: Most volunteers aren't solving core problems. *U.S. News & World Report, 122*(16), 26–33.

Glickman, L., & Caro, F. G. (1992). *Improving the recruitment and retention of older volunteers.* College Park, MD: National Eldercare Institute on Employment and Volunteerism.

Havighurst, R. J., Neugarten, B. L., & Tobin, S. S. (1968). Disengagement and patterns of aging. In B. L. Neugarten (Ed.), *Middle age and aging* (161–172). Chicago: University of Chicago Press.

Herzog, A. R., Kahn, R. L., Morgan, J. N., Jackson, J. S., & Antonucci, T. C. (1989). Age differences in productive activities. *Journals of Gerontology: Social Sciences, 44,* S129–S138.

Hinterlong, J. E., Morrow-Howell, N., & Sherraden, M. N. (2001). Productive aging: Principles and perspectives. In N. Morrow-Howell, J. E. Hinterlong, & M. N. Sherraden (Eds.), *Productive aging: Concepts and challenges* (pp. 3–18). Baltimore: Johns Hopkins University Press.

Holstein, M. (1992). Productive aging: A feminist critique. *Journal of Aging and Social Policy, 4*(3/4), 17–33.

Hunter, K. I., & Linn, M. W. (1980–81). Psychosocial differences between elderly volunteers and nonvolunteers. *International Journal of Aging and Human Development, 12,* 205–213.

Independent Sector. (1999). Giving and volunteering in the United States: Findings from a national survey. Retrieved February 6. 2001, from http://www.independentsector.org

Kuehne, V. S., & Sears, H. A. (1993). Beyond the call of duty: Older volunteers committed to children and families. *Journal of Applied Gerontology, 12,* 425–438.

Larson, R. (1978). Thirty years of research on the subjective well-being of older Americans. *Journal of Gerontology, 33,* 109–125.

Litigation Support Services. (1984, September). *Impact evaluation of the Foster Grandparent Program on the foster grandparents.* Washington, DC: ACTION.

Maddox, G. L. (1968). Persistence of life style among the elderly: A longitudinal study of patterns of social activity in relation to life satisfaction. In B. L. Neugarten (Ed.), *Middle age and aging* (pp. 181–183). Chicago: University of Chicago Press.

Marriott Seniors Volunteerism Study. (1991). Commissioned by Marriott Senior Living Services and United States Administration on Aging. Washington, DC: Marriott Senior Living Services.

Moen, P., Dempster-McClain, D., & Williams, R. (1992) Successful aging: A life-course perspective on women's multiple roles and health. *American Journal of Sociology, 97*, 1612–1638.

Morris, R., & Caro, F. (1996). Productive retirement: Stimulating greater volunteer efforts to meet national needs. *Journal of Volunteer Administration, 14*, 5–13.

Morrow-Howell, N., Hinterlong, J. E., & Sherraden, M. N. (Eds.). (2001). *Productive aging: Concepts and challenges*. Baltimore: Johns Hopkins University Press.

Morrow-Howell, N., Hinterlong, J. E., Sherraden, M. N., & Rozario, P. (2001). Advancing research on productivity in later life. In N. Morrow-Howell, J. E. Hinterlong, & M. N. Sherraden (Eds.), *Productive aging: Concepts and challenges* (285–311). Baltimore: Johns Hopkins University Press.

Musick, M. A., Herzog, A. R., & House, J. S. (1999). Volunteering and mortality among older adults: Findings from a national sample. *Journals of Gerontology: Social Sciences, 54B*, S173–S180.

Okun, M. (1994). The relation between motives for organizational volunteering and frequency of volunteering by the elderly. *Journal of Applied Gerontology, 13*, 115–126.

Peter D. Hart Research Associates. (1999). *The new face of retirement: Older Americans, civic engagement, and the longevity revolution*. New York: Author.

Riley, M. W. (1998). Response to successful aging. *Gerontologist, 38*, 151.

Riley, M. W., Foner, A., & Riley, J.W., Jr. (1999). The aging and society paradigm.

In V. L. Bengston & K. W. Schaie (Eds.), *Handbook of theories of aging* (pp. 327–343). New York: Springer.

Riley, M. W., Kahn, R. L., & Foner, A. (Eds.). (1994). *Age and structural lag: Societies' failure to provide meaningful opportunities in work, family, and leisure*. New York: John Wiley & Sons.

Rowe, J., & Kahn, R. (1998). *Successful aging*. New York: Random House.

Sherraden, M. N., Morrow-Howell, N., Hinterlong, J. E., & Rozario, P. (2001). Productive aging: Theoretical choices and directions. In N. Morrow-Howell, J. E. Hinterlong, & M. N. Sherraden (Eds.), *Productive aging: Concepts and challenges* (260–284). Baltimore: Johns Hopkins University Press.

Soo, Y. K., & Gong-Soog, H. (1998, December). Volunteer participation and time commitment by older Americans. *Family and Consumer Sciences Research Journal*, p. 146.

SRA Technologies. (1985, September). *Senior Companion Program Impact Evaluation*. Washington, DC: ACTION.

Sundeen, R. A. (1990). Family life course status and volunteer behavior: Implications for the single parent. *Sociological Perspectives, 33*, 483–500.

U.S. Bureau of the Census (1996). *Statistical abstract of the United States: 1996* (116th ed.). Washington, DC: U.S. Government Printing Office.

Van Willigen, M. (2000). Differential benefits of volunteering across the life course. *Journals of Gerontology: Social Sciences, 55B*, S308–S318.

Ward, R. A. (1979). The meaning of voluntary association participation to older people. *Journal of Gerontology, 34*, 438–445.

Wilson, J., & Musick, M. (1997). Work and volunteering: The long arm of the job. *Social Forces, 76*, 251–272.

6

Family Life

Roberta R. Greene

"Changes in the size, well-being, and diversity of the older population over the course of the late twentieth century are historically unprecedented" (Hudson, 1996, p. 33). The number of older adults will burgeon between the years 2010 and 2030, when the baby boomer generation reaches age 65. By 2030, there will be 70 million older adults, more than twice the number in 2000 (Administration on Aging, 2003). There is a growing dispute among policymakers about the implications of the aging of U.S. society. Much of the debate centers on whether the U.S. taxpayers can afford to continue paying for a range of programs and entitlements for the older population, as well as escalating health care costs. Policymakers increasingly are raising concern about how those who need social services and health care will be served.

Although these discussions have great importance for policy formation, it is essential to understand the age revolution within a broader context (Corman & Kingson, 1996). That expanded context embraces changes in attitudes toward aging, an increase in

empirically based gerontological knowledge, as well as alterations in family forms. Understanding the consequences of demographic change on intergenerational family relationships will become a major issue for social work practitioners (Bengtson, Giarrusso, Silverstein, & Wang, 2000).

Shifting the Focus of Social Work Practice

For centuries, the informal support of the family has been critical in the care of older adults. Although fulfilling a crucial need, formal social services have played a lesser role. With the longevity revolution, however, gerontologists are skeptical about what the future holds for the family of later years. Theorists who argue that the family has declined in importance over the 20th century question the viability of the "postmodern [family] life course" (Fuller-Thompson, Minkler, & Driver, 1997, p. 407). For example, Popenoe (1993) argued that the family has been "stripped down" to the bare essentials of childbearing and the provision of affection and companionship. Researchers ask, if the modern day family is already strained, will there be a continuation of high solidarity and intergenerational support among family members? How will the fluidity of age-appropriate roles affect family structures and the norms of intergenerational family reciprocity (Bengtson et al., 2000)?

The longevity revolution requires social workers to consider the changing nature of the U.S. family. The baby boomer generation—those born between 1946 and 1964—has had "unprecedented life experiences" (Maugans, 1994, p. 1) that will influence family function, structure, and expectations for intergenerational behavior. Baby boomers have experienced differences in the timing and tempo of human events (Corman & Kingson, 1996). They are the first generation raised in a postindustrial society with accelerated changes, the last generation raised by housewives, and the generation that took to the streets in the Vietnam and civil rights demonstrations of the 1960s and 1970s. Baby boomers tend to postpone marriage longer, have smaller families, have more dual career marriages, prevent pregnancy more often, and have higher rates of divorce than previous generations. In addition, there are more single parents and blended households among this group (Maugans, 1994). Furthermore, because of the falling birth rates, baby boomers will have a smaller pool of family members to care for them in their later years. These changes will require a reexamination of caregiving distributions to meet the changes in household, family, and kinship arrangements (Kiyak & Hooyman, 1999).

In addition, new knowledge about how people age and changes in attitudinal perspectives will alter the way that people approach their own aging experience. For example, Riley and Riley (2000) called for an age-integrated society in which learning, work, and leisure are integrated throughout the life course, whereas Uhlenberg (2000) contended that age integration is the way for older adults to remain productive throughout life. Middle-aged people themselves are expecting to live longer and lead more productive lives. According to the Administration on Aging (1997), 41 percent of people now working believe that they are at least somewhat likely to live to age 85; 23 percent believe that they are somewhat likely to live to age 90; and even 15 percent believe that they are at least somewhat likely to live to age 95. This stocktaking raises the question, "What societal expectations do we have for the last twenty-five years of life" (Fahey, 1996, p. 38)?

Another change among the baby boomer cohort will be their sense of economic security and productivity. Many of the boomer generation who are engaged in caregiving will be able to afford a direct pay model in which families hire and supervise their own aides. They may envision choices such as a respite voucher program or a general ability to select providers and programs (Feinberg & Whitlach, 1998). Many boomers anticipate that retirement—an evolving concept—will consist of a range of arrangements and activities or will involve second and third careers (Corman & Kingson, 1996). Others will be successful at updating technological skills and benefiting from home offices and flexible work hours (Silverstone, 1996).

Changes in attitude toward aging will affect people's help-seeking behaviors. For example, Silverstone (1996) hypothesized that many people who are approaching their older years will be much more aggressive and educated health care consumers and will have more confidence in their continuing ability to make decisions. Recent literature has also suggested that as people age and cannot maintain direct control of a particular function, they may still exercise or mediate control through others (Bandura, 1997; Smith et al., 2000). That is, they will determine whether they want or need a certain type of support. They will want to plan and to make choices, often with the input of family members (High, 1991). In a similar vein, Walsh (1999) pointed out that "the aging process is more variable and malleable than was long believed" (p. 318). She urged elders to make the most of their choices.

Aging research and practice began with a focus on disease and decline (Silverstone, 2000). However, later research drastically altered "the very foundations of existing paradigms regarding the elderly" (Scharlach & Kaye, 1997, p. xii). In thinking about the needs of older adults in the new millennium, Greene (2000) argued that the future population explosion does not necessarily mean that the number of stereotypically frail and dependent people will expand. Neither should it be assumed that these older adults will want and require the same services. This change in attitude will involve an increased focus on how to promote positive aspects of aging and how to help older adults maintain the capability to function in their environments as they age. Gerontologists increasingly understand that

> many people have the capacity in old age to free themselves from the societal expectations and roles that may have confined them earlier in their lives and to become more fully who they are. The goal of longevity should not be simply to extend the quantity of human years lived on this earth but to enable the inherent quality within human lives. (Jones, 1999, p. 1)

These various attitudinal, economic, and social forces, coupled with changes in family form, necessitate a reconstruction of social work strategies to meet the challenge of serving older adults and their families in the 21st century (Silverstone, 2000).

New Family Forms

Baby boomers have "set the records for a variety of living arrangements that reshaped the definition of families and household composition" (Wattenberg, 1986, p. 20). In a postmodern society, the family constellation goes beyond biological or genetic relationships (Stacey, 1996). The demographic, economic, and social changes of the 20th century have had important consequences for family structures and relationships. Most industrial countries, including the United States, have seen an extension of life expectancy and an increase in the number of people in their middle and older years. Multigenerational families of four and even five generations are now common (Golden & Saltz, 1997).

With the combination of longevity, decreased fertility rates, and higher rates of divorce, family structures have taken on a different shape. At the beginning of the 20th century, most families were shaped like a pyramid—with usually one elderly person at the top. The 21st century family is shaped more like a beanpole—long and thin, with great-grandparents still living, but with fewer members of their children's, grand-children's, and great-grandchildren's generations. In short, what was once a pyramid is now a beanpole (Hooyman & Kayak, 1996). Furthermore, all generations will share more time together than ever before in history.

The high rate of divorce has resulted in an intricate set of intergenerational relationships. For example, older people now may have biological children and grandchildren, stepchildren and stepgrandchildren, in-laws and former in-laws (Bengtson et al., 2000). Another change in the intergenerational family is that grandparents are raising grandchildren (Burnette, 1997; 1999; Weber & Waldrop, 2000). Nearly 4 million U.S. children live in households headed by grandparents (Lugaila, 1998). Researchers have found that more than one in 10 current grandparents has raised a grandchild for at least six months (Fuller-Thomson, Minkler, & Driver, 1997; Fuller-Thomson & Minkler, 2001). This increasingly common phenomenon is the result of parental death, incarceration, unemployment, and substance abuse. Teen pregnancy, family violence, and HIV/AIDS also play a role (Fuller-Thomson et al., 1997; Fuller-Thomson & Minkler). Social workers are increasingly establishing programs for this grandparent population.

Another important trend is the increasing heterogeneity of older adults. Minority populations are expected to increase to include close to half (47 percent) of the U.S. population by the year 2050 (Day, 1992). The larger and modified extended families of African American and Latino families may exhibit cultural differences in family reciprocity important to social work practice (Tennstedt & Chang, 1998). For example, caregivers are more likely than the general population to live with the care recipient and to provide care for more than one person (National Alliance for Caregiving and the Alzheimer's Association [NAC/AA], 1999; National Alliance for Caregiving and the American Association of Retired People [NAC/AARP], 1997). In addition, diversity may be categorized more broadly to include not only ethnicity and immigrant status, but also gender, race, education, income, upbringing, service in the Vietnam War, protest against the Vietnam War, work, and unemployment—all of which may affect family caregiving patterns and social services conditions (Light, 1988).

A Growing Conceptual Base: Professional and Family Caregiving

Models of geriatric health care are based on designs that promote optimal functioning among older adults. At the core of this care process are comprehensive assessments used to examine whether clients have the capacity to function successfully in their environment and to determine what resources are necessary to improve interpersonal functioning (Greene, 1989). The intent of the biopsychosocial assessment is to evaluate functional capacity or everyday competence—older people's ability to care for themselves, to manage their affairs, and to live independent, quality lives in their communities (Willis, 1991).

Because the incidence of acute and disabling illnesses rises sharply in later years, older adults continue to account for a disproportionate use of health care services. Policymakers are fearful that by the year 2030, growing numbers of frail elders with health limitations will require health and social services that outstrip the available delivery systems (Silverstone, 1996). In this context, the ability of older adults to maintain functional capacity is a core concern of geriatric social workers.

Another quintessential issue for geriatric social workers is the seminal question, what should adult children do for their dependent parent (Brody, 1985) or what should the nature of family reciprocity be—"the cyclical process of helping and being helped throughout life" (Bengtson et al., 2000, p. 9)? For the past 40 years, theorist and practitioner interest has focused on family caregiving—who needs care, who receives care, who provides care, what care is provided, the costs of care, and the impact of care on the caregiver (Cantor, 1992; Fuller-Thomson & Minkler, 2001; Wiener, 2003).

Family theorists who study the family of later years examine this question while focusing on the older person as a member of the family constellation (Greene, 2000; Silverstone & Burack-Weiss, 1983). As early as 1973, Boszormenyi-Nagy and Spark posited that "the major connecting tie between the generations is that of loyalty based on the integrity of reciprocal indebtedness" (p. 217). Their interest was in

the way that emotional bonds, interdependence, and the exchange of goods and services maintain family relationships between older parents and adult children. That is, how help is received and provided across generations (Maugans, 1994).

Parent care is not a developmental stage. Rather, parent care revolves around the interaction of parent–child issues of independence versus dependence throughout the life course. Brody (1985) cautioned social workers against adopting the myth that elderly parents received better care in the good old days:

> The truth to which the myth speaks is that adult children cannot and do not provide the same total care to their elderly parents that those parents gave to them in the good old days of their infancy and childhood. The roles of parent and child cannot be reversed in that sense. The good old days, then, may not be earlier periods in our social history (after all, the myth existed then too), but an earlier period in each individual's and family's history to which there can be no return. (p. 27)

This point of view, based on the theory of family development, emphasizes that family relationships are more than a combination of individual life cycles. Rather, family members' life stages are intertwined, and the effects of membership, including births, marriages, and deaths, introduce family change over time (Carter & McGoldrick, 1999).

Gerontologists also examine how families adapt when an older member needs care and how caregivers, particularly women, balance various family responsibilities (Brody, 1990). Recent research provides new insights into family caregiving. According to Tennstedt (1999), the relationship between an older adult's level of frailty and receipt of care is not a simple linear one. Rather, there is probably a threshold of impairment at which the amount of care increases substantially related to an increase in the number and scope of needs, necessitating a wider variety of help and more intensive care; a preference by elders for care by their families; the family's sense of responsibility for providing care; the greater ease of informal care to meet specific needs; or problems with access, availability, or limitations of formal services.

The amounts and types of assistance received may be associated with traditional gender and social roles. For example, older men may not know how to cook for themselves. Older adults usually continue doing the daily tasks with which they are familiar, however. Thus, it is important for social workers to prioritize services, which requires an understanding that "the demand" for services is related to both functional assessment and perceived need. Although it is commonly assumed that more caregiving tasks result in more caregiving distress, more recent analytical models have found that this is not the case (Yates, Tennstedt, & Chang, 1999). Rather, it is the problem behaviors, such as wandering or hitting, that cause caregiver burden.

Geriatric social workers need to consider factors that mediate such stress (NAC/AARP, 1997). It is not the amount of care that causes distress, but the caregiver's appraisal or perception of the caregiving. The greater the sense of control or confidence in one's caregiving responsibilities, the less stress (Szabo & Strang, 1999). Therefore, family caregiving requires more planning. Tennstedt (1999) suggested that research data be used to develop client profiles to target service to at-risk elders. In addition, geriatric social workers can devise services that are aimed at increasing a family's sense of caregiving competence.

Research findings also reveal that adhering to older adults' psychosocial preferences can lead to a higher level of satisfaction and a better quality of life. A study by Carpenter, Van Haitsma, Ruckdeschel, and Lawton (2000) indicated that these preferences encompass goals for personal growth and development, as well as preferences associated with self-preservation and function. Social workers can learn much more during their assessments about the relative importance or ranking of preferences, such as the trade-off between freedom and safety, or family's and friends' involvement in care. Moreover, such findings imply that gerontologists need to better understand how to assess preferences in several domains, such as social activities and privacy. In addition, they suggest that care recipients need to participate in the design and execution of their own care.

Augmenting Social Work's Practice Base

Social work practice with older adults and their families had a bumpy start. During the 1950s and 1960s, when psychoanalytic theory became the primary basis for assessing and intervening with individual social work clients, many practitioners subscribed to the view that older adults were poor candidates for social work treatment. Some practitioners did adopt aspects of the psychodynamic approach, such as facilitating reminiscence among older adults to improve their functioning (Greene, 1982; Pincus, 1970). However, many social workers thought that older adults needed only concrete services, such as those provided by Meals-on-Wheels or homemakers' clubs (Greene, 1989).

Family-centered practice models were slow to emerge, but the identification of the family as the client has had important ramifications for social work practice (Lowy, 1985). Various types of treatment interventions based on this conceptual premise have been successful. Practitioners who drew on systems theory strived to relieve family stress and explored the ways that the family of later years helps the older adult maintain the highest level of functional capacity.

The purpose of social work intervention with the family of later years continues to be to help family members adapt to changes in the older adult's biopsychosocial functioning. That is, practitioners mobilize the family system on behalf of the older adult (Greene, 2000; Silverstone & Burack-Weiss, 1983). In addition, practitioners deal with transitional tasks, such as retirement and widowhood, that may precipitate a crisis, and they direct their attention to past conflicts, roles, alliances, and communication patterns.

As ecological approaches emerged in the 1970s and 1980s, social work practitioners began to emphasize a healthy, realistic adaptation to problems in living (Kirschner, 1986). Social workers who use the ecological perspective as a conceptual framework continue to examine older clients' behavior as a multifaceted result of person–environment transactions at multiple systems levels (Bronfenbrenner, 1979; Greene & McGuire, 1998). This multisystemic approach allows practitioners to work with small-scale microsystems, such as families and peer groups; the connection between systems, known as mesosystems, such as the family and health care systems; exosystems, the connections between systems that do not directly involve the person, such as social security and Medicare; and macrosystems, or overarching large-scale systems, such as legal, political, and value systems. Clinical social workers use the ecological perspective today to conduct multilevel client assessments that will give them an understanding of how clients function within their total environment and allow them to employ a range of interventions for these clients (Table 6-1).

The ecological perspective underscores the need for social workers to promote everyday competence among older adults (Willis, 1991). Furthermore, an ecological view takes into account an older adult's functional capacity across the life course. To understand the life course, the social worker must address the client's functioning over time, the timing of family life events, and the historical and cultural changes associated with them. The attention to changing social conditions helps practitioners understand the older adult's present functioning, as well as family caregiving, within the context of life events (Hareven, 1982). Because stress in caregiving is often the reason that

Table 6-1

Geriatric Social Work with Older Adults and Their Families: Major Interventions

The social worker

- assesses the biopsychosocial functioning of the older adult.
- promotes competence and continued cognitive and social engagement
- identifies the family as the client system.
- deals with family reciprocity.
- supports and mobilizes family caregiving.
- enhances family solidarity
- attempts to reduce family stress.
- seeks resources from multiple social systems.
- uses the full continuum of care.
- helps clients access a mutually agreed upon level of appropriate care.
- respects and celebrates client diversity.
- encourages choice.
- fosters natural client strength and healing capacity

families seek social services, practitioners frequently continue to assemble the family when dealing with such difficulties. Social workers help families to cope with difficult life transitions, illness, or chronic impairments and to balance caregiving demands (Getzel, 1986).

Intervening with Families of Later Years

Today's social workers can draw not only on systems and ecological practice strategies, but also on techniques that promote the positive aspects of aging. The concept of the positive aspects of aging is an umbrella term that centers around individual and family strengths. It generally focuses on the ways that adults continue to adapt and or develop throughout the life course. Theorists have addressed the topic of wellness from a number of vantage points. For example, Greene and Blundo (1999) cri-

tiqued systems theory and suggested postmodern modifications that would help practitioners avoid problem-saturated descriptions of families and seek to understand their strengths. In addition, practitioners would explore a client's story within his or her culturally specific and personal history.

In a parallel vein, as Walsh (1998, 1999) pointed out, studies of adult development and family functioning reveal that families have a variety of adaptive mechanisms to help them successfully meet the challenges of later life. She indicated that flexibility in family structure, roles, and reactions to developmental tasks can play a vital function in exploring new options in old age. She prompted practitioners to foster family coping and adaptational process to improve families' ability to address disruptive life challenges.

Using the phrase salutogenesis orientation to encompass his study of how people naturally use their resources to strive for health, Antonovsky (1998) developed another positive approach to aging. He assumed that a family is a collective that employs its coping capacities to return to stability when faced with stressors such as chronic illness or disability. Similarly, gerontologists, such as Atchley (1999), developed continuity theory to examine how older adults adapt to changing situations. Such theorists provide practitioners with ideas for promoting competence among older adults by tapping natural coping mechanisms. The major research question is, what enables you to cope or what keeps you going? Atchley was impressed with the research finding that, irrespective of changes in health, a large proportion of older adults continue to show consistency in thinking patterns, activities, living arrangements, and social relationships. He used the term continuity strategies to refer to the means that older adults take to maintain life satisfaction despite disability. Such continuity was attributed to "coherence in psychological, behavioral, and social patterns of aging individuals" (Atchley, 1999, p. 8).

Other positive aging concepts include successful aging and resilience (Rowe & Kahn, 1998). Although successful aging has been of interest for a number of decades, a decade of research sponsored as part of the MacArthur Foundation Studies has renewed interest in this concept. Successful aging, according to Rowe and Kahn (1998), consists of three major factors: (1) avoiding disease by adopting a prevention orientation; (2) engaging in life by continuing social involvement; and (3) maintaining high cognitive and physical functioning through ongoing activity (Figure 6-1). Subsequently, Crowther et al. (2002) added maximizing positive spirituality. This shift in paradigm suggests that social workers should develop more programs that promote health and psychosocial well-being, as well as use assertive rehabilitation strategies.

A resilience-based orientation, a theoretical advance currently under way that builds on social work's strengths perspective, examines what factors contribute to successful outcomes in the face of a crisis or how people overcome the odds. The concept of resilience has a variety of meanings. According to Webster (1983), it refers to the ability to recover strength, spirits, and good humor. In social work, it pertains to people's ability to spring back after experiencing adverse stress or problems (Barker, 1995). Although originally applied to children and youth, the term resilience is increasingly being applied to older adults; it may substitute for the associated concepts of competence—a person's ability to overcome stress and to perform adequately to live in his or her environment—and self-efficacy—a person's belief that he or she can accomplish certain tasks (Lewis & Harrell, 2002).

The resilience approach has become sufficiently sophisticated to provide ideas for highly useful intervention strategies (Fraser, Richman, & Galinsky, 1999). For example, Walsh (1998, 1999) has used the research of the last two decades and her own clinical experiences to substantiate the fact that families are resilient, that they have the ability to overcome adversity. She has suggested that practitioners stay in tune

Figure 6-1

Components of Successful Aging

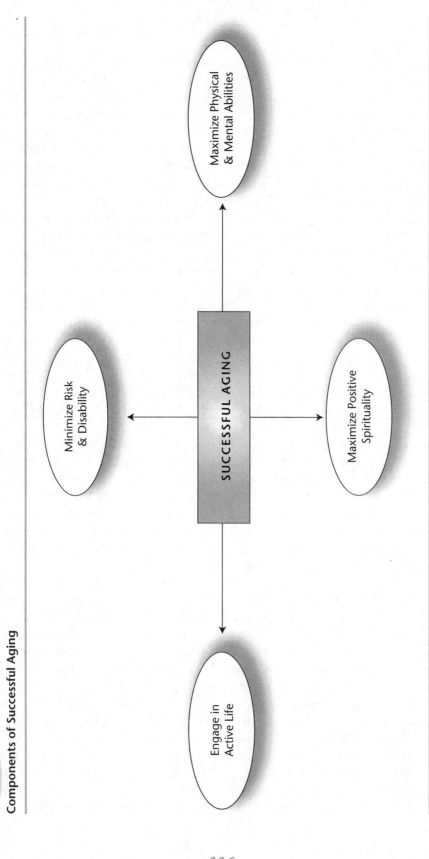

Source: Crowther, M. R., Parker, M., W., Achenbaum, W. A., Larimore, W. L., & Koenig, H. G. (2002). Rowe and Kahn's model of successful aging revisited: Positive spirituality—The forgotten factor. *Gerontologist, 42,* 613–620. © 2002 Gerontological Society of America. Reprinted with permission of the publisher.

to a family's naturally healing capacity. Social workers who foster family resilience focus on a family's intrinsic strengths and resources that allow them to better meet life crises (Carter & McGoldrick, 1999). In addition, these practitioners examine the match between family strengths and the family's specific circumstances. That is,

> family resilience describes the path a family follows as it adapts and prospers in the face of stress, both in the present and over time. Resilient families respond positively to these conditions in unique ways, depending on the context, developmental level, the interactive combination of risk and protective factors, and the family's shared outlook. (Hawley & DeHaan, 1996, p. 293; Greene, 2002)

Practitioners who use a resilience orientation see the capacity for growth and the potential to engage in self-righting behavior in every family. Moreover, such practitioners see every intervention as a potential means to prevent further problems and to reduce family stress. The concept of resilience is important to the perceptions of the family of later years and their ability to meet the stress of family caregiving. The resilience perspective recognizes that, although stress puts an extra burden on family life, families are inherently prepared to maintain their equilibrium.

Conclusion

Certainly, there will be more frail and disabled clients for social workers to serve in the new millennium. There also will be a sizable number of older adults who will be suitable candidates for innovative interventions. The "positive aspects of aging" points of view are particularly important as social workers revisit their role in working with the new aged and their intergenerational families. It is necessary to match a client with needed services and care along a full continuum of care (Figure 6-2). Wellness programs and preventive services must play a more central role, encompassing a range of activities along a continuum of functional capacity—from those with the most to those with the least capacity (Beaver & Miller, 1992; Greene, 1993; Vourlekis & Greene, 1992).

Both problem prevention and health promotion require social workers to rethink their approach to assessment, using "the social work principle of basing the level of care on the individual's functional capacity—from those who are most independent to those who are least independent" (Vourlekis & Greene, 1992, p. 15). To provide the most concentrated services to the most frail or physically or mentally challenged people, practitioners must think of a far-reaching spectrum of services, ranging from preventive and supportive services to nursing home and hospice care (Vourlekis & Greene, 1992; Greene, Kropf, & Pugh, 1994; Hooyman, Hooyman, & Kethley, 1981). Furthermore, practitioners must evaluate care needs by using client triage, a process in which the most frail or physically and mentally challenged clients receive the most intense service. This process must be accompanied by an understanding that clients can reverse frailty and regain strength. In this way, social workers can meet the challenges of those most in need.

Figure 6-2

Five Continuums for Elderly People

1. Continuum of need

Independent (little or no need)	Moderately dependent	Dependent (multiple needs)

2. Continuum of services

Health promotion and disease prevention	Screening and early detection	Diagnosis and pretreatment evaluation	Treatment	Rehabilitation: Skilled nursing services	Continuing care and hospice

3. Continuum of service settings

Own one's residence	Friend or relative's residence	Congregate living situation	Subacute care facility (for example, day hospital)	Acute care facility (for example, hospital)	Skilled long-term care facility (for example, nursing home)	Continuing care and hospice

4. Continuum of service providers

Nonservice	Self-care	Family and friends (support network)	Paraprofessionals	Professionals

5. Continuum of need

Single discipline	Multidisciplinary	Interdisciplinary

SOURCE: Hooyman, N., Hooyman, G., & Kethley, A. (1981, March). *The role of gerontological social work in interdisciplinary care.* Paper presented at the annual program meeting of the Council on Social Work Education, Louisville, KY. © Council on Social Work Education. Reprinted with permission.

References

American Association of Retired Persons. (2003). *Beyond 50.03: A report to the mation on independent living and disability*. Washington, DC. Available at www.aarp.org

Antonovsky, A. (1998). The sense of coherence: An historical and future perspective. In H. I. McCubbin, E. A. Thompson, A. I. Thompson, & J. E. Fromer (Eds.), *Stress, coping, and health in families* (pp. 3–20). Boston: Allyn & Bacon.

Atchley, R. C. (1999). *Continuity and adaptation in aging*. Baltimore: John Hopkins University.

Bandura, A. (1997). *Self-efficacy: The exercise of control*. New York: W. H. Freeman.

Barker, R. L. (1995). *The social work dictionary*. Washington, DC: NASW Press.

Beaver, M. L., & Miller, D. (1992). *Clinical social work practice with the elderly* (Rev. ed.). Homewood, IL: Dorsey Press.

Bengtson, V. L., Giarrusso, R., Silverstein, M., & Wang, H. (2000). Families and intergenerational relationships in aging societies. *Hallyn International Journal of Aging, 2*(1), 3–10.

Boszormenyi-Nagy, I., & Spark, G. (1973). *Invisible loyalties*. New York: Harper & Row.

Brody, E. (1985). Parent care as normative family stress. *Gerontologist, 25*, 19–29.

Brody, E. (1990). *Women in the middle: Their parent care years*. New York: Springer.

Bronfenbrenner, U. (1979). *The ecology of human development*. Cambridge, MA: Harvard University Press.

Burnette, D. (1997). Grandparents raising grandchildren in the inner city. *Families in Society, 78*, 489–499.

Burnette, D. (1999). Custodial grandparents in Latino families: Patterns of service use and predictors of unmet needs. *Social Work, 44*, 22–34.

Cantor, M. (1992). Families and caregiving in an aging society. *Generations, 16*, 67–70.

Carpenter, B. D., Van Haitsma, K., Ruckdeschel, K., & Lawton, M. P. (2000). The psychosocial preferences of older adults: A pilot examination of content and structure. *Gerontologist, 40*, 335–348.

Carter, B., & McGoldrick, M. (Eds.). (1999). *The expanded family life cycle: Individual, family, and social perspectives*. Boston: Allyn & Bacon.

Corman, J. M., & Kingson, E. R. (1996). Trends, issues, perspectives, and values for the aging of the baby boom cohort. *Gerontologist, 36*, 15–26.

Crowther, M. R., Parker, M. W., Achenbaum, W. A., Larimore, W. L., & Koenig, H. G. (2002). Rowe and Kahn's model of successful aging revisited: Positive spirituality—The forgotten factor. *Gerontologist, 42*, 613–620.

Day, J. C. (1992). Population projections of the United states, by age, sex, race, and Hispanic origin: 1992 to 2050. *Current population reports* (Series P25, No. 1092). Washington, DC: U.S. Government Printing Office.

Fahey, C. J. Msgr. (1996). Social work education and the field of aging. *Gerontologist, 36*, 36–41.

Feinberg, L. F., & Whitlach, C. J. (1998). Family caregivers and in-home respite options: The consumer-directed versus agency-based experience. *Journal of Gerontological Social Work, 30*(3/4), 9–28.

Fraser, M. W., Richman, J. M., & Galinsky, M. J. (1999). Risk, protection, and resilience: Toward a conceptual framework for social work practice. *Social Work Research, 23*, 129–208.

Fuller-Thomson, E., Minkler, M. (2001). American grandparents providing extensive child care to their grandchildren: Prevalence and profile. *Gerontologist, 41*, 201–209.

Fuller-Thompson, E., Minkler, M., & Driver, D. (1997). A profile of grandparents raising grandchildren in the United States. *Gerontologist, 37,* 406–411.

Getzel, G. S. (1986). Helping elderly couples in crisis. In C. H. Meyer (Ed.), *Social work with the aging* (2nd ed., pp.157–170). Silver Spring, MD: National Association of Social Workers.

Golden, R., & Saltz, C. C. (1997). The aging family. *Journal of Gerontological Social Work, 27*(3), 55–64.

Greene, R. R. (1982). Life review: A technique for clarifying family roles in adulthood. *Clinical Gerontologist, 2,* 59–67.

Greene, R. R. (1988). A life systems approach to understanding parent–child relationships in aging families. *Journal of Family Psychotherapy, 5*(1/2), 57–69.

Greene, R. R. (1993). Public information, prevention, and health promotion. In S. Finckel, C. Dye, A. Garcia, M. Gatz, R. R. Greene, D. P. Hay, M. Smyer, & M. J. Wykle (Eds.), *Report of the Interdisciplinary Coordination Group on Mental Health and the Elderly.* Washington, DC: National Institute of Mental Health.

Greene, R. R. (2000). Serving the aged and their families in the 21st century: Using a revised practice model. *Journal of Gerontological Social Work, 34*(1), 41–62.

Greene, R. R. (2002). (Ed.). *Resiliency: An integrated approach to practice, policy, and research.* Washington, DC: NASW Press.

Greene, R. R., & Blundo, R. (1999). Postmodern critique of systems theory insocial work with the aged and their families. *Journal of Gerontological Social Work, 31*(3/4), 87–100.

Greene, R. R., Kropf, N., & Pugh, K. L. (1994). Planning health education for older adults: The use of health model and interview data. *Gerontology and Geriatric Education, 15*(2), 3–18.

Greene, R. R., & McGuire, L. (1998). Ecological perspective: Meeting the challenge of practice with diverse populations. In R. R, Greene & M. Watkins (Eds.), *Serving diverse constituencies: Applying the ecological perspective* (pp. 1–28). New York: Aldine de Gruyter.

Hareven, T. K. (1982). The life course and aging in historical perspective. In T. K. Hareven & K. J. Adams (Eds.), *Aging and life course transitions: An interdisciplinary perspective* (pp. 1–26). New York: Guilford Press.

Hawley, D. R., & DeHaan, L. (1996). Toward a definition of family resilience: Integrating life-span and family perspectives. *Family Process, 33,* 283–298.

High, D. M. (1991). A new myth about families of older people. *Gerontologist, 31,* 611–623.

Hooyman, N. R., Hooyman, G., & Kethley, A. (1981, March). *The role of gerontological social work in interdisciplinary care.* Paper presented at the Council on Social Work Education Annual Program Meeting, Louisville, KY.

Hooyman, N., & Kayak, H. (1996). *Social gerontology* (4th ed.). Needham Heights, MA: Allyn & Bacon.

Hudson, R. B. (1996). The changing face of aging politics. *Gerontologist, 36,* 33–35.

Jones, A. H. (1999). Literary perspectives on ageing. *Literature and Ageing, 354,* p.1.

Kirschner, C. (1986). The aging family in crisis: A problem in living. In C. H. Meyer (Ed.), *Social work with the aging* (2nd ed., pp. 149–156). Silver Spring, MD: National Association of Social Workers.

Kiyak, N., & Hooyman, N. (1999). Aging in the twenty-first century. *Hallyn International Journal of Aging, 2*(1), 56–66.

Light, P. C. (1988). *Baby boomers.* New York: W. W. Norton.

Lewis, J. S., & Harrell, E. B. (2002). Resilience and the older adult. In R. R. Greene (Ed.), *Resiliency: An integrated approach to practice, policy, and research,* (pp. 277–292). Washington, DC: NASW Press.

Lowy, L. (1985). *Social work with the aging.* New York: Longman

Lugaila, T. (1998). Marital status and living arrangements: March 1997. *Current population report series, P20–506.* Suitland, MD: U.S. Census Bureau.

Maugans, J. E. (1994). *Aging parents, ambivalent baby boomers: A critical approach to gerontology.* Dix Hills, NY: General Hall.

National Alliance for Caregiving and the Alzheimer's Association (NAC/AA). (1999). *Who cares? Families caring for people with Alzheimer's disease.* Bethesda, MD: Author.

National Alliance for Caregiving and the American Association of Retired Persons (NAC/AARP). (1997). *Family caregiving in the U.S.: Findings from a National survey.* Bethesda, MD: Author.

Pincus, A. (1970). Reminiscence in aging and its implications for social work practice. *Social Work, 15,* 47–53.

Popenoe, D. (1993). American family decline, 1960–1990: A review and appraisal. *Journal of Marriage and the Family, 55,* 527–555.

Riley, M. W., & Riley, J. W. (2000). Age integration: Conceptual and historical background. *Gerontologist, 40,* 266–269,

Rowe, J. W., & Kahn, R. L. (1998). *Successful aging.* New York: Pantheon Books.

Scharlach, A. E., & Kaye, L. W. (Eds.). (1997). *Controversial issues in aging.* Boston: Allyn & Bacon.

Silverstone, B. (1996). Older people of tomorrow: A psychosocial profile. *Gerontologist, 36,* 27–32.

Silverstone, B. (2000). The old and the new in aging: Implications for social work practice. *Journal of Gerontological Social Work, 33*(4), 35–50.

Silverstone, B., & Burack-Weiss, A. (1983). *Social work practice with the frail elderly and their families.* Springfield, IL: Charles C Thomas.

Smith, G., Kohn, S. J., Savage-Stevens, S., Finch, J. J., Ingate, R., & Lim, Y. (2000). *Gerontologist, 40,* 458–468.

Stacey, J. (1996). *In the name of the family: Rethinking family values in the postmodern age.* Boston: Beacon Press.

Szabo, V., & Strang, V. R. (1999). Experiencing control in caregiving: A national profile. *Gerontologist, 27,* 677–683.

Tennstedt, S. (1999, March 29). *Family caregiving in an aging society.* Paper presented at the U. S. Administration on Aging Symposium: Longevity in the New American Century, Baltimore.

Tennstedt, S., & Chang, B. H. (1998). The relative contribution of ethnicity vs. socioeconomic status in explaining differences in disability and receipt of national care. *Journals of Gerontology: Social Sciences, 53B*(2), 861–870.

Uhlenberg, P. (2000). Introduction: Why study age integration. *Gerontologist, 40,* 261–308.

Vourlekis, B., & Greene, R. R. (1992). *Social work case management.* New York: Aldine de Gruyter.

Walsh, F. (1998). *Strengthening family resilience.* New York: Guilford Press.

Walsh, F. (1999). Families in later life: Challenges and opportunities. In E. A. Carter & M. McGoldrick (Eds.), *The expanded life cycle: Individual, family, and social perspectives* (pp. 307–324). Boston: Allyn & Bacon.

Wattenberg, E. (1986). The fate of baby boomers and their children. *Social Work, 31,* 20–28.

Weber, J. A., & Waldrop, D. P. (2000). Grandparents raising grandchildren: Families in transition. *Journal of Gerontological Social Work, 33*(2), 27–46.

Webster, N. (1983). *New universal unabridged dictionary*. New York: Simon & Schuster.

Wiener, J. (2003). The role of informal support in long-term care. In J. Brodsky, J. Habib, & M. Hirschfiel (Eds.), *Key policy issues in long-term care* (WHO Collection on Long-Term Care, pp. 3–24). Geneva: World Health Organization.

Willis, S. L. (1991). Cognition and everyday competence. In K. W. Schaie (Ed.), *Annual Review of Gerontology and Geriatrics* (vol. 11, pp. 80–109). New York: Springer.

Yates, M. E., Tennstedt, S., & Chang, B. H. (1999). Contributors to and mediators of psychological well-being for informal caregivers. *Journals of Gerontology: Psychological Sciences, 54B*(1), 12–22.

Vital Involvement: A Key to Personal Growth in Old Age

Helen Q. Kivnick

Worldwide technological, economic, and demographic changes are forcing a reconsideration of the period of life referred to as old age—in all domains of individual functioning and at every level of societal organization and participation. In particular, the formidable extension of the individual life span and the expansion of the size of the overall population of elderly people require a reconceptualization of social work practice with individuals in this life period. The foundation of social work rests on the notion that human behavior takes place in a mutual interaction with the social environment (human behavior and the social environment; HBSE). This dual attention to individual development and to the social environment, as well as to the reciprocal influences between these entities, constitutes a solid basis for adapting social work practice modalities in order to optimize the personal development of elderly people. That is, social workers can help promote indi-

vidual life strengths and psychosocial health as older individuals participate in such diverse levels of social systems as the family, the geographic community, activity- and age-based social groups, the residential community, the political system, and more.

In presenting vital involvement as a construct that links the elderly individual with the social environment, HBSE theory provides a basis for practice that promotes strength and growth in both. Rather than focusing simply on personal growth in old age or on societal changes that are necessary if elderly people are to achieve their individual potential, the principle of vital involvement promotes social work practice with the goals of optimizing the quality of every individual's long life in the context of a society that is increasingly multigenerational and multicultural, and in a way that enables elderly people to make ongoing contributions to the social systems in which they live and from which they are drawing support.

Human Behavior and the Social Environment

Social work educators cite the need for an HBSE basis to social work practice (Schneider & Netting, 1999; Tracy & Pine, 2000). As a group, however, social workers too often fall short of using HBSE theory to guide the development of practice modalities, approaches, and activities that best serve the multidimensional interests of clients and their environments. In particular, they fail to build on what HBSE theory teaches about the inextricability of person and environment. This failure is not surprising, in that theorists seeking to explain human behavior as it occurs in the social environment tend to emphasize either the person or the environment—but not both.

These emphases resemble the images produced by a movie camera. Theorists who emphasize the person (for example, Erikson, Freud, Piaget, Gilligan, Kohlberg, Baltes) bring into clear focus the specific personal dynamics or processes (for example, psychosocial, psychosexual, cognitive, moral, behavioral) that they seek to explain. To a greater or lesser extent, these theorists refer to the role of the environment in the development of human behavior. But even when they mention the environment, it remains, as in a close-up film frame, blurred and indistinct. It is present, to be sure, but only as an all but featureless background. As theorists focus on individual dynamics, so practice modalities grounded in such theory make use of interventions to improve these dynamics. For example, psychoanalytically oriented psychotherapy focuses on altering pathological psychodynamics; cognitive–behavioral treatment teaches clients new internal cognitions. The construct of selective optimization and compensation developed by Baltes (1991) illustrates this individual focus, as directed explicitly toward older adults.

On the other hand, theorists who emphasize the environment (for example, Bronfenbrenner, Lewin, Carter and Anderson, McGoldrick) make the environment their photographic "figure" and the person their "ground." These theorists bring into clear focus the structure and dynamics of multiple levels of the environment in which a given person lives. They may clarify the components of social systems and the relationships among them as part of their focus on one environmental system (for example, family, neighborhood) or another. Or, explicitly attending to old age, they may identify such system features as structural lag (Fried, Freedman, Endres, & Wasik, 1997; Riley & Riley, 1994) or pervasive ageism (Neugarten, 1984) as problems requiring resolution. In these theories, however, individual persons and their internal dynamics remain blurred, as a film hero sitting at a desk blurs when the camera moves back to focus on the details of the portraits hanging on the wall behind him. The HBSE approach offers social workers a vision for beginning to bring these oppositely focused theories into a productive balance and for using this balance in practice that promotes well-being in both person and environment.

Principles of Life Cycle Development

The construct of vital involvement emerges from the most recent formulations of Erikson's life cycle developmental theory (Erikson, Erikson, &

Kivnick, 1986; Kivnick, 1993; Kivnick & Jernstedt, 1996; Kivnick & Murray, 2001). The theory describes eight psychosocial themes as an underlying framework upon which people actively—though not necessarily consciously—build their lives. Three re-articulated principles clarify the cyclical process through which an individual interacts with the environment: (1) process in time, (2) dynamic balance of opposites, and (3) vital involvement. In this process, the individual develops a unique set of strengths and weaknesses that influence the choices, responses, and engagements that, in turn, influence subsequent development.

Process in Time

On Figure 7-1, each row represents a period in life's time (for example, infancy, older adulthood). Each column on the figure represents a psychosocial theme (for example, trust and mistrust, integrity and despair). According to the principle of process in time, each of the eight themes is the focus of psychosocial activity at a particular period or stage. However, **all** themes are perpetually in operation—even when they are not focal. The developing person reworks infancy's trust and mistrust, for example (Figure 7-1, Box 1), throughout life while struggling to maintain hope and acknowledge misgiving in a way that both builds on earlier experience and responds to current circumstances—while simultaneously concentrating on whatever theme is focal (Figure 7-1, Boxes 9, 17, 25, 33, 41, and 49). This tension remains meaningful in older adulthood (Figure 7-1, Box 57), as the elderly person relies on a lifetime of faith to balance realistic mistrust in a world that becomes increasingly un-

familiar and in a future that grows ever more uncertain.

Dynamic Balance of Opposites

According to the principle of dynamic balance of opposites, each psychosocial theme includes two opposing tendencies, both of which are essential, in some measure, to psychosocial health. For example, healthy resolution of school age's focal tension between industry and inferiority requires the child to balance emerging competencies and feelings of industriousness with ever-present reminders that there is still much to learn. Healthy balancing of older adulthood's focal tension between integrity and despair requires an ongoing adaptation to current losses and deteriorations, as well as to environmental supports and obstacles. It also requires a reconciliation of the commissions and omissions of a lifetime, and a weaving together of past and present into a life tapestry whose warp clearly extends into the future, however uncertain.

The dynamic balance of opposites principle helps clarify the significance of some differences in culture, gender, race, sexual preference, physical ability, and more. Variation is great—across groups, over historical time—in defining appropriate thematic balances. Nonetheless, the thematic content itself crosses boundaries. LaVern, for example, might find it easier to relinquish commitments and responsibilities that she now finds unsatisfying, if her cultural environment assigned specific role behaviors to elderly people. In a society in which self-esteem depends largely on individual instrumentality, she finds both her sense of self and her image in the eyes of others extremely

Figure 7-1

Psychosocial Themes at Various Periods of Life

Older Adulthood	57	58	59	60	61	62	63	64 Integrity & Despair WISDOM
Middle Adulthood	49	50	51	52	53	54	55 Generativity & Self-absorption CARE	56
Young Adulthood	41	42	43	44	45	46 Intimacy & Isolation LOVE	47	48
Adolescence	33	34	35	36	37 Identity & Confusion FIDELITY	38	39	40
School Age	25	26	27	28 Industry & Inferiority COMPETENCE	29	30	31	32
Play Age	17	18	19 Initiative & Guilt PURPOSE	20	21	22	23	24
Toddlerhood	9	10 Autonomy & Shame/Doubt WILL	11	12	13	14	15	16
Infancy	1 Basic Trust & Mistrust HOPE	2	3	4	5	6	7	8

Source: Erikson, E. H., Erikson, J. M., & Kivnick, H. Q. (1986). *Vital involvement in old age.* New York: W. W. Norton. Adapted with permission from W. W. Norton, Inc.

Box 7-1

Violet lives alone in a small two-room apartment in a subsidized senior housing complex in a part of the country where winters are very cold and very long. She moves hesitantly, with a walker that she regards as almost more of an obstacle than a help. Her mind wanders, and she has a difficult time focusing on thoughts long enough to enjoy most conversation. She frequently turns on the television, but she loses interest almost immediately. When she tries to read, she finds that unless she is instantly engrossed in whatever she picks up, she does not care to concentrate. It takes considerable effort to accomplish basic maintenance activities, and she has begun to wonder whether she should move into a nursing home or assisted living facility, where she will not have to worry about how much longer she will be able to care for herself. Violet has always been a religious woman, and she greatly misses attending church regularly. She is also troubled at her thoughts of "giving up," fearing that they may reflect an unacceptable loss of faith. Her one consistently meaningful occupation is praying along with television mass each morning, which she describes as an ongoing involvement in religious practice and a regular expression of her lifelong commitment to God.

vulnerable to older adulthood's decreasing capacities. With little sense of appropriate later-life balances for industry and inferiority, and for identity and confusion, for example, she is afraid that if she gives up long-time commitments, she will be worthless to herself and to those around her.

Similarly, gender can influence the dynamic balance of opposites. Irene, for example, is an older woman who has always taken pleasure in friendships based on telephone conversations. As an element of her long-time balance between intimacy and isolation, the telephone represents a way that she is accustomed to "being with" others even when she is physically alone. This past experience enables her to maintain social participation (a component of balancing intimacy and isolation) in the face of physical disability, in a way that comparably situated older men may find all but impossible.

Vital Involvement

According to the principle of vital involvement, a person enacts each psychosocial theme—each pair of opposing tendencies—through characteristic behaviors, activities, and attitudes. Life's activities, experiences, feelings, and attitudes may all be understood as part of balancing (that is, reworking, preworking, working on) one theme or more. Psychosocial themes constitute meaningful structures for linking the psychological (related to internal feelings and capacities) and the social (related to the external, interpersonal environment in which the psychological self exists).

Vital involvement is defined as a person's meaningful engagement with the world outside the self, a process of "being in relation" to elements of the environment (for example, people, materials, animals, ideas, institutions,

Box 7-2

LaVern has spent a lifetime working hard at being "in charge of" and "responsible for." When her first husband proved to be an alcoholic, she assumed financial as well as emotional responsibility for him and the children. When she was widowed, she joined a variety of committees through which she organized activities and provided care for those in need. Now remarried, she cares for an invalid husband. She sits on her senior community's resident council, and she volunteers in at least one service activity per day. When an extended family member needs advice or assistance, LaVern is the first one to be called. Her posture is military straight; she wears a hat whenever she steps outside her apartment. She has a strong perception of herself as a competent and responsible person. She is terrified at the prospect of someday having to rely on someone else for help. And she panics at minor experiences of forgetfulness, unable to tolerate even a small lapse in control. She acknowledges, a bit surprised, that she does not derive deep satisfaction from any of her volunteer projects, but that she dare not let anything go.

sounds) that is essential to doing internal psychosocial work and to enjoying its resulting psychosocial health. In contrast to superficial interaction, vital involvement implies ". . . an active state keeping awake . . . a readiness to develop those patterns of interaction that are ready" (Erikson, Erikson, & Kivnick, 1986, p. 44), but that may not yet have been actualized. Vital involvement typifies an individual's engagement with whatever he/she finds meaningful. Every instance of vital involvement may not be a life changing experience. But all vital involvement carries the possibility of initiating deep, lasting psychosocial change (Kivnick & Murray, 2001, pp. 18–19).

Vital involvement gives meaning to the internal processes of psychological growth and development. It is the mechanism through which the person and the environment interact with one another, through which the person incorporates outside experience and in-

fluence into the integrated self. It is also the mechanism through which the person expresses that self to exert influence on the outside world. Vital involvement is the process through which the individual relates to others, participates in the community, contributes to society, and exercises social change. It is through vital involvement with elements of the environment that the person accomplishes the lifelong developmental work of balancing all eight psychosocial themes. Through relationships, encounters, and activities, the person essentially enacts currently focal thematic balances in terms of a unique set of environmental circumstances and modifies those balances as the circumstances demand.

We exercise "our being alive by stimulating the environment as it stimulates us; for as we become vitally involved, we are also challenging the environment to involve us in its convincing ways" (Erikson, Erikson, &

Kivnick, 1986, p. 33). Unlike ordinary activity and interaction, vital involvement implies a depth of engagement that carries with it the possibility of personal change (Kivnick & Murray, 2001). It may be understood as an expression of the empowerment that Minkler (1996) promoted as a concept to tie together notions of political economy, humanistic gerontology, feminist perspectives, and cultural diversity. Shifting from traditional notions of "power over" to alternative notions of "power with" (Browne, 1995), and from traditional goals of personal independence to feminist goals of interdependence (Gilligan, 1982), vital involvement is a process through which elderly people use their own values, commitments, and interests to develop interactions with the community. Such vital involvement stands in stark contrast to a process through which a powerful social service system and its workers obtain for powerless elderly people those services that they deem appropriate.

The construct of vital involvement encompasses social work's dual emphases on person and on environment. It is compatible with the feminist notion that individual strength and resilience are meaningful primarily in a relational context, in an ongoing process of give-and-take (Jordan, 1991). Moreover, it invokes the notions of ongoing, life cycle development for every client.

Minkler (1996) noted that within the broad framework of the political economy of aging, the intersection of race, class, and gender powerfully influences the distribution of resources. That is, an elderly person's race and gender are likely to have a strong influence on

Box 7-3

Until they retired, Celia and her husband ran a small-town newspaper in the vicinity of the family farm. After retirement, they moved to the city to be in the middle of the social and political events that they had been writing about for so long. He did organizing work for one union. She wrote position papers for another. When she began to lose strength in her hands, she bought a computer and taught herself to use it so that she could continue to write. Her muscular and neurological deterioration progressed. Her husband fell and broke his hip while trying to help her up from a fall. He did not recover. Celia dresses in clothes that she can store, neatly folded, in piles on her late husband's bed; she cannot reach a closet rod or open a bureau drawer. She still writes position papers for the union. And she has begun to write what she hopes will become instructive little essays about lessons learned in a marriage that was long, loving, and by no means tranquil. She moves about on a motorized cart. Every day she is thankful for the coffee shop in her building that allows her to "get out" to meet friends and for the skyway system (enclosed walkways) that gives her year-round access to museums and libraries. She acknowledges that when she can no longer transfer herself to and from the toilet, she will probably have to move into a nursing home. "I can deal with that," she says, matter-of-factly. "As long as they let me keep my computer, I can deal with being anywhere."

her or his options for the vital involvements that enhance or diminish not only quality of life, but also survival itself. Clearly, social work practitioners must work to rectify the social and economic inequalities that threaten the health and well-being of certain groups of elderly people—and of "youngers" as well. However, social workers must not let these inequalities blind them to the very real strengths that exist in members of disadvantaged groups. The disproportionate responsibility of African American older women for raising grandchildren and great-grandchildren, along with caring for elderly relatives (Burton, Dilworth-Anderson, & Bengtson, 1992; Minkler, 1996), for example, does not invalidate the strength of the intergenerational bonds that often develop in the context of this externally imposed family configuration. Neither does it eliminate the personal growth and richness that these women may experience in the process of caregiving. These vital involvements are the product of individual strengths and resilience, and of cultural values and traditions, although they emerge in circumstances of disadvantage and discrimination. As we work to eliminate the latter, we must celebrate and perpetuate the former.

For elderly people, social workers are challenged to maximize "the remaining or new potentials of the last interactions [along with] the vital (if paradoxical) involvement in the necessary disinvolvements of old age" (Erikson, Erikson, & Kivnick, 1986, p. 33). They are challenged to use old age as "prime time" (Freedman, 1999). How can social work practice optimize psychosocial health among the new aged? And how

can practitioners do that in a way that enables everyone (new aged, old aged, not yet aged) reciprocally to optimize the quality of the social environment?

Strengths-Based Perspective

In their benchmark paper, Weick and colleaguess (1989) introduced a strengths perspective in which social workers approach clients in a spirit of collaboration, with particular concern for strengths and competencies. First, they work to identify client strengths. Then they strive to develop ways to use these client resources in building life solutions. Since its introduction, this perspective has come to emphasize two primary elements: (1) empowering clients and (2) building on client strengths (Saleebey, 1996, 1997). This perspective does not encourage the ignoring of client problems, but it "demands instead that they [problems] be understood in a larger context of individual and communal resources and possibilities" (Saleebey, 1992, p. 171). The strengths perspective emphasizes client self-determination and the participation of both client and practitioner in a search for those personal and environmental forces that can meaningfully enhance the client's life. It emphasizes the power of individuals to heal themselves, to right their own life course, by taking appropriate advantage of resources that exist in the environment. It also allies clients and practitioners around movement toward positive possibility. This powerfully motivating alliance is fundamentally different from one in which the goal is merely to move away from problems and difficulties.

Using community resources seizes opportunities for ordinary people to be vitally involved with one another. Emphasizing the competencies of clients, along with identifying corresponding opportunities in the environment, can help elicit and strengthen personal capacities in practitioners as well as in those initially identified as clients; by exercising these strengthened capacities, each person can contribute to strengthening the environment as a whole (Sullivan, 1997). The development of these connections enhances both clients and community—both persons and environment—as they stimulate one another's strengths (Benard, 1997; Saleebey, 1997). As Husock (1992) observed, this approach has much in common with that of the settlement house, which helps people through community participation and through involvement with a broad cross-section of the population. Programs are presented without being identified as solutions to problems, thus eliminating artificial distinctions between needy and helper, and enabling all interested participants to benefit.

Traditional versus Strengths-Based Perspective

In keeping with the dominant medical model, two axes broadly define the field of concerns that social work traditionally addresses (Figure 7-2). The vertical axis identifies the content of specific concerns as ranging from the personal (for example, functional abilities, injuries, diseases, motivations) to the environmental (for example, transportation, climate, community resources). The horizontal axis characterizes any specific concern along a continuum of degree ranging from problem (for example, disability, risk factor, disease) to

strength (for example, asset, protective factor). The farther left a concern falls on this horizontal axis, the more serious the problem.

Traditional social work focuses on concerns that fall in the two left quadrants. The goal is to diminish the severity of concerns, represented by moving any given problem away from its original position on the left of the horizontal axis toward a new, less serious position farther to the right on this same axis. A physiological concern is identified as a problem and then handled through assessment, diagnosis, and intervention (for example, treatment, health care services, environmental manipulation) that ideally lessen the severity of the problem until, at the point of intersection with the vertical axis, it ceases to be a problem altogether. Psychosocial problems are similarly addressed. Within this traditional model, social work seeks to help clients solve problems, that is, move to a state of functioning without problems. But this traditional model does not explicitly attempt to **maximize** client functioning, which would involve movement beyond the vertical axis and into the right-hand quadrants that represent strengths.

In our own lives, we would probably regard such de facto striving to achieve a state of emptiness—a state without problems or strengths—as somewhere between laughable and appalling. For our loved ones and ourselves we strive for excellence, for maximum strength, ability, and achievement. Simply being free of problems may be a starting point, but it certainly is not a goal that most people strive for in their own lives. Why, then, do social workers so persistently

Figure 7-2

Field of Concerns Traditionally Addressed by Social Work

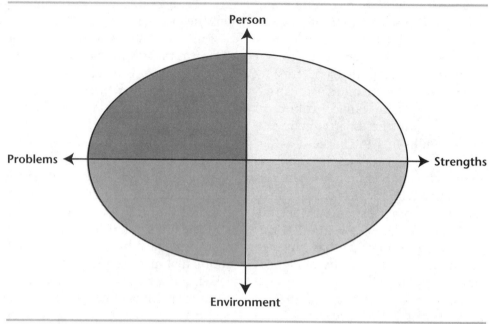

identify such emptiness as the aim of their work with elderly clients?

Scholars and practitioners have begun to use the strengths perspective in working with such disparate populations as people with chronic and persistent mental illness (Sullivan, 1997), consumers of public social services (Bricker-Jenkins, 1997), older adults (Fast & Chapin, 1997; Stoffel, Kivnick, & Hanlon, 2000), inner-city schoolchildren (Benard, 1997; Mills, 1995), juvenile offenders (Brendtro & Ness, 1995; Clark, 1998; Corcoran, 1997), adult criminal offenders (Gilgun, 1996), people with physical disabilities (Holmes, 1997), and those with substance abuse problems (Rapp, 1997). Regardless of the client population or specific intervention strate-

gies, strengths-based social work builds a foundation for change by fostering (in both practitioner and client) a favorable view of the client, enabling the client first to see and then to move beyond his or her problems and diagnoses, encouraging the client to exercise existing skills and competencies, supporting the development of further client strengths, and meaningfully linking client capacities to needs and supports in the immediate community. As seen on Figure 7-2, all five of these steps move beyond the negative, left-hand side of problem-focused practice to operate, quite explicitly in terms of client strengths, environmental supports, and potential client contributions to the community, in the figure's positive, right-hand quadrants.

Vital Involvement in Social Work with Elderly People

The primary goal of gerontological social services has long been to enable elderly clients to remain "independent" or "in the community" for as long as possible. This focus dates from an era in which people spent most of their adult life working and caring for family (Laslett, 1989) and in which old age constituted predominantly a few years of dependence and decrepitude between work and death. Such relatively recent constructs as the "third age" (Laslett) and the "new aged" (McCallum & Geiselhart, 1997) reflect the emergence of an historically unique, widely expectable, postretirement period characterized by health, activity, relative freedom from obligation, and opportunity for personal fulfillment and generational trusteeship. Thus, the original goal of gerontological services is seriously outmoded.

When elderly people constituted a relatively small fraction of the overall population and old age consisted of a few years at the end of the life cycle, it may have made sense for services to concentrate on enabling elderly people to stay, for as long as possible, outside residential facilities that are expensive, restrictive, and, in most ways, entirely different from the places that any resident has previously chosen to live. However, elderly people now constitute a sizable fraction of the overall population, and ordinary individuals can expect to spend a decade (often more than one) in the period referred to as "old age." Especially in view of these altered proportions, it is essential for senior social work to address far more than residential location and access to compensatory services.

Both for elderly people who require some form of long-term care and for those who remain more self-reliant, psychosocial well-being is a crucial resource that can play a role in the adaptivity that Baltes and his colleagues (Baltes & Baltes, 1990; Baltes, Wahl, & Reichert, 1991) have described as so much a part of successful aging. Even those who disagree with the assertion that personal identity is created by actions, by projects that contribute to the community (Woodward, 1988), or with the view that the process of life review itself gives a final shape to identity (Butler, 1963) must acknowledge that successful aging depends on each elderly person's lifelong pattern of strengths, abilities, values, and purposes. Understanding these patterns and enabling the elderly person to adapt them to current circumstances can maximize that success. Social workers must learn to broaden their notion of elderly people' resources beyond such traditionally assessed variables as physical health, socioeconomic status, and social support. They must include in their inquiry the vitality, the grit, and the underlying commitment to values that constitute the infinite resource of the human spirit. As individual elderly people, as family members, as professionals, and as a whole society, they must respect this spirit, understand its dynamics, nurture it, and learn to use it to fullest advantage—not only for elderly individuals themselves, but also for the nested ecological systems (Bronfenbrenner, 1979) in which they live.

To promote individual growth in later life, it is necessary to tap into the personal values and lifelong commitments that guide all people as they use their time, solve their problems, and, ultimately, live out (or last through) their "aged" years (Kivnick & Murray, 1997). Each elderly person's values and commitments will, finally, determine whether she or he will continue to grow through vital involvement with facets of the community, maintain a narrowly circumscribed existence with the help of support services received in a community-based residence, exercise meaningful personal strengths after moving to a residential facility where necessary support services are easily delivered, or simply receive necessary support services by moving to a traditional residential facility. Vital involvement and associated psychosocial growth and development need not remain outside the nursing home door. Far more important than *where* an elderly person lives is the vital involvement promoted by *how* the elderly person lives.

Assessment

Exploration, assessment, and planning constitute the first phase of the social work helping process (Hepworth, Rooney, & Larsen, 2002). Practitioners and scholars acknowledge serious negative ramifications of attending only to client problems; possible negative effects include reinforcement of the client's initial low self-image; danger of the problem focus becoming a self-fulfilling prophecy; interference with the social worker's recognition of a client's potential for growth; and underestimation of a client's existing strengths, pre-intervention history of growth and development, and intervention-based progress in the direction of personal strengths, abilities, and dreams.

More than two decades of research (Gomez, Zurcher, Farris, & Becker, 1985; Maluccio, 1979; Presley, 1987; Toseland, 1987) and conceptual development (Cowger, 1994, 1997; Saleebey, 1997) confirm the importance of client strengths, goals, hopes, growth, and satisfaction to the outcome of social work practice. Nonetheless, many clinicians continue to practice assessment in terms of three primary foci: (1) the client's view of the problems or concerns that led to the social worker, (2) legal mandates that influence the client–social worker relationship, and (3) potentially serious concerns related to the client's health or safety—each of which directs client and social worker attention to problems, disabilities, dangers, and potential negative consequences (Hepworth et al., 2002). This lag in practice development is dangerous for the well-being of elderly people, who are vulnerable to overwhelmingly negative stereotyping by themselves and others, as a result of a lifelong socialization in the monolithic view of old age as dependence and disability; the inescapable presence of physiological deteriorations, psychosocial losses, and chronic medical conditions; and the relatively recent and still tenuous societal acknowledgment that old age includes the potential for individual growth and contribution.

Cowger (1994) argued that "the role of the social worker . . . is to nourish, encourage, assist, enable, support, stimulate, and unleash the strengths within people [and] to illuminate the strengths available to people in their own environments" (p. 264), and that an initial assessment of client strengths is essential to mobilize the personal competencies that will create change.

Why have social workers persisted in emphasizing client problems and disabilities in the face of research, ideology, and practice data that clearly indicate the need for greater breadth? Kivnick and Murray (2001) answered this question by pointing to an historical link to the medical model, an agency-based encouragement for practitioners to regard client strengths and assets as indications to direct professional attention elsewhere, and the lack of a consensually accepted language for discussing client strengths. They also identified structural and systemic characteristics that make it necessary for social workers, perhaps more so than other professionals, to continue concentrating on elderly clients' problems and weaknesses (for example, mandated standardized assessments, service and reimbursement eligibility). This misplaced concentration cannot continue to dominate social work practice if social workers are to succeed in their professional goal of facilitating the development of strong, healthy elderly people in a society that is similarly strong and healthy.

Cowger (1994) and Kivnick and Murray (2001) offered tools for social workers to use in implementing processes in which the client and the social worker cooperate to understand the client's whole story—including strengths as well as weaknesses, triumphs as well as defeats, dreams as well as despairs. Building on a two-axis model (horizontal: environmental versus personal; vertical: strengths versus deficits), Cowger directed practitioners to work with clients of all ages in the quadrant of personal strengths, focusing on cognition, emotion, motivation, coping skills, and interpersonal skills.

For each of these psychological strengths, Cowger suggested a number of examples intended to guide client and professional in their collaborative exploration (1997).

Kivnick and Murray (2001) drew from conceptual research on older adult role models (Kivnick, 1995; Kivnick & Jernstedt, 1996) and on practice-based research on case management in community-based long-term care (Kivnick, 1991, 1993) to develop a 10-item strengths assessment interview (see appendix B, p. 241). Derived entirely from research on elderly people, this tool is designed explicitly to engage elderly clients. The open-ended interview questions guide both elderly client and social worker in thinking and talking meaningfully about the diverse life strengths around which the elderly individual has built her or his long life. Inseparable from the elderly person's history of vital involvement in the world, these strengths took shape as the elderly person experienced environmental supports and obstacles in everyday interactions with people, ideas, objects, organizations, and more. Emerging, they helped structure the person's "gifts" in a lifelong process of give-and-take.

Personal losses, disabilities, needs, and risks disrupt this process of give-and-take—as do changes in the environment and its diverse social and physical systems. All of these interfere with an elderly person's taking in essential matter, energy, and information. They also interfere with contributions that have helped the elderly individual define a unique, personal ecological niche. Personal life strengths deteriorate further as a result of disuse; the life strengths' environmental supports diminish further as a result of corresponding neglect. It takes more than identifying and compensating for specific losses to restore an appropriate ecological balance. It is essential also to work with the client to identify the values, hopes, dreams, and capacities (that is, the life strengths) that are critical to this balance.

Intervention

The cooperative exploration and assessment of an elderly person's needs and strengths lead quite naturally into the planning, strategizing, implementing, and progressing of the intervention phase. Just as assessed obstacles and problems inform social work intervention, so must assessed strengths play a role in planning and implementing intervention. It is important that vital involvement remain integral during the move from assessment to intervention, for intervention is the heart and soul of social work. Once personal dreams have been identified, they must be translated into goals. Strategic plans must be developed for achieving these goals. Intervention plans and contracts must go beyond the professional delivery of devices and services, and client acceptance of those assistances to include the elderly person's vital involvement in making progress toward personal goals. Progress must reflect a personal engagement that runs deeper than using devices, receiving services or completing tasks. In a practice grounded in vital involvement, it is the social worker's role to ensure that interventions foster strengths in the client, in the environment, and in the links between them.

Emphasizing vital involvement helps social workers and elderly clients alike develop a balanced approach, addressing obstacles along with assets, problems along with strengths, losses along with opportunities. Indeed, the construct of vital involvement makes it possible to move beyond simply matching needs with available services and assisting clients with the resolution of existing problems. Both of these activities remain necessary, but they are most powerful when they enable clients to live meaningful lives in their communities. Rather than continuing to produce all-too-familiar "case plans" or "care plans," promoting vital involvement encourages social workers to collaborate with clients in designing "life plans."

In addition to structuring care and services for elderly clients, practitioners must focus the social work process on two additional phenomena: (1) the ways that elderly people use allocated care and services to optimize personal meaning and growth, and (2) the ways that such use strengthens and enriches the environments in which individual elderly people live and from which they receive supports. Irene not only eventually agreed to accept the services available from the Association for the Blind, but also expanded her role with the association from one of "service recipient" to one that included "volunteer." That is, she made productive use of services provided, and she provided service that helped strengthen the association in return.

Case Work with Individuals. Social workers serve elderly clients in diverse settings and in a wide variety of roles. In all of these, attention to vital involvement can promote the reciprocal

Box 7-4

Irene, mentioned earlier, was referred to public senior services for help in adapting to progressive blindness. In her right eye, she has a detached retina and suffers from macular degeneration. A recent fall resulted in the loss of her left, "good" eye and its replacement with a prosthesis. Before the fall, she had moved into a large, suburban house with her granddaughter and great-granddaughter. She had sometimes felt painfully isolated from the friends and acquaintances that she enjoyed in her long-time urban neighborhood. She feels increasingly helpless and unhappy since the fall. She now needs assistance with such basic daily activities as walking, shopping, bathing, and using the telephone.

Irene's initial interviews with the case manager focused on enumerating her difficulties and on identifying possible assistive devices, such as bathroom bars, a bath bench, a hand-held shower, a large-button telephone, sturdy shoes, and new glasses. Each of these would help mitigate one cause for her feelings of helplessness. But none seemed to point her in the direction of personally meaningful competence.

In a strengths assessment, Irene explained to the case manager that she had sold her urban home and bought this house with her granddaughter because her great-granddaughter needed to move out of the city, and this was a way she could help. She and her granddaughter share financial and maintenance responsibilities for the household. Irene also expressed a great pride in her 30 years as a professional bookbinder, noting that she has always loved both the reading and the physical qualities of books. As she thought about it, she suddenly realized that bookbinding has a great deal in common with the embroidery that she has done since childhood. (Neither Irene nor the case manager would have thought to include this vital involvement information in their work together without an assessment tool that elicited it.)

Together, Irene and the case manager began to realize that minimizing the obstacles posed by sudden and increasing blindness was the first—rather than the final—step in her continuing to live the life that she has created for herself. Although undoubtedly changed, that life is not yet over. Along with arranging for appropriate assistance, they began to brainstorm about how she would like to live, not just survive. What would she like to be doing? Learning? Creating? Feeling? With whom would she like to be visiting? How could they build on her lifelong interests and abilities to enable her to continue the experiences that are, as they have always been, central to the meaning of her life?

growth of person and social environment. Social work clinicians provide counseling and psychotherapy to elderly people and their families. As case managers, social workers conduct assessments and monitor progress, work with families, access outside services (for example, health care, nutrition, personal care, linguistic assistance), make referrals, and determine eligibility. When they facilitate social support to help a woman recover from a shattered hip,

Box 7-5

Irene initially hesitated to contact the Association for the Blind. Like many proudly self-sufficient individuals, she had no wish to identify herself with an agency or with a group of people characterized by disability. However, while discussing her love of books, she and the case manager began to think of this association more as a possible tool for her re-engaging with reading than as a support group for the visually impaired. That is, they began to see the association as a resource for Irene's vital involvement.

Fortunately, the person who initiated Irene's first telephone conversation from the association was someone who also loved to read, and Irene found herself talking about books and stories with the caller. She soon expressed eagerness to receive the equipment and media for talking books—in contrast to her earlier reluctance even to consider using these devices. Almost immediately, she enjoyed the talking books. As time passed, she also came to look forward to discussing these books with similarly avid readers from the association. She eventually volunteered with the association, making initial telephone contact with elders like herself who had active minds and wide-ranging interests, and for whom newly failed vision loomed as a sentence of helplessness, stagnation, and despair.

they are likely to increase both the pace and the degree of her recovery (Kempen, Scaf-Klomp, Ranchor, Sanderman, & Ormel, 2001). When they help her learn to navigate her apartment in a new wheelchair, they help her regain a measure of mobility. When they work with her so that she can continue from the wheelchair activities that she has always enjoyed, social work clinicians go beyond immediate problem solving to help her revive her vital involvement.

Agency Programming. Social workers in community multiservice agencies arrange such on-site services as transportation and translation, coordinate multiple agencies to deliver programs, monitor service reimbursability, and make referrals. They may also be involved in implementing programs, supervising other staff, and coordinating elements of client programming and staff training and development. In addition to helping to meet elderly clients' basic needs for a daily hot meal, for social contact outside the home, and for the language and culture translation that is especially important for immigrants, staff at these agencies could help promote diverse vital involvements among elderly participants.

For example, research indicates that elderly people who work as aides or volunteers in early child care programs nurture the young children in a way that complements the instrumentality of trained teachers (Larkin & Newman, 2001). Even without formal training and support in preschool education, elderly people can add a familial element to the daily lives of preschool participants, enrich the professional experience of teachers, enhance their own feelings of competence and community participation, and improve the

Box 7-6

Cooking is an occupation through which Ana has long exercised competence, experienced creativity, expressed her identity, and delighted her family. She has always loved to cook. She knows that she is good at it. She has always gone to the kitchen and cooked, mixing ingredients without having to think about them, when one of the children was in trouble or when she had to make a rent payment that she could not afford. She realizes, as her shoulders relax and a smile spreads across her face in discussing the topic, that she has always felt like herself while cooking. The fact that this activity nurtures those who love her helps her maintain reciprocity with family members in the face of new disabilities and dependencies.

Ana's case manager seeks to arrange for this woman's relatives to be available to supplement basic personal care, home care, and meal preparation services. But an adult son is less reluctant to stop by and replace light bulbs, for example, when he anticipates an affectionate visit with Mom and a plate of his favorite cookies than he is if he knows that he will also have to commiserate at length with her loneliness and boredom or defend himself against attacks of abandonment. His daughter may well telephone her grandmother to request recipes or to invite herself over to make *tamales* or *julekaka* when her sense of her grandmother continues to include interests to be shared and cultural traditions to be learned. Telephone calls are likely to become less frequent and more wholly dutiful if the adult son feels an overwhelming resentment about his obligations to his mother or if the granddaughter finds herself lacking common ground with the grandmother whom she had always enjoyed as an energetic guide to new experiences and generationally distant worlds. When the elder woman remains vitally involved, contact with her continues to enrich family and friends, enabling them to continue to provide assistance and support without becoming irreversibly depleted. This kind of intergenerational family involvement is easiest in ethnic communities (for example, Latino; Hmong) in which families are traditionally large and deem elder care a privilege as well as a responsibility.

quality of community-based service. This kind of structured activity facilitates the vital involvement of older adults in intergenerational nurturing. In turn, this nurturing improves elderly people' own feelings of well-being, enhances important agency services, and contributes to overall agency quality.

Existing service programs have likely been designed to compensate for client deficits. Simultaneous attention to client assets and to community involvement holds great promise for increasing the impact of compensatory service programs and for introducing creative programming to promote growth and development in both participants and their community. The Muse Workshops at The Center in Clay, New York, offer multicultural folk art programs for seniors (Town of Clay, n.d.). In disciplines such as prose and poetry writing, drawing, and painting, the workshops encourage elderly people to explore diverse cultures and to re-involve themselves in artistic expression. Elderly muses also work with children and with each other, both to enhance general understanding of multicultural values and idioms, and to increase proficiency in expressive arts. Clearly, participation in Muse Workshops enriches the elderly people in a way that simply receiving a hot lunch cannot accomplish. The creative, intergenerational structure of the workshop program expands the enrichment to children, to The Center, and to the town in which they all live.

Agencies that are educational or artistic in purpose also sponsor programs that support older people's involvement in the arts. Research supported by the American Music Conference has demonstrated that active music making reduces loneliness and depression among elderly people. Through Operation Reach Out, the St. Croix River Valley Arts Council encourages arts participation and appreciation among area elderly people, and also promotes the work of area elderly artists (Center for Creative Aging, n.d.). The council distributes a free newsletter, providing regularly updated information about shows and performances in the community and featuring the work of elderly artists. In addition, the council displays the work of these senior artists.

The Roots & Branches Theatre (http://www.fegs.org/news_events/news/rootbranches/haym2.swf) integrates New York City seniors over the age of 65 with college arts students at New York University to create, rehearse, and perform a major play each year. Work-shops are held in the fall, a script is constructed and rehearsed over the winter, and springtime performances are given at senior centers , and other community venues. Since 1976, Liz Lerman's Dance Exchange has made dance and movement participation accessible to elderly people across a spectrum from novices who have never done formal "dance" or "movement" through retired dance professionals. Levels of involvement range from weekend workshops for beginners to a national, intergenerational performance company. At Roots & Branches and at the Dance Exchange (http://www.danceexchange.org), programs promote physical and psychosocial strength in participating elderly people—related not only to the theater and dance activities themselves, but also to intergenerational understanding and communication. In addition, these groups' performances allow participants to contribute to the community by providing the live arts experiences that stimulate vitality and excitement in audiences and performers alike.

Although artistically diverse programs like these are not necessarily the creations of social workers, they exemplify the kinds of multilevel strength promotion that can result from vital involvement by older people. Seniors who participate certainly experience personal growth. Their involvement enriches other participants—often across several generations. Public showings and performances help break down generational and cultural barriers, replacing them with understanding and respect. Public performances also enrich those elderly people who may not yet be ready to participate in the expressive arts, but who are quite ready to support their counterparts from the audience. These creative aging programs and others stimulate both individual and community development in a way that social workers are, almost by definition, trained to build into professional practice in every agency.

Hospitals and Nursing Homes. Hospital-based social workers provide short-term individual and family support, and they carry out discharge planning. As nursing homes accept larger numbers of short-stay patients, discharge plan-

ning becomes a bigger and bigger part of hospital and nursing home social workers' job responsibilities. Such planning, like the individual casework discussed earlier, currently focuses largely on accessing services and assistive devices, determining eligibility, and identifying resources for clients' future use. Also like individual casework, discharge planning must expand its scope to include vital involvement for exercising the elderly client's strengths and hopes. This vital involvement will support the elderly person's long-term growth in and contribution to the community into which she or he is discharged.

Box 7-7

Carter Catlett Williams (personal communication, November, 1998) described one woman's arrival at a nursing home established as part of a nationwide network promoting nursing home culture change that emerged in 1995 (Pioneer Network, n.d.). Like many residents, this woman was moving to the nursing home as a last resort, and she experienced the move as an admission of defeat. She had always been strong and competent. Widowed, she had lived on her own for years. Rather than receiving care, she had given care, serving as a source of strength and support for family, friends, and neighbors. Like many women of her cohort, she was known for her cooking, and she took pride in using her skills in the kitchen to nurture others. By the time of her admission, however, she required assistance with all of her activities of daily living (ADLs), and her speech was so severely impaired that she could barely make herself understood. Still, she resented this move.

This nursing home was designed as a collection of "neighborhoods," each consisting of several private rooms that opened off a shared kitchen and living room area. These common spaces were intended for resident use and created to be both attractive and practical. The new resident paid only superficial attention when she was shown her room and her bathroom. But she could not resist the kitchen. Surfaces, drawers, and appliances were low and easily reached. Floor space readily accommodated wheelchairs and walkers. The atmosphere was bright and inviting. She smiled in spite of herself and, speech impairment notwithstanding, proclaimed, "I thought I was coming here to die. Now I see that I've come here to *live.*" She might as well have said, "I've come here to cook!" For this woman, living was unthinkable without vital involvement in cooking, and it was suddenly clear that this nursing home community wanted to support her in doing both.

Box 7-8

With the unexpected death of my father, it quickly became apparent that my mother's Alzheimer's disease was already moderately advanced. Osteoarthritis, rheumatoid arthritis, scoliosis, atrial fibrillation, Parkinson's disease, low blood pressure, lactose intolerance, and severe hearing loss were just some of the additional conditions that led social work staff in the Meadowood retirement community, outside Philadelphia, to determine that she needed to move immediately into the community's nursing home unit. Creative, curious, and relentlessly retentive (Kivnick, 1995), my parents had over 45 years transformed an ordinary eight-room ranch house into a gallery that displayed intergenerational family photographs; artwork and crafts collected from around the world; and their own original objects of glass, wood, copper (Dad's), needlepoint, bargello, crewel, knitting, and sewing (Mom's). Moving from that home into a two-bedroom apartment roughly three years earlier had required them to dispose of roughly two-thirds of their collection. Now Mom was moving (if things worked out in the best of ways) into a single, small room that would have to accommodate whatever belongings she continued to own.

Like most facilities, the Meadowood Health Center has no locked storage space for nursing home residents. My brothers and I had little time to identify those few objects that would be most meaningful to Mom in the room that would now be home—objects that could engage her in personal memories, in moments of self-recognition, or in new experiences of interest. But Mom had never spent many of her waking hours in the bedroom. We could not imagine her voluntarily living in a bedroom for the rest of her life. Neither could we imagine her feeling "at home" in common spaces with walls that were bare or decorated with commonplace prints.

We proposed to the Health Center administrator that we hang much of the artwork from Mom and Dad's apartment in the hallway outside her room. This artwork included her needlepoint copies of Vasarely paintings, framed embroidery from the Middle East, a Chinese scroll, a Japanese fan, a sand painting from the American Southwest, a Scandinavian tapestry, the Picasso and Roualt prints that had hung in our living room since my childhood. We reasoned that these pieces could certainly help Mom feel more comfortable in a new environment that was bound to be shocking. We also suggested that they might be more engaging for other residents and for staff than the haphazardly chosen pictures that were currently scattered on the walls. The administrator and her colleagues agreed, and so we launched what they called the "Art Sharing" project.

Mom's artwork now hangs in the hallway outside her room, along with a sign identifying the pieces as hers, and the project is facilitywide. On the day we hung the pictures, house-keeping staff stopped me to say that they would look forward to spending time on this hall. Residents gathered while the pictures went up, asking Mom specific questions to which she responded with a surprising measure of her once-characteristic authority. For a moment, despite her newly bereft status, she was a celebrity.

Mom does not always recognize her own hall. Most of the time, she does not acknowl-edge the nursing home as "home." But she does stop as she moves up and down the hall, sometimes, to smile at the Kabuki actors whose expressions made her laugh from the moment that she bought the poster. I do not know what she is thinking when she looks at her needlepoint of Don Quixote and Sancho Panza, just beyond where her hall branches off from the main lounge. I do know that she is looking. She is not sleeping or dozing in her wheelchair. Her expression is not blank. She is not crying out in agitation.

Is Mom's dementia progressing less rapidly than it might if we had not created Arts Around? Probably not. Are other residents less confused or in less pain? I doubt it. Does interesting artwork on the walls relieve staff of the burdens of low salary, distasteful job tasks, and inconsistent appreciation? I do not think so. But to the extent that familiar artwork in the halls engages Mom in anything outside the "chutes and ladders" of her degenerating mind, she retains some connection to the world. To the extent that residents are confronted with interesting art when they glance at the walls, they enjoy frequent opportunities for the personal engagement that the arts offer us all. Art in the halls introduces positive sensory stimulation into a physical environment that is more often experienced as somewhere between sterile and noxious. And to the extent that staff use her pictures as a basis for making small talk with Mom, they are personalizing interactions that too often have no basis but instrumentality.

Other residents and their visitors occasionally stop and look at one or another of Mom's pieces. New staff quickly identify Mom with her artwork; they make a point of coming into her room to see what she has on the walls inside. And sometimes I notice them looking at the walls as they walk through Mom's hall—not staring toward the window at the end and the outside beyond.

For longer stay nursing home residents, social workers process admissions, conduct pre-admission screens, do adjustment work with residents and families, access supplementary services, monitor financial reimbursement, and encourage socializing and participation in activities. Although much of inpatient practice focuses on accessing services and solving problems, attention to vital involvement can lead to creative programming that flows down from agency leadership; percolates up from individual residents; and, in both directions, enriches elderly residents, nursing home staff, family members, and the entire nursing home community.

Housing and Day Treatment. In senior high-rises, retirement communities, and continuous care communities, social work staff help individual residents with adjustment and service referrals, assist with service access and reimbursement, and facilitate such specialized assessments as an occupational therapy evaluation of apartment safety or a physical therapy assessment of readiness to participate in a particular exercise program. They may also collaborate with other staff in designing communitywide wellness and activity programming, as well as in forming multidisciplinary teams for assessment, intervention, and monitoring. In one high-rise in Portland, Oregon, a longtime resident had grown too frail to participate in regular programming. This woman had, for years, planted a rose bush in memory of each resident who died. Attentive staff recognized the value of this activity—to the woman, to all building residents, and to the building community as a whole—and

on her return from one particular hospitalization, they made a plan with her to continue this practice despite her physical deterioration.

In day treatment programs, social workers are part of the multidisciplinary teams that design and conduct group activities, access and deliver on-site services, and arrange for appropriate off-site services. Social workers are likely to retain primary responsibility for senior and caregiver support groups. In view of often overwhelming disabilities among those who need day treatment, staff are pressed to mitigate elder and caregiver stress by providing as many services as possible. The vital involvement through which each participant experiences the unique human process of psychosocial growth and development may be lost in this press for services. Without vital involvement, the interpersonal connections that constitute the essence of community may also be lost.

Conclusion

Across the United States, existing programs and creative intervention strategies promote a diversity of vital involvements among elderly participants. Beyond the relatively limited arena of formal programming, individual elderly people and their families frequently exercise vital involvement as a natural adaptation of lifelong relationships to the vicissitudes of aging and disability.

The construct of vital involvement was formulated to describe a process inherent in epigenetic psychosocial development throughout the life cycle (Erikson et al., 1986). As the process

Box 7-9

A team of artists, caregivers, and elder dementia patients developed a program called Time Slips (n.d.) to use creative storytelling to promote meaningful communication with people who have Alzheimer's disease. In Milwaukee, Wisconsin, and in New York City, intergenerational teams of day program staff, patients, and trained undergraduate storytelling facilitators participated in weekly workshops through which even extremely reticent elders "blossomed out of silence" and into creative communication. Group stories wove together personal memories, historical and cultural references, and illness-related quips. The stories gave rise to a photographic art installation and a play staged in New York City in November 2001. As with Arts Around, confused elder Time Slips participants experienced vital involvement with a world outside their personal ruminations. In so doing, they created a process that enriches the other group participants, and that creeps out, tendril by tendril, to connect lives meaningfully across time and barriers.

that mediates between person and environment, vital involvement is integral to everyday mental health (Kivnick, 1993). Targeted programs reactivate this process in elderly people and social environments where a focus on problems ignores growth and allows strength to atrophy. But the process has always been part of lifelong development and of individual creativity. Although some may dismiss existing life cycle theory as irrelevant to realizing human potential among the new aged (Cohen, 2000), the theory-based construct of vital involvement inextricably ties healthy development to personal creativity at every age.

Growth promotion programs and strategies have emerged from such disciplines as occupational therapy, recreational therapy, psychology, nursing, physical therapy, activities therapy, horticulture, music, art, dance, drama, writing, faith practice, and more—in addition to social work. Vital involvement's reciprocity, and its being interwoven

with life strength and development, allows it to encompass the essential goals and values of each of these professions. In so doing, it sheds light on the full range of human strengths in elderly clients and in their various social and structural environments, regardless of the setting in which any given elderly individual may live or any given professional may work.

Social work's fundamental concern with person, environment, and their interconnections makes the vital involvement construct uniquely understandable to and usable by social workers. This construct complements the field's ongoing work with individual clients. It also directs practitioner attention to the environment as a source of supports to be provided, as well as obstacles to be overcome. Social workers can promote vital involvement in elderly people not only by accessing existing services, but also by creating new supports (for example, programs, linkages, institutions) that connect members of all generations in positive, productive ways. In case management, supervision, and training, social work practice can be structured to take advantage of vital involvement's inherent dualities, reciprocities, and positive orientation.

An understanding of vital involvement can enable practitioners, administrators, and policymakers to broaden the range of existing senior programs and to expand participation in these programs, thus maximizing personal growth and development among elderly people. It can also lead to the development of new policies and new programs in a variety of settings. Finally, it can encourage social workers to conduct their individual and family lives in ways that promote contributions of elder people to one another, to their families, and to the neighborhoods, facilities, and community agencies within which we will all live out our old age.

References

American Music Conference. (n.d.). Retrieved November 11, 2001, from http://www.amc-music.com/.

Baltes, M. M., Wahl, H., & Reichert, M. (1991). Successful aging in long-term care institutions. In K. W. Schaie & M. P. Lawton (Eds.), *Annual review of gerontology and geriatrics* (Vol. 11, pp. 311–337). New York: Springer.

Baltes, P. B. (1991). The many faces of human ageing: Toward a psychological culture of old age. *Psychological Medicine, 21*, 837–854.

Baltes, P. B., & Baltes, M. M. (1990). Psychological perspectives on successful aging: The model of selective optimization with compensation. In P. B. Baltes & M. M. Baltes (Eds.), *Successful aging: Perspectives from the behavioral sciences* (pp. 1–34). New York: Cambridge University Press.

Benard, B. (1997). Fostering resiliency in children and youth: Promoting protective factors in the school. In D. Saleebey (Ed.), *The strengths perspective in social work practice* (2nd ed., pp. 167–182). New York: Longman.

Brendtro, L. K., & Ness, A. E. (1995). Fixing flaws or building strengths? *Reclaiming Children and Youth: Journal of Emotional and Behavioral Problems, 4*(2), 2–7.

Bricker-Jenkins, M. (1997). Hidden treasures: Unlocking strengths in the public social services. In D. Saleebey (Ed.), *The strengths perspective in social work practice* (2nd ed., pp. 133–150). New York: Longman.

Bronfenbrenner, U. (1979). *The ecology of human development*. Cambridge, MA: Harvard University Press.

Browne, C. (1995). Empowerment in social work practice with older women. *Social Work, 40*, 358–364.

Burton, L., Dilworth-Anderson, P., & Bengtson, V. (1992). Creating culturally relevant ways of thinking about aging and diversity: Theoretical challenges for the 21st century. In E. P. Stanford & F. M. Torres-Gil (Eds.), *Diversity: New approaches to ethnic minority aging* (pp. 129–140). New York: Baywood.

Butler, R. (1963). The life review: An interpretation of reminiscence in the aged. *Psychiatry, 26*, 65–76.

Center for Creative Aging. (n.d.). Retrieved November 1, 2001, from http://www.center-for-creative-aging.org.

Clark, M. D. (1998). Strength-based practice: The ABC's of working with adolescents who don't want to work with you. *Federal Probation, 62*(1), 46–53.

Cohen, G. D. (2000). *The creative age: Awakening human potential in the second half of life*. New York: Avon Books.

Corcoran, J. (1997). A solution-oriented approach to working with juvenile offenders. *Child and Adolescent Social Work Journal, 14*, 277–288.

Cowger, C. D. (1994). Assessing client strengths: Assessment for client empowerment. *Social Work, 39*, 263–268.

Cowger, C. D. (1997). Assessing client strengths: Assessment for client empowerment. In D. Saleebey (Ed.), *The strengths perspective in social work practice* (2nd ed., pp. 59–73). New York: Longman.

Erikson, E. H., Erikson, J. M., & Kivnick, H. Q. (1986). *Vital involvement in old age*. New York: W.W. Norton.

Fast, B., & Chapin, R. (1997). The strengths model with older adults: Critical practice components. In D. Saleebey (Ed.), *The strengths perspective in social work practice* (2nd ed., pp. 115–132). New York: Longman.

Freedman, M. (1999). *Prime time: How baby boomers will revolutionize retirement and transform America*. New York: Public Affairs.

Fried, L. P., Freedman, M., Endres, T., & Wasik, B. (1997). Building communities that promote successful aging. *Western Journal of Medicine, 167*, 216–219.

Gilgun, J. F. (1996). Human development and adversity in ecological perspective, Part 1: A conceptual framework. *Families in Society, 77*, 395–402.

Gilligan, C. (1982). *In a different voice: Psychological theory and women's development*. Cambridge, MA: Harvard University Press.

Gomez, E., Zurcher, L. A., Farris, B. E., & Becker, R. E. (1985). A study of psychosocial casework with Chicanos. *Social Work, 30*, 477–482.

Hepworth, D. H., Rooney, R. H., & Larsen, J. A. (2002). *Direct social work practice: Theory and skills* (6th ed.). Pacific Grove, CA: Brooks/Cole.

Holmes, G. E. (1997). The strengths perspective and the politics of clienthood. In D. Saleebey (Ed.), *The strengths perspective in social work practice* (2nd ed., pp. 151–164). New York: Longman.

Husock, H. (1992, Fall). Bringing back the settlement house. *Public Interest*, pp. 53–72.

Jordan, J.V. (1991). The meaning of mutuality In J.V. Jordan, A.G. Kaplan, J.B. Miller, I.P. Stiver, & J.L. surrey (Eds.), *Women's growth in connection: Writings from the Stone Center* (pp. 81–96). New York: Guilford Press.

Kempen, G.I.J.M., Scaf-Klomp, W., Ranchor, A. V., Sanderman, R., & Ormel, J. (2001). Social predictors of recovery in late middle-aged and older persons after injury to the extremities: A prospective study. *Journal of Gerontology; Social Sciences, 56B*(4), S229–S236.

Kivnick, H. Q. (1991). *Living with care; caring for life: The inventory of life strengths*. (Available from Long-term Care DECISIONS Resource Center, School of Public Health, University of Minnesota, Minneapolis, MN 55455)

Kivnick, H. Q. (1993). Everyday mental health: A guide to assessing life strengths. *Generations, 17*(1), 13–20.

Kivnick, H. Q. (1995). Save it. In M. Cruikshank (Ed.), *Fierce with reality: An anthology of literature about aging* (p. 172). St. Cloud, MN: North Star Press.

Kivnick, H. Q., & Jernstedt, H. L. (1996). Mama still sparkles: An elder role model in long-term care. *Marriage and Family Review, 24*(1/2), 123–164.

Kivnick, H. Q., & Murray, S. V. (1997). Vital involvement: An overlooked source of identity in frail elderly people. *Journal of Aging and Identity, 2*, 205–223.

Kivnick, H. Q., & Murray, S. V. (2001). Life strengths interview guide: Assessing elder clients' strengths. *Journal of Gerontological Social Work, 34*(4), 7–32.

Larkin, E., & Newman, S. (2001). Benefits of intergenerational staffing in preschools. *Educational Gerontology, 27*, 373–385.

Laslett, P. (1989). *A fresh map of life: The emergence of the third age.* London: Weidenfeld and Nicolson.

Liz Lerman Dance Exchange (n.d.). Retrieved October 19, 2001, from http://www.danceexchange.org/.

McCallum, J., & Geiselhart, K. (1997). *Australia's new aged.* St. Leonards, New South Wales, Australia: Allen & Unwin.

Maluccio, A. (1979). Perspectives of social workers and clients on treatment outcome. *Social Casework, 60*, 394–401.

Mills, R. (1995). *Realizing mental health.* New York: Sulzberger & Graham.

Minkler, M. (1996). Critical perspectives on ageing: New challenges for gerontology. *Ageing and Society, 16*, 467–487.

Neugarten, B. L. (1984). *Age or need? Public policies for older people.* Beverly Hills, CA: Sage Publications.

Pioneer Network. (n.d.). Retrieved November 19, 2001, from http://www.pioneer network.net/index.cfm/fuseaction/showHomePage.cfm.

Presley, J. H. (1987). The clinical dropout: A view from the client's perspective. *Social Casework, 68*, 603–608.

Rapp, R. (1997). The strengths perspective and persons with substance abuse problems. In D. Saleebey (Ed.), *The strengths perspective in social work practice* (2nd ed., pp. 77–96). New York: Longman.

Riley, M. W., & Riley, J. W., Jr. (1994). Age integration and the lives of older people. *Gerontologist, 34*, 110–115.

Roots & Branches. (n.d.). Retrieved November 1, 2001, from http://www.fegs.org/news_events/news/rootbranches/haym2.swf.

Saleebey, D. (1992). Conclusion. In D. Saleebey (Ed.), *The strengths perspective in social work practice* (pp. 169–179). New York: Addison-Wesley Longman.

Saleebey, D. (1996). The strengths perspective in social work practice: Extensions and cautions. *Social Work, 41*, 296–305.

Saleebey, D. (1997). *The strengths perspective in social work practice* (2nd ed.). New York: Longman.

Schneider, R. L., & Netting, F. E. (1999). Influencing social policy in a time of devolution: Upholding social work's great tradition. *Social Work, 44*, 349–357.

Stoffel, S., Kivnick, H. Q., & Hanlon, D. (2000, November). *Vital involvement groups: Piloting an approach to personal strength in old age.* Paper presented at the meeting of the Gerontological Society of America, Washington, DC.

Sullivan, W. P. (1997). On strengths, niches, and recovery from serious mental illness. In D. Saleebey (Ed.), *The strengths perspective in social work practice* (2nd ed., pp.183–197). New York: Longman.

TimeSlips. (n.d.). Retrieved October 1, 2001, from http://www.timeslips.org/

Toseland, R. (1987). Treatment discontinuance: Grounds for optimism. *Social Casework, 68*, 195–204.

Town of Clay. (n.d.). Retrieved October 28, 2001, from www.townofclay.org.

Tracy, E. M., & Pine, B. A. (2000). Child welfare education and training: Future trends and influences. *Child Welfare, 79*, 93–113.

Weick, A., Rapp, R. C., Sullivan, W. P., & Kisthardt, W. (1989). A strengths perspective for social work practice. *Social Work, 34*, 350–354.

Woodward, K. (1988). Reminiscence, identity, sentimentality: Simone de Beauvoir and the life review. In R. Disch (Ed.), *Twenty-five years of the life review: Theoretical and practical considerations* (pp. 25–48). New York: Haworth Press.

Spiritual and Religious Life

James W. Ellor

"Years may wrinkle the skin, but to give up interest wrinkles the soul."

Douglas MacArthur

Since the dawn of time, humanity has turned to God or gods to explain the unknown, the scary, the basis for creation, and the answers to the 'greatest mysteries of life and death. For many hundreds of years in Western Europe, the only theory of explanation for creation and life came from Christian Scripture as interpreted by the church. Over the past 150 years, Western societies have moved toward more scientific and humanistic interpretations or explanations of human existence. During this time, the importance of religious and spiritual interest has fluctuated both in society in general and within specific groups or geographic locations. In the experience of the current cohort of older adults, historians have suggested that society has become progressively less interested in spiritual matters (Blazer & Palmore, 1976) and more invested in science. Yet, for this same cohort, surveys continue to suggest that 80 percent of older adults actively attend church, syna-

gogue, or temple (Gallup, 1994). Frequently, seniors find religion and spirituality more important than the social worker who listens to their concerns.

Positive or successful aging finds its way into the nomenclature of social work through sociological studies of lifestyle. Studies of positive lifestyle have moved from subjective, or ideal, discussions, such as those articulating utopian communities, to more scientific investigations of life satisfaction and behavioral outcomes. Positive aging in the current form addresses the question, "What is the goal or ideal form of aging?" For too long, the social work literature has emphasized the negative aspects of aging and has supported the pathology-based medical model of aging, which links positive aging to a lack of health pathology or chronic illness. Positive aging offers an ideal of healthy aging that can inspire personal growth. However, the basis for positive aging is an attitude toward life, rather than an absence of illness or physical problems. Positive aging offers a goal for such practice concepts as clinical assessment and intervention, and it forms the basis for positive program development.

A Theory of Spiritual and Religious Positive Aging

Three terms have emerged in recent years in the field of gerontology: wellness, successful aging, and positive aging. Although these terms are not mutually exclusive, each is used somewhat differently, often by different groups of professionals.

The term "wellness" emerged from the field of prevention. Often associated with adolescents and addictions, prevention is an approach to help individuals avoid certain self-destructive behaviors. Because aging is not something to be prevented, wellness has become a lifestyle approach to help people avoid some of the problems that commonly develop in aging. Often emanating from health educators, wellness generally focuses on physical aging and disease prevention.

Professionals who struggle with the issues of happiness in aging, with particular emphasis on the length of life, use the term "successful aging." With older adults living longer, they believe that some aspects of prevention can be used to enhance longevity.

As understood in this chapter, the term "positive aging" draws from both prevention and successful aging, but the emphasis is on the person's attitudes as much as on the behaviors and practices used to enhance longevity. Positive aging may not mean a long life. Rather, positive aging reflects individuals' capacity to adjust their attitude toward life in order to make the most of the years that they have.

Rowe and Kahn (1998) noted that one perspective on successful aging is genetic, in that length of life is a combination of genetics and lifestyle. However, what wellness, successful aging, and positive aging have in common is the need to adjust lifestyle to provide greater happiness. Numerous research studies, as well as personal anecdotes from seniors, suggest the truth of the statement, "when you have your health, you have everything." Yet, when health fails, positive aging can be an important factor, because it reflects an approach to life that sees the good in life, not just the deficits. Thus, positive aging reflects not only a wellness perspective to lifestyle, but also an attitude adjustment toward life that is able to find ultimate meaning in everyday existence.

Religion versus Spirituality

In the individual and community quest for meaning in human existence, as well as in their quest for the ultimate meaning of life, religion and spirituality play an important role. The term *religion,* as defined by Koenig, McCullough, and Larson (2001), referred to "an organized system of beliefs, practices, rituals, and symbols, designed (a) to facilitate closeness to the sacred or transcendent (God, higher power, or ultimate truth/reality); and (b) to foster an understanding of one's relationship and responsibility to others in living together in a community" (p. 18). Organized religions first emerged more than 6,000 years ago. They reflect both the nature of the organizations and the beliefs held by these groups (Figure 8-1).

Figure 8-1

Model for Positive Aging Programming in a Clinical Setting

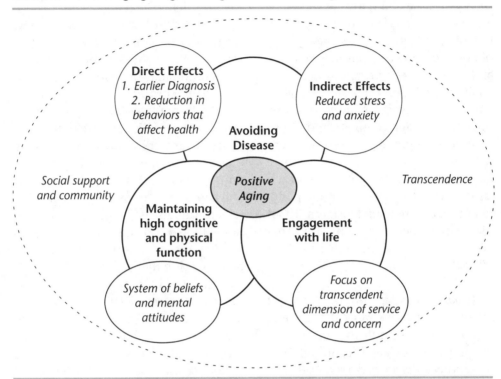

ADAPTED FROM Rowe, J. W., & Kahn, R. L. (1998). *Successful aging.* New York: Pantheon, p.39. Koenig, H. G.. (1997). *Is religion good for your health?* Binghamton, NY: Haworth Press, pp. 67, 80.

In contrast, spirituality is unique to each individual. Koenig and associates (2001) defined *spirituality* as "the personal quest for understanding answers to ultimate questions about life, about meaning, and about relationship to the sacred or transcendent, which may (or may not) lead to or arise from the development of religious rituals and the formation of community" (p. 18). Religion and spirituality are not mutually exclusive. Rather, each has its place within the other. It is generally thought, however, that an individual can be spiritual without being religious, but cannot be religious without being spiritual. This personal spirituality of

nature and the inner self may not find support in common beliefs and organizations. For many, the concept of Divine intervention and the mysteries of the work of God's spirit explain the impact of religious and spiritual matters on positive aging. The very belief in God and the spirit is indeed critical; yet, research in this area suggests that even without a belief in the miraculous, religion and spirituality are important to positive aging.

Holistic View of Later Life

Studies by Koenig (1997), Dorsey (1993), and Levin (1993) have begun to build a database of scientific studies of positive aging that reflect a holistic view of later life. When drawn together with the theory of successful aging developed by Rowe and Kahn (1998), these studies of the role of religion suggest a *new* theory of positive aging (see Figure 8-1). Rowe and Kahn defined *successful aging* as "the ability to maintain three key behaviors and characteristics: avoiding disease, maintaining high cognitive and physical functioning, and active engagement with life" (p. 38). Each of these three factors is important by itself, but each also relates to the other. Rowe and Kahn, reflecting on Abraham Maslow's (1954) hierarchy of needs, hypothesized that avoiding disease is the most basic of these three.

Avoiding Disease. Although medical science has demonstrated that genetic factors play a significant role in the major diseases of later life, lifestyle and the choices that a person makes also play an important role. Avoiding disease and disability is the goal of disease wellness. Health experts know that reducing stress also reduces high blood pressure and the diseases that stem from it. For example, eating fatty foods can lead to high cholesterol levels, which can contribute to circulatory diseases. Many people ignore the early signs of disease. Elevated blood pressure, for example, may not cause pain or dysfunction until it becomes heart disease. By the time the person recognizes the heart disease, he or she has become a patient who needs a physician to help fight the disease. The goal of wellness is to avoid becoming a patient. Early intervention and lifestyle change can lengthen life and avoid the discomforts and expense of medical treatment. Most people would agree that avoiding health problems enhances the experience of aging.

To accomplish the goals of wellness for most seniors in Western society, a focus on lifestyle is critical. Genetic background may predispose a senior to one of the chronic illnesses that commonly plague later life. Yet, a positive attitude toward life can help that senior cope with any chronic disease. This may mean strict compliance with the recommendations of a physician. But it may also mean the senior's perspective toward the disease. A positive attitude not only toward the disease, but also toward life, is important. It starts by remembering that each day is precious and that life is in and of itself a gift. Because it is not always easy to maintain a positive attitude toward life, the social support of family and community also plays a key role.

Koenig and Cohen (2002) suggested that religious and spiritual factors have both direct and indirect effects in the prevention of disease. Among the direct effects is the important area of early detection of disease. Religious teachings, particularly those of Hinduism and the three major religions of Abraham—Judaism, Christianity, and Islam—all teach the sanctity of life and respect for the human body. In the words of the Christian tradition, the body is a "temple of the Holy Spirit" (I Corinthians 6:19 [Revised Standard Version]). Consistent with this tenet from Scripture, Koenig (1997) cited research indicating that religious people may be more compliant with the recommendations of medical professionals. A second direct effect noted by Koenig (1997) is that religious commitment affects health by "discouraging behaviors such as excess alcohol and drug use, smoking, risky sexual behaviors, and several other activities that adversely affect health" (p. 80). Studies by Koenig (1997) suggest that, in particular, rates of alcohol and cigarette smoking are lower for religious individuals than for the general population. These direct effects on longevity offer avenues in which religious affiliation influences wellness and makes positive aging possible.

Koenig (1997) pointed to the indirect effect of reduced stress and anxiety provided by what both Koenig and colleagues and Pargament (1990) referred to as "religious coping." Koenig (1997) noted that there is "a link between religiousness, social support, and mental health." This link is evident in the social support offered by religious groups, as well as in the perspective on life offered by traditional religion, particularly religions that describe a God who is higher than humanity and reliable in looking after the world. This benevolence is seen as comforting at times of distress. With religious coping, the individual can see a *human tragedy* and reframe it as *God's will,* in this way reducing some of the stress of the situation. Religious support and coping can be documented both in mortality and in suicide studies (Koenig, 1997). One need only listen to seniors talk about how they have managed emotionally through difficult times. They commonly say that they derive comfort from faith in a higher power that walks with them through these events.

Maintaining High Cognitive and Physical Function. The third and final factor articulated by Rowe and Kahn (1998) is maintaining high cognitive and physical function. The balance of life between cognitive impairments—common among older adults—and potential physical diseases, and the ability to overcome these deficits of aging come from a combination of genetics and attitude. Although science does not completely know why one person develops Alzheimer's disease and the next person does not, it is clear that those people who continue to be challenged to maintain high cognitive and physical function able to avoid these deficits longer. Rowe and Kahn (1998) found that "research has three reassuring messages on the subject of maintaining function in old age: first, many of the fears about functional loss are exaggerated; second, much functional loss can be prevented; and third, many functional losses can be regained" (p. 42). For example, the myths of cognitive dysfunction abound in the community. Although some seniors do suffer from Alzheimer's disease and other associated disorders, Rowe and Kahn went on to say that, "in Alzheimer's disease, as in so much else about aging, genes are not destiny. How we live also determines how we age" (p. 43).

Religion plays a part in maintaining function through its system of beliefs and mental attitudes. Beliefs in such things as an afterlife are reflected in discussions about how to live one's life. Beliefs in the nature of the body are projected into a motivation for health care, as well as into prohibitions against such things as excessive alcohol consumption, smoking, and suicide. Koenig (1997) noted, "The research to date, then, appears to show that people who are more religious are physically healthier and tend to live longer than those who are not religious" (p. 93). As important, or even more so than the basic impact of belief, is the role of religion in providing meaning in life. Through transcendence, both with the Divine and between people, religions offer a fundamental source and rationale for ultimate meaning.

Staying Actively Engaged in Life. Rowe and Kahn (1998) pointed to a second factor for successful aging—engagement with life. In this regard, they described two factors: positive relationships with others and the feeling of making a contribution to society. For most people, an active engagement in life leads to greater well-being. Havighurst, Neugarten, and Tobin (1963) were the first to recognize the importance of active engagement in their development of the activity theory of aging. Both for the provision of mutual support and for a greater sense of well-being, transcendent behaviors of caring, reflected in various activities, can offer the individual a sense of purpose and meaning in life. This transcendent theme is clearly an important aspect of religion.

From the perspective of religion and spirituality, transcendence is understood to exist both between God and humanity, as well as between person and person. This transcendence is critical to the development of meaning as understood by the psychologist Viktor Frankl (1969) and by the theologian Paul Tillich (1967). Existential authors have agreed that transcendence is the heart of meaning. Frankl noted, "Existence is not only intentional but also transcendent. Self-transcendence is the essence of existence" (p. 50). Without self-transcendence, there can be no way to discover and fully grasp meaning. Senior center and recreation therapy staff can testify that it is possible for people to be engaged in many activities without finding meaning in them. Without meaning, activities are simply motions and actions. Engagement with life reflects the deep human need for meaning and well-being. Koenig and Futterman (1995) reported that between 1974 and 1995, "there had been 23 studies of the relationship between religiousness and well-being among older adults. In 21 of these studies, investigators found that people who were more religious had greater well-being." By staying active in religion, particularly when that involves other people of like-minded faith, such as members of a religious congregation, seniors are participating in transcendent activities and in that allow for engagement in meaningful aspects of life.

Roles of Religion and Spirituality in Successful Aging

Key to all the roles of religion and spirituality in all three areas of successful aging are two elements: the social support of a caring community and transcendent meaning. Religious organizations provide a group identity that offers social support. Studies by Veroff, Kulka, and Douvan (1981) have indicated that after family, clergy are the first individuals turned to in times of crisis. These studies showed that when seniors turn to those outside the family for support, they seek assistance from clergy 39 percent of the time, from their physician 21 percent of the time, and from social workers 3 percent of the time (Veroff et al., 1981).

Beyond help-seeking patterns, religious congregations offer numerous social services, groups, and social opportunities (Tobin, Ellor, & Anderson-Ray, 1986). Worship, Bible study, women's or men's groups, and all of the other activities and services give the individual the opportunity to be part of a caring community that offers support, both informally and formally. Koenig (1997) noted, "Well known are the physical health effects of strong social support, better mental health, healthier lifestyles, avoidance of alcohol and smoking, early recognition of disease and greater compliance with treatment, and these have been increasingly linked to religious beliefs and practices" (pp. 93–94).

Transcendent meaning also ties all three aspects of successful aging together with the spiritual. Frankl (1969) and Tillich (1967) struggled with the translation of the word spirit or in German, *Geist*. Frankl suggested that any European, when confronted with the word *spirit,* would need to ask which type of spirit. Where Tillich made the distinction between *Geistlich* and *Geistig* in his writing by talking about spirit with a lower-case "s" and Spirit with a capital "S," Frankl made no such distinction. Bulka (1979) noted that

> the translators of Frankl's works used the term spirituality loosely, thus distorting the precise meaning that is evident from the German. Frankl, in his own English writings, carefully avoids this misuse by using the terms "'noölogical'" and "'noëtic,'" to differentiate the psychological and psychic,

respectively, and to distinguish the spiritual dimension in its religious sense. (p. 17)

For Frankl (1969), the spiritual aspect of the person is the *noölogical* dimension. In short, Frankl perceived the traditional psychological concept of self-transcendence as this noölogical quality of interpersonal concern. Frankl (1975) noted, "the noölogical dimension may rightly be defined as the dimension of uniquely human phenomena" (p. 13). It is within this dimension that Frankl understands "man's search for meaning" (p. 13). It reflects human relationships to one another and to the Divine, not the religious understanding of the transcendent relationship between humanity and the Divine. This explanation of the noölogical dimension offers social workers a clue in helping clients to find meaning, as it suggests that transcendence must be present. Therefore, meaning is found in the social context of reaching out to others and being reached by others.

Logotherapy

Although logotherapy, the therapeutic approach developed by V. Frankl, focuses on the distinctly human aspects of life, it borders on the religious. Frankl (1975) viewed religion as a human phenomenon, which the therapist must perceive as positive. However, he is clear that psychotherapy is not religion. Transcendence at the human level reflects the capacity to care about others more than one necessarily cares about oneself. "Frankl insists that the essence of the human endeavor is self-transcendence" (Bulka, 1979, p. 94). The ability to transcend constitutes the noëtic aspect of the person. Frankl (1967a) wrote:

> Man transcends his environment toward the world; but more than this, he also transcends his being toward an ought. When he does this, he rises above the level of the somatic and the psychic and enters the realm of the genuinely human. This reality is constituted by a new dimension, the noëtic, the dimension of the spirit. (p. 134)

In this way, the human spirit, *Geistig*, reflects many of the values for human interaction that are found in religion. Frankl noted: "truly, self-transcendence is the essence of human existence" (p. 134). Meaning is not an intrapsychic philosophical concept. Rather, it is a critical aspect of spirituality that points to humanity's fullest capacity for "being."

Frankl (1963) described "the striving to find a meaning in one's life as the primary motivational force in man" (p. 154). Three key concepts elucidate the importance of meaning: "freedom of the will," "the will to meaning," and "the meaning for life" (Frankl, 1969, p. 16). Frankl acknowledged that the body can be placed in bondage, but the therapeutic value of logotherapy lies in the understanding that each person has a freedom of will. In other words,' even though the body can be held in chains, no one can take away the individual's right to choose his or her attitude toward the world. Individuals have a freedom to choose value orientations, a freedom to choose transcendence over the primacy of the self. This freedom resides, however, in the context of responsibility toward oneself and others.

Frankl (1969) said that the motivation to choose the transcendent values comes from what he called the will to meaning. According to Bulka (1967), the will to meaning "may be seen as the mediating principle between the human being, the 'subject,' and the world of values, the 'object'" (p. 48). Human beings are free to choose and have the capacity to will toward meaning. Frankl was clear that the will to meaning is a spiritual act. He frequently contrasted the will to meaning with the pleasure principle of Sigmund Freud or the will to power principle of Alfred Adler, which suggests that the primary motivation of humanity is to strive toward pleasure or power, respectively. The drive to pleasure and the will to power, in Frankl's view, are self-defeating. The more an individual pursues either of them, the more he or she is alienated from others. This type of isolation leads to greater anxiety—not the fulfillment of "being." Frankl (1967a) put it this way: "My own reaction to this theorizing is that I would not be willing to live for the sake of my 'defense mechanisms,' much less to die for the sake of my 'reaction formations'" (p. 54).

In logotherapy, life has an unconditional meaningfulness that is always available to grasp. As illustrated by Frankl's (1967b) many examples, meaning is there to be found. However, no one can give meaning to someone else. Meaning is realized through values that are available if an individual chooses to grasp or see them. "Meaning is what is meant by a person who asks me a question, or by a situation which, too, implies a question and calls for an answer" (Frankl, 1969, p. 62). It is the product of a triad of creative, experiential, and attitudinal values. These attitudinal values are further defined by reflection on the individual's values toward pain, guilt, and death (Frankl, 1969, p. 73).

This concept of the spiritual suggests that "rather than being concerned with any inner condition, be it pleasure or homeostasis, man is oriented toward the world out there, and within this world, he is interested in meanings to fulfill, and in other human beings" (Frankl, 1969, p. 73). The freedom of the will can challenge suffering to determine how the individual will view the suffering. Meaning can be found, even in tragedy. It is this human capacity to will to meaning that truly sets humanity aside from other life forms.

Although the spiritual or noëtic aspect of humanity reflects the transcendent nature of human existence, Frankl (1967a) pointed out the human capacity to will to understand God. Meaning at the human level is down to earth. However, Frankl also described "some sort of meaning that is 'up in heaven,' as it were; some sort of ultimate meaning" (p. 143). He noted that "the more comprehensive the meaning, the less comprehensible it is" (p. 143). This ultimate meaning eludes scientific definition, but can be found in religion. Frankl (1975) defined religion as man's search for ultimate meaning (p. 13). He went on to explain that religion guides the individual to find the ultimate meaning in life. If this is true, he added, belief and faith are another way of saying trust in an ultimate meaning. Frankl noted, "Once we have conceived of religion in this way—that is, in the widest possible sense—there is no doubt that psychiatrists are entitled also

to investigate this phenomenon, although only its human aspect is accessible to a psychological exploration" (Frankl, 1975, p. 13).

Positive Aging in Counseling

To promote positive aging, counseling must take into account the role of an individual's attitude toward life by using three basic principles: counseling should be holistic, should adopt the strengths perspective, and should be open to the religious and spiritual transcendent attitudes of the individual. Both theory and the literature have addressed traditional holism since Adler introduced the concept of holism in his work. For Adler, holism suggested that it is not possible to dissect the person into physical or emotional segments. Rather, the elements of a person are interrelated. Westberg suggested that holism does not define the dimensions of the person; it only ensures the inclusion of the spiritual in the equation. Most therapists today who wish to include the spiritual understand four dimensions: physical, social, emotional, and spiritual. Each dimension offers a different explanation of the human experience. Holism suggests the interaction of these dimensions. The articulation of the specific dimensions and their interactions are key to understanding the nature and needs of the whole person.

In the past, social workers faced some risk if they included the spiritual dimension in their clinical practice. With the recent inclusion of the spiritual into the approved curriculum of the Council for Social Work Education, however, the exile of the spiritual dimension has ended, and all social workers are now free to explore ways to fully understand and include the religious and spiritual dimension in practice. This same principle is being illustrated by President George W. Bush's Office of Faith-Based and Community Initiatives, which is mandated to address the earlier misunderstandings of the separation of Church and State that can be corrected in government.

For all those who use the positive aging approach in counseling, it is essential to remember that inclusion of the spiritual dimension does not imply the exclusive use of the spiritual. Holistic approaches see all four dimensions as critical. Thus, approaches that exclude the spiritual or include the spiritual to the exclusion of the other dimensions are all equally problematic. In the case of the former, the social worker is missing an important aspect of the transcendent in the client's life. In the latter, the social worker has lost his or her grounding in the very nature of being human. Positive aging is an approach that involves the whole client. It includes the strengths of clients, as well as those aspects of human existential existence that may plague their lives.

Because positive aging reflects the strengths of the individual, not just the deficits or pathologies, social workers can find a parallel in the strengths perspective (Saleebey, 1992). Clinebell (1979) first described this concept as growth counseling. In either the strengths perspective or growth counseling, the social worker begins the assessment by discovering both the strengths and weaknesses of the client. One of the key strengths is in the individual's spiritual and religious involvement and commitment. Strengths perspective advocates (Saleebey, 1992) have noted that positive assessment should include not only assessment for the *Diagnostic and Statistical Manual of Mental Disorders* (American Psychiatric Association, 1994) pathologies, but for a similar set of strengths.

Finally, clinical assessment should include the spiritual needs of the individual. In clinical practice, such an assessment involves three areas: (1) modeling of the ideal, (2) transcendent relationships with a higher power, and (3) social support. Modeling of the ideal reflects the assessment of religion as an element in coping behaviors and the meaning. As noted earlier, Koenig and colleagues (1988) and Pargament (1990) suggested that both religion and personal spirituality are useful as primary and secondary coping mechanisms. Religion and personal spirituality often assist an individual in reframing catastrophic situations. Pargament illustrated this when he said,

> Religious beliefs can contribute to the sense of integrity and continuity between what has been and what is. While other aspects of the self (e.g. physical and social) are often disrupted by disease processes and social events such as widowhood, religious beliefs offer a more stable contextual framework that lends steadiness to the life of the elderly person. (p. 195)

Social support is also critical. The common elements of religious beliefs and, at times, ethnicity among members of religious groups bring a social support that both enhances social function and offers a path for the discovery of meaning. The need for spiritual support in a social context is evident in the acts, thoughts, and feelings of many of the people who are served by the helping professions. Often without the knowledge of the counselor, psychiatrist, or other human service worker, religious congregations offer emotional and spiritual comfort. These services can parallel the work of the helping professional, or they can work against their efforts. Practitioners can be sure of the impact of the work of the religious group only if they are fully aware of it and interact with it at least in a marginal way.

Counseling in the context of positive aging then builds on the model by encouraging the avoidance of disease, an engagement with life, and the maintenance of high cognitive and physical function. In this context, counseling focuses both on the client's actions and on the client's attitude toward life. This assessment and intervention strategy involves support for the individual's use of religious coping behaviors, an examination of his or her search for meaning in life through transcendence, and the provision of social support. In terms of strengths perspective strategies, this approach sees the spiritual and religious aspects of the individual as important aspects of his or her overall strengths.

Positive aging may not imply a long life. Rather, it implies a meaningful one. The avoidance of disease may facilitate the search for meaning, but the greatest challenge may be in finding meaning for the person who has a chronic illness or is dying. Social workers should understand that there are two rules for this search for meaning. First, they must believe that meaning is always out there; it is critical for the senior to share this belief. Second, they cannot give meaning to the older adult. In short, the client must conduct the search for meaning. The role of the social worker is to facilitate the process. It is not to achieve some type of insight or analysis. Key to this process is the ongoing support of the client's attitude toward life as a gift. To find meaning in life is often to identify first the source of ultimate meaning and then to see how this transcendent source has been modeled or used in the client's everyday life.

Positive Aging Programming

Program options that promote positive aging also follow the model (see Figure 8-1). Both religious congregations and non-sectarian agencies that include religious and spiritual programming can offer strategies for promoting healthy aging, engagement with life, and maintenance of high cognitive and physical functioning, while promoting the search for transcendent meaning. First, it is necessary to understand that programs in religious congregations and those in nonsectarian agencies start from different assumptions.

In religious congregations, many of the programs are informal. They may not have "intake" procedures, or care files, but they do provide important programming that offers meaning for those who take advantage of it. Depending on the religious tradition, women's groups, men's clubs, Bible studies, and prayer groups all potentially offer meaningful opportunities for social support.

In community agencies and senior centers, a different challenge faces programmers. Generally, the participants are not all from a single religious tradition. In this case, interfaith approaches are essential. Opportunities for social support that involves the search for meaning and spirituality will differ from one tradition to the next. What people have in common are their community context and their search for spirituality. Religion tends to separate clients, while spirituality will draw them together. Seniors are receptive to positive aging's focus on maintaining a positive attitude in the search for meaning and transcendence, which includes both the language of spirituality and the support of the group. Senior center programs that reflect on the meaning of the personal life journey, using the principles that have been described, are one example. Groups that address topics such as grief or caregiver support should also follow these principles.

Conclusion

Positive aging as reflected in this religious and spiritual model points the social worker toward basic principles for both clinical practice and program generation. At the heart of this model is the understanding that positive aging is holistic and focuses on the attitude of the individual. The emphasis is not only on living longer. Rather, the emphasis is on developing an attitude toward living life, such as it is, to the fullest. To understand living is to find meaning through transcendence and spiritual support. Positive aging does not require the social workers who as-

sist seniors to be religious or spiritual themselves, but it requires them to listen to the religious and spiritual needs of their clients. Support of positive aging comes through the search for transcendent meaning.

References

American Psychiatric Association. (1994). *Diagnostic and statistical manual of mental disorders* (4th ed.). Washington, DC: Author.

Blazer, D., & Palmore, E. (1976). Religion in a longitudinal panel. *Gerontologist, 16,* 82–84.

Bulka, R. P. (1979). *Work, Love, Suffering, Death: A Jewish/Psychological Perspective through Logotherapy.* Northvale, NJ: Jason Aronson.

Clinebell, H. (1979). *Growth counseling: Hope-centered methods of actualizing human wholeness.* Nashville, TN: Abingdon Press.

Dossey, L. (1993). *Healing words: The power of prayer and the practice of medicine.* New York: HarperCollins.

Frankl, V. (1963). *Man's search for meaning: An introduction to logotherapy.* New York: Washington Square Press.

Frankl, V. (1967a). *Psychotherapy and existentialism: Selected papers on logotherapy.* New York: Washington Square Press.

Frankl, V. (1967b). *The Doctor and the Soul: From psychotherapy to logotherapy.* New York: Bantam Books.

Frankl, V. (1969). *The will to meaning: Foundations and applications of logotherapy.* New York: New American Library.

Frankl, V. (1975). *The unconscious God.* New York: Washington Square Press.

Gallup, G. H. (1994). *Religion in America* [Suppl.]. Princeton, NJ: The Gallup Poll.

Havighurst, R. J., Neugarten, B. I., & Tobin,

S. S. (1963). Disengagement, personality and life satisfaction. In P. Hansen (Ed.), *Age with a future.* Copenhagen: Munksgaard.

Koenig, H. G. (1997). *Is religion good for your health?* New York: Haworth Press.

Koenig, H. G., & Cohen, H. J. (Eds.). (2002). *The link between religion and health: Psychoneuroimmunology and the faith factor.* New York: Oxford University Press.

Koenig, H. G., & Futterman, A. (1995). *Religion and health outcomes: A review and synthesis of the literature.* Paper presented at the Conference on Methodological Approaches to the Study of Religion, Aging, and Health. Washington, DC: National Institute on Aging.

Koenig, H. G., McCullough, M. E., & Larson, D. B. (2001). *Handbook of religion and health.* London: Oxford Press.

Koenig, H. G., Smiley, M., & Gonzales, J.A.P. (1988). *Religion, health, and aging.* New York: Greenwood Press.

Levin, J. S. (1993). *Religion in aging and health: Theoretical foundations and methodological frontiers.* Beverly Hills: Sage Publications.

Maslow, A. H. (1954). *Motivation and personality.* New York: Harper & Row Publishers.

Pargament, K. (1990). God help me: Toward a theoretical framework of coping for the psychology of religion. *Research in the Social Scientific Study of Religion, 2,* 195–224.

Rowe, J. W., & Kahn, R. L. (1998). *Successful aging.* New York: Pantheon Books.

Saleebey, D. (1992). *The strengths perspective in social work practice.* New York: Longman.

Tillich, P. (1967). *Systematic theology.* New York, Harper & Row.

Tobin, S. S., Ellor, J. W., & Anderson-Ray, S. M. (1986). *Enabling the elderly: Religious institutions within the community service system.* Albany: State University of New York Press.

Veroff, J., Kulka, R. A., & Douvan, E. (1981). *Mental health in America: Patterns of help-seeking from 1957–1976.* New York: Basic Books.

Education and Learning

E. Michael Brady

Lifelong Learning

In the century between America's Civil War and the early years of the Vietnam War, nearly all formally organized education centered on children and youth. Lifelong learning—except for a few triumphant examples, such as the assimilation of immigrants, agricultural extension, the Lyceum and Chautauqua movements (Knowles, 1977), and the public library system—had been marginal in the overall educational picture.

In recent years, however, with the United States rapidly aging in its demographic profile, attention has begun to shift. What had been a severe bias toward children and youth in the provision of educational programs and services has begun to ameliorate. At the turn of the new millennium, lifelong learning for adults occupies the attention of local public schools (for example, preparation for a general equivalency diploma [GED], adult basic education, enrichment programs), post-secondary education (for example, extension education, continuing professional education, degree opportuni-

ties for all ages), business and industry, health and human services, the corrections system, and just about every sector of the economy. In the words of Cross (1981), we have indeed become "a learning society."

Lifelong learning—both formal and informal—has gained increasing popularity among middle-aged and older adults. Participating in classes, workshops, and other organized educational programs plays an important role for many in the flexible life course. And there are a nearly infinite variety of ways that adults engage in educational activities. Learning may or may not be institutionally sponsored, may or may not be group-oriented, may or may not be fee-based, may or may not be taught by trained instructors, may or may not even be in "real time." Today, if one can imagine a situation in which adults are actively engaged in learning, it probably exists.

As recently as 1960, only a few educational institutions offered programs specifically designed for people over the age of 50. The limited number of programs that were in operation were experimental in nature and had no basis in scientific research. By the late 1960s, however, scholars were exploring the link between aging and intellectual development, the wants and needs of mature individuals, and effective practices for working with older learners. By the mid-1970s, programs designed for older learners were proliferating, and the subspecialty of "educational gerontology" had even emerged on the scene (Peterson, 1990).

In a seminal article published in the first volume of the first scientific journal specifically dedicated to educational gerontology, Moody (1976) traced the history of changing attitudes toward older adults and the value of education in their lives. He identified four stages, each with its own underlying presuppositions that professionals and educators held about older adult education. In the first stage, the primary attitude was one of rejection of older adults. Because older adults were viewed at this time, for the most part, as economically and social obsolete, the contention was that it would be a waste of time and financial resources to provide them with educational programs.

The second stage in the development of attitudes toward lifelong learning in later age was an emphasis on social services to address the problems and needs of older people. Educational opportunities were considered to be one of a number of social services that government and private agencies could provide to assist needy elderly people. With the focus on providing access and opportunity, older adults passively received services rather than learning the skills necessary to initiate new programs. In Moody's view, many of these social service programs led to the segregation of older adults, mostly because they were designed to keep people "busy" rather than to genuinely help people improve their lives.

This attitude changed with the third stage, participation. The presupposition here was that older adults should be encouraged to actively continue in the mainstream of community life and to develop self-sufficiency—the mindset being that the knowledge and skills of these older adults become instrumental in helping them to overcome personal and societal problems. Finally, Moody (1976) theorized that the fourth and final stage of self-actualization emphasizes psychological growth and spiritual concerns as the major goal of educational programs for older adults. Based on Maslow's theory (Maslow, 1968) of the hierarchy of needs, self-actualization can be realized only through a combined psychological and spiritual quest for meaning and insight.

Although the first stage in Moody's (1976) typology has more or less completely passed from the scene (gratefully), there are strong elements of the other three stages in contemporary practice. Variations often depend on the situation and the functional status of the learners. Self-actualization is often the primary goal in programs for and with the well and mobile older adult, especially when practiced in higher education settings, but participation models are in wide use within public school–based adult education enrichment programs. Finally, a more needs-based and service approach may be the dominant model in, for example, retirement communities and nursing homes—if learning programs exist at all.

Public Policy and Older Adult Education

The change in societal attitudes toward lifelong learning has had an impact on federal and state policies. The first major development occurred with the Older Americans Act of 1965 (P.L. 89-73). This important piece of "Great Society" legislation provided a means for funding training and research at colleges and universities, which created new educational opportunities for older adults and extended workplace training, multidisciplinary graduate programs, and research in addressing the needs and wants of older learners.

A critical event in the policy history of lifelong learning took place in 1971 with the White House Conference on Aging. This national event had a significant impact on the attitudes of educators and gerontologists. Education received special attention at the conference, which called for increased funding and staffing to provide educational programs for older adults in both the public and private sectors. The main spokesperson for older learner issues at this conference, University of Michigan Professor Emeritus Howard Yale McClusky, asserted that education is a basic right for all people. Learning is continuous and, hence, is one of the primary ways of enabling older people to live a full and meaningful life. It is also one of the most effective means to help empower elderly people to make wholesome and meaningful contributions to society (McClusky, 1971).

Congress enacted the Older Americans Comprehensive Services Amendments of 1973 (P.L. 93-29) in 1973 to strengthen the Older Americans Act.

This act placed the Administration on Aging (first established as part of the original Older Americans Act of 1965) under the U.S. Department of Health, Education, and Welfare. In addition, it created both the Federal Council on Aging and the National Information and Resource Clearinghouse for the Aging. Under this act, state governments received grants for special library and education programs for older adults. In addition, the Administration on Aging supported research and training for personnel to work with older adults.

States also began to develop policies in support of older adult education. Beginning in the 1970s, centers on aging were founded in a number of land grant and research universities. State-supported institutions of higher education began to offer reduced-fee or tuition-free enrollment opportunities to older residents. Although specific rules vary widely between states and, in some cases, even within states (by level of institution), Manheimer, Snodgrass, and McKenzie (1995) found that all but six states had some tuition waiver or reduction program in tax-supported institutions of higher education.

Although there has been movement in public policy for lifelong learning, it is substantially weaker than public policy for health, housing, transportation, human services, and other areas that address the needs of older people. This lack of substantial progress in the development of policy was the focus of criticism by Peterson and Masunaga (1998), who argued that the overall record for government's promotion of education for older learners is lackluster. Statutes (for example, the "Lifelong Learning Act of 1976" [Higher

Education Act, 1976]) have been enacted, but remain essentially underfunded or not funded at all. States indeed have adopted policies allowing older adults free access to classes. But in most cases, institutions of higher education do not receive any state aid for teaching these students, so there is no incentive for them to promote these programs actively. In the words of Peterson and Masunaga (1998):

> Policy for older adult education is seriously limited, but sorely needed. The lack of policy has held back the development of the field, reduced its impact, and allowed the development of a diverse and uncoordinated set of instructional programs. Leadership is needed in order to reverse this situation, but none is visible yet. In this rapidly aging society, the need exists for educational innovations delineated by Moody twenty years ago—serious older adult educational programs with a focus on the third and fourth stages, that is, participation of older adults in society and older adults' self-actualization. Productive aging of an individual reflects productive functioning of the society, and vice-versa. (p. 60)

In the end, it is fair to say that most of the innovative work that has been done in older adult education has derived less from public policy initiatives than from creative, entrepreneurial, and visionary individual practitioners and institutions.

Learning Ability

The adage "you can't teach an old dog new tricks" haunts both instructors of adults and older learners themselves as they encounter adult learning situations. The older staff member who chooses to retire rather than learn the company's new computer system or the young professor, fresh out of graduate school, who secretly believes her older students will never meet the intellectual challenges that she is prepared to offer them have an abiding presence in our culture. This powerful myth—that adults lose their ability to learn as they age—although it has never been substantiated in the literature, nonetheless prevails.

Whereas the purpose of earlier generations of cognitive research may have been to measure decrements attributable to the aging process, most current research focuses on discovering the shape of cognitive change. Notwithstanding age-related decrements in speed of processing or short-term memory functioning, research in older adult learning recognizes that normal aging does not usually involve a simultaneous decline in all cognitive functions. As with all other aspects of human aging, however, there is a wide range of individual differences in the pattern of cognitive change in later life.

Multidimensional Intelligence

One of the major conceptualizations that has made a substantial difference in the way that educators think about the ability to learn is the theory of multidimensional intelligence. Before the 1960s, most researchers and educational practitioners considered intelligence to be a singular construct. Cattell (1963, 1987) and Horn (1976, 1985) took a different approach, theorizing that there are two basic types of intelligence, each with multiple constitutive factors. "Fluid" intelligence is the ability to perceive complex relations, to remember events and ideas over the short term, and to engage in concept formation, reasoning, and abstraction. This construct is measured by tests (which are usually timed) for rote memory, basic reasoning, figural relations, and memory span. For the most part, there has been general agreement that fluid intelligence is innate and peaks in early adulthood. At best, it remains stable throughout adulthood into later age, and in some cases—usually involving the functions of sensory perception and short-term memory—it declines.

"Crystallized" intelligence originates in acculturated information, those sets of skills and pieces of information that people learn as part of growing up in any given culture, such as verbal comprehension, vocabulary, general knowledge, and the ability to evaluate experience. In the absence of pathology, crystallized intelligence grows across the life span. The amount of growth depends on many factors, including cognitive ability, breadth of experiences, and both the quantity and quality of learning activities.

A far different, yet equally useful, expression of the multidimensionality of intelligence lies in the work of Gardner (1983). From his perspective, the concept of intelligence has been too narrowly limited to the realm of logical and linguistic abilities, primarily by the way that intelligence has been measured (that is, psychometrically). Rather, he argued, "there is persuasive evidence for the existence of several relatively autonomous human intellec-

tual competencies . . . that can be fashioned and combined in a multiplicity of adaptive ways by individuals and cultures" (Gardner, pp. 8–9). By researching a number of sources, including prodigies, brain-damaged individuals, and normal children and adults, Gardner (1999) originally identified seven different forms of intelligence (an eighth was recently added). These multiple intelligences are

1. linguistic (the ability to think in words and to use language to express and appreciate complex meanings)
2. logical–mathematical (the ability to calculate, quantify, consider propositions and hypotheses, and carry out complex mathematical operations)
3. spatial (the capacity to think in three-dimensional ways: to perceive external and internal imagery, to recreate and modify images, and to decode graphic information)
4. bodily–kinesthetic (the ability to manipulate objects and the development of finely tuned physical skills)
5. musical (a special sensitivity to pitch, melody, rhythm, and tone)
6. interpersonal (the capacity to understand and interact effectively with others)
7. intrapersonal (a high degree of self-awareness and the use of this self-understanding in planning and directing one's life)
8. naturalist (the ability to recognize important distinctions in the natural world, such as flora and fauna)

Gardner (1983) argued that although most people possess the full spectrum of intelligences, each individual has distinctive cognitive features and combines these multiple intelligences in highly personal ways. One implication of Gardner's research has been that traditional programs, which focus on a preponderance of linguistic and mathematical functions, may not be the most effective means of education. The theory of multiple intelligences has won great support among K–12 educators and has begun to influence adult education as well (Merriam & Caffarella, 1999).

Noncognitive or Environmental Factors

Of particular import for social workers and adult educators considering the potential of lifelong learning in later age is the role of noncognitive or environmental factors, such as education, professional and personal experience, and lifestyle choices. Fry (1992) wrote that "the intellectual abilities and learning effectiveness of older people are not merely genetically programmed, but are influenced by exogenous factors such as self-knowledge, motivation, and expectancies" (p.305). Schaie (1994) described the following noncognitive variables as providing positive influences on the ability to learn:

- being without cardiovascular and other chronic diseases
- living in favorable environmental circumstances
- having an above-average education and a history of occupational pursuits involving high complexity and low routine

- living on an above-average income in an intact family
- participating in activities typically available in complex and intellectually stimulating environment

Other factors that contribute to healthy cognitive functioning in later life include having a flexible personality in middle age, marriage to a spouse with high cognitive status, satisfaction with one's accomplishments in midlife and early old age, and recent participation in formal (that is, organized courses of study) and/or informal learning activities (Fisher & Wolf, 1998; Jarvis, 2001; Merriam & Caffarella, 1999).

The conclusion consistently reached in the literatures of cognitive psychology, adult education, and educational gerontology is that older adults can and do learn. They may not learn as quickly or as abstractly as they did when they were younger. But a healthy older adult can learn with a richness of nuance, depth, and reflection that may be possible for only the rarest of young adults. And the best of all learning is rooted in the older individual's needs and interests.

Why Participate? Need and Motivation

There is a long history of research on issues related to learning needs and motivation to participate in educational programs in the general adult education literature. In an important early study, Houle (1961) developed a theory of motivation in response to the question, why participate? In general terms, he found that adults take part in learning activities for reasons that are goal-oriented (for example, solving a specific problem, achieving a personal or professional objective), activity-oriented (for example, participating for the sake of the activity itself and/or for the social interaction associated with the learning experience), and learning-oriented (for example, seeking knowledge for its own sake). Although motivation is a complex matter and there is a good degree of overlap between these three basic factors in Houle's research, by far the most common reason for participation is goal-oriented.

More than a decade later, Morstain and Smart (1974) studied motivation among 611 adults taking evening credit courses in a college in New Jersey. Their six-factor model modestly extended the typology that Houle (1961) had developed:

1. social relationships—Some learners participate in order to make new friends and engage in social interaction.
2. external expectations—Some learners are complying with the wishes or directives of someone else with authority (for example, a supervisor at work).
3. social welfare—Some learners have an altruistic orientation; they participate because they want to serve others or their community.
4. professional advancement—Some learners participate for job enhancement or professional advancement.
5. escape/stimulation—Some learners participate in education as a

way of alleviating boredom or escaping home or work routine.
6. cognitive interest—Some learners are participating, like Houle's "learning-oriented" people, for the joy of learning itself.

The most well-known model for expressing the learning needs of older people dates back to McClusky's (1974) background paper on education written for the 1971 White House Conference on Aging. Originally describing these needs in a four-factor model—coping, expressive, contributive, and influence needs—McClusky later edited his theory to include a fifth construct—transcendence needs.

The most basic reason that older people participate in educational activities (both formal and informal) is to meet the fundamental needs of survival and coping. Some people require remedial education designed to overcome weaknesses or omissions in their formal education of childhood and youth. Such programs would include the development of reading and writing skills, instruction in English as a second language, or consumer education designed to help the learner deal with the daily decisions necessary for survival in a complex and challenging environment. In addition to these, coping needs might include learning to adjust to the normal physical changes that occur with aging or learning to adapt to the social and psychological changes that accompany the death of a spouse or losses associated with retirement.

Much like those with a "cognitive interest" described by Morstain and

Smart (1974), and those who are "learning-oriented" described by Houle (1961), the expressive learners described by McClusky (1971) are people who participate in educational activities for the sake of learning itself. The reward for involvement is intrinsic to the activity, and interest alone is sufficient motivation for participation. Enjoyment results from the physical or social activity, from the spontaneity involved, and from the exhilaration of achieving the "aha" of learning. For many older people, there was not ample time earlier in their lives for such experiences. Retirement has provided them with the freedom and leisure to pursue intellectual interests without concerns for seeking practical application. The internationally known Elderhostel program, lifelong learning institutes (about which more will be said later in this chapter), and numerous other elder education programs are, in good part, responses to the expressive learning needs of older people.

The contributive category in the needs typology of McClusky (1971) originates in the altruistic desire of most people to assist others. The service provided may be in the form of volunteerism with local hospitals, churches, schools, nursing homes, or countless other agencies. Whatever the avenue of service, the resource of time, skills, and perspective can be of extensive value to older people and to the entire community. Education can be the means by which older people identify their potential contributions, mobilize resources, and direct their time and service in the most meaningful manner. As Peterson has written, education has a "role in developing and directing the contributive impulse. Without knowledge of the available opportunities for service, people often waste precious energy and become discouraged about the value of their contribution" (McClusky, 1983, p. 137).

The ability to influence, the fourth category in McClusky's (1971) original formulation, relates to the capacity for developing leadership skills in later life and, ultimately, for enhancing the older adult's role as citizen in influencing larger social and political issues. Education can help elderly people identify their own strengths for leadership, develop group process skills, and assist in evaluating the results of social change initiatives. Although the opportunities in political organizations, community groups, service organizations, educational institutions, and other venues are great, for the most part these are highly complex organizations that require sophisticated knowledge if the participant is to be an effective agent for change.

Several years later, after discussion and critique by colleagues, McClusky (1974) added a fifth category to his older learner needs typology—transcendence needs. These are needs for gaining a deeper understanding of the meaning of life, for reviewing what one's life has been like, and for confronting the issues that frequently arise when a person is approaching the final stages of life. Although transcendence needs are evident at all ages across the human life span, they are perhaps most imperative in the later years when death is clearly in view and cannot be as easily put aside. Late age, as Manheimer (1999–2000) has written, is "a philosophical time of life." There are layers of questions to explore. Education can be and often is an important partner as older adults make these existential odysseys.

Older Learner Preferences

A major study sponsored by the American Council on Education focused attention on the learning preferences of a sample of U.S. residents ages 55 and older. In this study, Lamdin and Fugate (1997) analyzed data from 860 people who had participated in learning programs offered by the American Association of Retired Persons, Elderhostel, Institutes for Learning in Retirement, and other providers of education for elderly people. The following is a briefly stated demographic profile of this research sample:

- 67.2 percent of the respondents were women.
- 94.1 percent were white.
- 80 percent were between the ages of 65 and 79.
- 82 percent were retired from paid employment (with nearly one-half reporting annual incomes of more than $40,000).
- 81 percent had at least two years of college.
- 37 percent had graduate degrees.

This profile of participants in elder education programs correlates highly with findings from other research on older learners (Brady, 1984; Manheimer et al., 1995; Peterson, 1983).

One line of investigation in the American Council on Education study was the nature of subject areas preferred by older learners (Lamdin & Fugate,

1997). The most highly preferred area of study was "music, art, dance, and arts-related crafts." This was followed in rank order by (1) travel-based or travel-related programs, (2) literature and drama courses, (3) politics/foreign affairs, (4) history/genealogy, (5) health/nutrition, (6) philosophy/religion, (7) computers, (8) finances, and (9) sports/leisure studies. It is not surprising that there is a strong preference for the general category of "expressive needs" represented in these specific content/subject areas.

Another survey item in this national study addressed learning styles and preferences. Findings were that the older generation is still a print-based media one. Also, older learners are highly social, preferring to learn in the company of others in group meetings, classes, workshops, and discussion groups (Lamdin & Fugate, 1997).

Selected Programs

The options for participation by older learners in formally organized programs are infinitely more numerous and more varied today than even a generation ago. Most local school districts have adult education programs that are widely accessible because of their relatively low cost and geographic proximity. Learners may take classes to earn credit toward a diploma, to prepare for the national GED examination, or to improve their professional skills; some may take classes for the purposes of recreation and personal development. In the latter category, typical public school adult education catalogues advertise classes in arts and crafts, poetry writing, ethnic cooking, literature discussion groups, and a myriad of subjects that are typically of interest to learners in the local community. An especially popular course these days is an introduction to computers, an area in which older people have begun to show interest. (There has been a current trend to offer computer classes especially designed for older learners in order to assuage their anxiety about "competing" with younger, presumably more technologically savvy, students.) Older people's interests in computers range from basic electronic mail functions for the purpose of communicating with grandchildren to financial software and advanced programming applications.

Public libraries continue their longstanding mission to serve the community as a whole—from preschoolers to the oldest citizens—meeting their informational needs, facilitating the learning of subjects undertaken in formal education, and encouraging reading and learning as a recreational activity and as a constructive use of leisure time. For many years, special programs from public and state libraries have provided services to the aging via bookmobiles, cable television, and books-by-mail delivery. Regular, on-site programs enable older adults to participate in discussions, to view films, to hear lectures, to learn from arts and crafts demonstrations, and to take part in other life enrichment programs. Many libraries have established partnerships with local senior centers, retirement communities, and nursing homes where they take resources directly to older people. "Talking books," large-print editions, and closed-captioned videos are important learning resources for elderly people with sensory impair-

ments. Finally, part of the mission of many librarians and volunteers is to make visits to the homebound in order to help meet their learning needs (Manheimer, 1995).

An increasingly well-known older learner program, which will celebrate its 30th anniversary in 2005, is Elderhostel. Combining the two concepts of "elder" and "hostel" (that is, low-cost accommodations while traveling), this program began as a modest experiment in summer programming at the University of New Hampshire and has grown into an international program serving more than 250,000 enrollees each year. There are currently Elderhostel programs in 90 countries, with the vast majority located in the United States and Canada. Courses are short-term—typically one week in length in the United States, two to three weeks overseas—and may take place on college and university campuses, conference centers, resorts, museums, summer camps, historical sites, and other venues where classes can be held. The curriculum is based primarily in the liberal arts tradition, and classes are taught by college faculty or other local experts. In 1992, Elderhostel introduced service learning programs in which participants provide volunteer service to worthy causes in cooperation with well-established public service organizations (for example, Habitat for Humanity). A national administrative office governs the fees, and the program's policy from its inception has been to keep costs lower than those of commercial travel programs (consistent with the "hostel" tradition). Scholarships are available for low-income individual, but they are seldom requested. One perennial problem with Elderhostel—and nearly all other elder learning programs—is the tendency to attract an audience of highly educated, middle and upper-middle class, white professionals. Outreach efforts and attempts to broaden the appeal of these programs to racially and economically diverse populations have, for the most part, been unsuccessful. Elderhostel has an informative and well-detailed Web site at www.elderhostel.org.

Similar to Elderhostel in that they are college-based, but substantially different in other important ways, are lifelong learning institutes (LLIs). The first LLI was the Institute for Retired Professionals, founded in 1962 by a group of retired teachers at the New School for Social Research in New York. Similar institutes were developed at Syracuse University in 1975, and at Harvard University and Duke University not long after. Today, there are more than 400 LLIs in the United States. A majority of these otherwise autonomous programs are linked by a national network administered by Elderhostel in Boston, Massachusetts; approximately 250 of the 400 programs belong to this network. The Elderhostel Institute Network hosts conferences, produces a newsletter, and facilitates communication between institutes via a computer listserv.

Lifelong learning institutes are usually self-managed, making their own decisions about program guidelines, courses, membership fees, and other administrative issues. The host institution may or may not have a substantial financial investment in the operation of the LLI. Typically, the college or university host offers classroom space, modest office accommodations for staff, and telephone/fax/computer facilities. Teachers are generally volunteers recruited from the ranks of the LLI membership (Brady, Holt, & Welt, 2003). In addition to peer-facilitated classes, which almost invariably meet during the day, many LLIs sponsor special lectures, exhibits, travel experiences, and social events for their members.

One recent "success story" among LLIs is the Osher Lifelong Learning Institute at the University of Southern Maine in Portland. Founded in 1997 by a small group of university staff and members of the community, what at the time was called Senior College grew at exponential rates. For the first semester of operation, only four classes were planned because of modest start-up expectations. However, enrollment was so large that one of these classes, a course on world religions taught by a local rabbi (who was also the chairman of the Senior College Board of Directors), had more than 100. Within several years, the institute's membership had grown to more than 800, and a typical semester involved 35 to 40 courses. The curriculum offers courses ranging from the history of opera, an exploration of *The Book of Psalms,* and the history of the Age of Napoleon to basic physics, the geopolitics of Latin America, and the psychology of drug abuse.

Teachers take an active and creative approach in these short-term (eight weeks at two hours per class) non-credit courses. In the *Psalms* course, learners not only read and analyze biblical passages, but also actually write their own psalms. Learners write and perform a drama in the theater class, they draw watercolors in the art class, and they craft memoirs in the life story class. This active learning approach has already resulted in two learner-initiated publications—one a book of spiritual reflections and the other a creative magazine (with plans for annual publication).

With strong community support throughout the entire Southern Maine region, a Maine state legislator introduced a bill in the winter of 2000 to authorize a statewide expansion of Senior College. The legislature established a $150,000 line-item in the University of Maine system's budget explicitly to spread the Senior College mission throughout the State of Maine. This money, in part, was used to hire a full-time director. Not long after this statewide initiative was under way, Bernard Osher, a California businessman with Maine roots, gave a significant endowment to Senior College to assist in its expansion and to establish a research program. The newly named Osher Lifelong Learning Institute at the University of Southern Maine has subsequently worked to build a network of senior colleges throughout the State of Maine. Whereas in the middle 1990s there were no LLIs in Maine, today there are 15 serving more than 5,000 older learners.

Role of Social Work in Older Adult Education

There are a variety of ways in which professional social workers can support lifelong learning as one important factor in vital and productive aging. An agenda for social workers may include the following:

- Become aware of elder learning opportunities in the local and regional community. Be knowledgeable about these resources in order to be a useful counselor and broker of information.
- Educate elderly clients to the value of later-life learning. Help them to locate educational programs that may be of interest to them or useful in the management of their day-to-day lives. Help to raise the awareness levels of clients and colleagues about tuition waiver/reduction programs that are nearly always underadvertised and underused.
- Work to recruit people of low or moderate incomes and from racially and ethnically diverse backgrounds to participate in local public school adult education or LLIs as learners, facilitators, office staff, and advisory board members.
- Engage in action research to examine the specific barriers to participation in lifelong learning among elderly people in the local community. Work closely with providers of educational programs to remove these barriers.
- Establish collaborative relationships with local schools and institutions of higher education that offer lifelong learning programs. Work with leaders in these organizations for more aggressive development and distribution of scholarships for low-income elderly people who, in many cases, would benefit substantially from participation in adult education.
- Establish alliances and coalitions to work toward increased funding for learning opportunities for elderly people.

- If working as a social worker in a facility that does not have education as its primary mission (for example, a long-term care facility, continuing care retirement community, community-based human service agency), help colleagues to understand that lifelong learning can have widely ranging influences in an older person's life and that elderly learners' interests and needs are broad and diverse. Advocate for expansion of learning opportunities within these settings.

Quoting Aristotle, Lowy and O'Connor (1986) argued that "education is the best provision for old age" and ought to, in fact, be considered a basic human right. The profession of social work, with its long tradition of human rights advocacy, might consider adding lifelong learning to the list of rights for which humane public policy and responsive institutional programs should be developed.

In conclusion, later life, much like youth, adolescence, and early maturity, is a time ripe with opportunity for growth, learning, and what Moody (1988) described as "abundance." The relatively new and uncharted territory of education and learning in the later years holds great promise for the productive aging of tens of millions of U.S. elderly people and for our society as a whole.

References

Brady, E. M. (1984). Demographic and educational correlates of self-reported learning among older students. *Educational Gerontology, 10,* 25–38.

Brady, E. M., Holt, S. R., & Welt, B. (2003). Peer teaching in lifelong learning institutes. *Educational Gerontology, 29,* 851–868.

Cattell, R. B. (1963). Theory of fluid and crystallized intelligence: A critical approach. *Journal of Educational Psychology, 54*(1), 1–22.

Cattell, R. B. (1987). *Intelligence: Its structure, growth, and action.* Amsterdam: North-Holland.

Cross, K. P. (1981). *Adults as learners: Increasing participation and facilitating learning.* San Francisco: Jossey-Bass.

Fisher, J., & Wolf, M. A. (Eds.). (1998). *Using learning to meet the challenges of older adulthood* (New Directions for Adult and Continuing Education, No. 77). San Francisco: Jossey-Bass.

Fry, P. S. (1992). A consideration of cognitive factors in the learning and education of older adults. *International Review of Education, 38,* 303–325.

Gardner, H. (1983). *Frames of mind.* New York: Basic Books.

Gardner, H. (1999). *Intelligence reframed: Multiple intelligences for the 21st century.* New York: Basic Books.

Higher Education Act, P.L. 94–482, 90 Stat. 2083 (1976). Title 1, Part B (Life Learning Act).

Horn, J. L. (1976). Human abilities: A review of research theory in the early 1970s. In M. R. Rosensweig & L. W. Porter (Eds.), *Annual review of psychology* (Vol. 27, pp. 437–485). Palo Alto, CA: Annual Reviews.

Horn, J. L. (1985). Remodeling old models of intelligence. In B. B. Wolman (Ed.), *Handbook of intelligence: Theories, measurements, and applications.* New York: John Wiley & Sons.

Houle, C. (1961). *The inquiring mind.* Madison: University of Wisconsin Press.

Jarvis, P. (2001). *Learning in later life: An introduction for educators and carers.* London: Kogan Page.

Knowles, M. (1977). *A history of the adult education movement in the United States.* Huntington, NY: Robert E. Krieger.

Lamdin, L., & Fugate, M. (1997). *Elderlearning: New frontiers in an aging society.* Phoenix: American Council on Education/Oryx Press.

Lowy, L., & O'Connor, D. (1986). *Why education in the later years?* Lexington, MA: Lexington Books/D.C. Heath.

Manheimer, R. (1995). *The second middle age: Looking differently at life beyond 50.* Detroit: Visible Ink Press.

Manheimer, R. (1999–2000). A philosophical time of life. *Generations, 23,* 15–20.

Manheimer, R., Snodgrass, D., & McKenzie, D. (1995). *Older adult education: A guide to research, programs, and policies.* Westport, CT: Greenwood Press.

Maslow, A. (1968). *Toward a psychology of being.* New York: Van Nostrand.

McClusky, H. Y. (1971). *Education: Background and issues.* Washington, DC: White House Conference on Aging.

McClusky, H. Y. (1974). Education for aging: The scope of the field and perspectives for the future. In Stanley M. Grabowski & W. Dean Mason (Eds.), *Learning for aging,* Washington, DC: Adult Education Association.

Merriam, S., & Caffarella, R. (1999). *Learning in adulthood* (2nd ed.). San Francisco: Jossey-Bass.

Moody, H. R. (1976). Philosophical presuppositions of education for old age. *Educational Gerontology, 1*(1), 1–16.

Moody, H. R. (1988). *Abundance of life: Human development policies for an aging society.* New York: Columbia University Press.

Morstain, B. R., & Smart, J. C. (1974). Reasons for participation in adult education courses: A multivariate analysis of group differences. *Adult Education, 24*(2), 83–98.

Older Americans Act of 1965, P.L. No. 89–73, 87 Stat. 60.

Older Americans Comprehensive Services Amendments of 1973, P.L. 93-29, 87 Stat. 59. (Also known as Title VIII of the Higher Education Act).

Peterson, D. (1983*). Facilitating education for older adults.* San Francisco: Jossey-Bass.

Peterson, D. (1990). A history of the education of older learners. In R. H. Sherron & D. B. Lumsden (Eds.), *Introduction to educational gerontology* (3rd ed., pp. 1–21). New York: Hemisphere.

Peterson, D. A., & Masunaga, H. (1998). Policy for older adult education. In J. C. Fisher & M. A. Wolf (Eds.), *Using learning to meet the challenges of older adulthood* (New Drections for Adult and Continuing Education, No. 77, pp. 55–60). San Francisco: Jossey-Bass.

Schaie, K. W. (1994). The course of adult intellectual development. *American Psychologist, 49,* 304–313.

10

"We Are the Most Free to Take the Risks Required": Activism among Elderly People

Sandra S. Butler

"An increasing number of us are outraged about the injustice and dehumanization we see and are ready to work for basic societal change. After all, we are the most free to take the risks required" (Kuhn, 1976, p. 87). These words were written more than a quarter of a century ago by the late Maggie Kuhn, retired social worker and founder of the Gray Panthers. A true spokesperson for senior activism, Kuhn encouraged elderly people to regard their experience as a positive good and as leverage for constructive social change and advocacy:

> Our goal is to use our freedom, our experience, our knowledge of the past, our ability to cope and survive, not just for free bus fares or tax rebates for people over 65, although we need these benefits. We want to work as advocates for the larger public good, as public citizens and responsible consumers. (p. 89)

Kuhn laid out four roles that activist elderly people—and the professionals who work with older adults—must play if they are to confront the "sickness of our society" (p. 92) and focus on social change: advocate, social critic, tester of new models and lifestyles, and public citizen. "As wrinkled radicals and liberated old people, we can testify that our roles empower us and hopefully release new power and energy in the places where we live as liberators, social critics, responsible consumers, and public citizens" (p. 96).

Activism and advocacy by older adults can enhance and enrich their lives, while also creating positive social change. Social reconstruction, in which elderly people define their personal competence and exert control over their lives, provides a framework for reversing the negative cycle of the social breakdown that society often imposes on elderly people. Through an empowerment-based practice model, social workers can assist elderly people in building on their strengths and in locating opportunities for activism in their lives. Although activism may not be appealing to all elderly people, it is clearly an empowering activity for some, just as it is for individuals of any age.

Social Breakdown Syndrome and Reconstruction Theory

Kuypers and Bengtson (1973) introduced a theory of social breakdown as a sensitizing model to explain the relationship between the elderly population, whose social system may be contracting, and the broader social environment within which they live. This social breakdown syndrome (SBS) was first introduced in relation to people with mental illness, but Kuypers and Bengtson adapted the theory to describe the situation of the elderly in our society. The seven steps originally associated with SBS were

1. precondition of susceptibility
2. dependence on external labeling
3. social labeling as incompetent
4. induction into a sick, dependent role
5. learning of skills appropriate to the new dependent role
6. atrophy of previous skills
7. identification and self-labeling as "sick" or inadequate (Kuypers & Bengtson, 1973, p. 187)

Rice (1992) consolidated these steps further to explain the negative changes in the self-concept of the aged population:

- Our society brings about role loss, offers only sparse normative infor-

mation and guidance, and deprives the elderly of reference groups, so they lose the sense of who they are and what their roles are.
- Society then labels them negatively as incompetent and deficient.
- Society deprives them of opportunities to use their skills, which atrophy in the process.
- The aged accept the external labeling, identify themselves as inadequate, and begin to act as they are expected to act, setting the stage of another spiral. (p. 444)

Social reconstruction theory provides an approach to change the system and break the SBS cycle (Kuypers & Bengtson, 1973; Long & Holle, 1997; Rice, 1992). The theory has three components. First, social reconstruction theory defines competence as successful social role performance. An expanded view of "productive aging"— in which an emphasis on wisdom, experience, creativity, volunteerism, and humanitarianism replaces the emphasis on work as the primary source of worth—is crucial. Elder activism provides one social role through which many elderly people attain competence. Second, social reconstruction theory emphasizes structural change that would ensure adequate health care, housing, and financial security so that elderly people are freed to pursue personal meaning and expression in later life (Long & Holle, 1997). This pursuit of personal expression could well be through activism, whether for improvement in the lives of elderly people or for other causes. Third, social reconstruction theory speaks directly to the ability of older adults to exert control in their lives. The premise of this final component is that the locus of control must be internally based (that is, within the older adult) and not externally based (Kuypers & Bengtson, 1973). Elderly people must be empowered to determine the political and social policies that affect them (Rice, 1992). According to this theory, self-worth in old age is directly equated to the ability to maintain power and engage in self-determination (Long & Holle, 1997).

Empowerment-Oriented Practices

As described by Cox and Parsons (1993), empowerment-oriented practice with elderly individuals provides a practice model that parallels social reconstruction theory. It recognizes that elderly people may experience various levels of powerlessness in our society as they age. This loss of power may be multifaceted and may be the result of both personal losses—such as physical decline, mental decline, or loss of support systems—and socially constructed losses—such as retirement, role loss, or age discrimination. In countering the varied losses of power, empowerment-oriented practice aims to increase personal efficacy and improve knowledge and skills for critical analysis of one's personal situation in order to take action to attain collective goals (Cox & Parsons, 1993).

The empowerment process comprises four key components. The first involves attitudes and beliefs, such as self-efficacy and an internal locus of control. The second component requires the validation of collective experiences. Knowledge and skills for critical thinking make up the third

component and lead to the fourth component: action (Cox & Parsons, 1993). It is this culmination of the empowerment process that is manifested in senior activism.

> Through the empowerment process, individuals are able to develop action strategies and cultivate the resources, knowledge, and skills necessary to influence internal and external structures. Psychologically, they learn to assume responsibility for action. Behaviorally, they become willing and able to act with others for the attainment of common goals and social change. (Cox & Parsons, 1993, p. 38)

One of the ultimate goals of the empowerment process is participation in the policy arena. Social workers engaging in empowerment-oriented practice with elderly people facilitate client engagement in social action to influence policies at the local, state, and national levels. Cox and Parsons (1993) suggested five aspects of this facilitation for the social work practitioner: (1) overcoming resistance to involvement in the policy-making process; (2) obtaining and sharing information about policies, both existing and proposed; (3) becoming familiar with and sharing knowledge about the policy process and policymakers; (4) developing and sharing analytical frameworks for understanding policies; and (5) acquiring and passing on practical knowledge about how to influence policy. The familiar adage, "the personal is political," comes into play in promoting elder activism. "The focus of the empowerment-oriented practice model on the political dimension of personal problems provides a vehicle for elderly people's meaningful involvement in the creation of an environment more responsive to their needs" (Cox & Parsons, 1993, p. 260). Moreover, elderly people engage in social and political activism related to a broad range of issues, many of which fall outside the realm of their specific personal "needs."

In her discussion of ways to develop a just community care policy, Estes (1999) suggested the "empowerment imperative" as an alternative to current approaches, which tend to produce and reinforce dependency. "This alternative involves a commitment to the design and evaluation of social interventions that enhance the capacity of the old and chronically ill for self-esteem, personal control, individual and social involvement, and *social action*" (p. 139, emphasis added). Among Estes' suggestions for improving personal control by elderly people in everyday life is the "creation of organizations and advocacy groups that serve the self-defined needs of elderly people" (1999, p. 140)—in other words, opportunities for senior activism.

Political Behavior among Elderly People

It is well-known by politicians and the public at large that people over age 65 have a high rate of political activity, at least in terms of voting. Although it is often assumed that senior citizens have homogeneous political attitudes and vote as a bloc, research has shown repeatedly that elderly people are as heterogeneous in their voting behaviors and political attitudes as are young and middle-aged adults (Binstock, 1997; Binstock & Day, 1996). Economic, racial, ethnic, gender, and social diversity remain as distinct in old age as in

younger generations and is evident in elderly people' political attitudes and choices (Binstock, 1991). Nonetheless, interest in politics appears to increase with age; among all age groups, older adults report the highest interest in public affairs and political campaigns (Binstock & Day, 1996).

In 1992, individuals ages 65 and older reported the highest rate of voter registration (78 percent) of any age group. In that same year, 70 percent of older U.S. citizens voted, compared with 58 percent of people ages 25 to 44 (Treas, 1995). Moreover, in the presidential elections from 1980 through 1996, the participation of U.S. citizens over age 65 was nearly three times that of the youngest voters (18- to 20-year-olds). Although voting participation declines for individuals older than age 75, these older citizens were still more likely to have voted than people younger than 35 in such elections (Hooyman & Kiyak, 1999). Beyond voting, elderly people participate in nonelectoral political activity, such as writing letters and making telephone calls to public officials. Some forms of political activity, such as vigorous protest activity, campaign work, and meeting attendance appear to decline with age (Binstock & Day, 1996).

Several authors have outlined the barriers to activism and advocacy among elderly people. Berger's (1976) lament that advocacy is not a technique widely subscribed to by senior citizens may still ring true today, although he wrote the following 25 years ago:

> Because of their inability to identify shared interests, their failure to recognize that they share a commonality

of fate, the low incidence of group identification among seniors, and the negative images connected with age which are common even today, the task of developing a sense of group identity and cohesiveness among seniors is a difficult one. (p. 13)

Berger further submitted that because many elderly people live alone, are impoverished, and may feel rejected by society, it is difficult to instill a belief that collective action on their part can produce desired changes.

Pratt (1976), in his book tracing the rise of the "gray lobby" in the United States, also discussed the difficulties of mobilizing the older population. He documented several factors that contribute to the difficulty of organizing elderly people. For example, health problems are more frequent than among younger people and may affect the quality of participation. There is a high rate of turnover in senior clubs, which is related to health issues. A low income and the uncertainty of future financial needs lead to a reluctance among elderly people to pay dues or make long-term commitments. Finally, in a "culture that teaches its members that economic and health problems are rightfully to be met through individual effort, attempts to meet problems collectively through united action are typically viewed with suspicion" (Pratt, 1976, p. 41).

On the other hand, Trela (1976) suggested that high achievers—generally, white men—who arrive at low-status old age experience a role inconsistency that can lead to political activism. In his research comparing political activism in age-graded associations (that is,

organizations whose membership criteria include age) with that in associations of mixed ages, Trela discovered a higher degree of activism in the age-graded organizations. He postulated that age-graded associations may activate political feelings grounded in age status and that political expression may best come about through mingling with one's peers. Although, as Trela (1978) noted, research has consistently shown that individuals from lower socioeconomic groups are less likely to participate in politics than those from higher-income groups, the importance of socioeconomic status in determining political involvement (Trela, 1978) appears to lessen with age and disappear completely in age-graded organizations.

A plausible explanation of this is that the salience of age status is raised while the sociological pressures of other central life statuses become relatively less potent determinants of political attitudes and behaviors. It appears that formal age-graded contexts activate the values and beliefs of a political generation and the resultant homogeneous socio-political environment is relatively free of cross pressures and invidious class distinctions that impede involvement in political affairs by the lower classes. (Trela, 1978, p. 343)

Old Age Interest Groups

The politics of aging began in the early 20th century with the formation of several groups advocating old age pensions—the American Association of Old Age Security, the American Association for Labor Legislation, and the Fraternal

Order of Eagles. The Great Depression brought the better known social movements of older people, such as the Ham and Eggs Group and the Townsend Movement—the best known group of this time, representing more than 2 million older people (Torres-Gil, 1993). Although these groups are given credit for providing an impetus for the passage of the Social Security Act, they are not given credit for its formulation or implementation. "Their greatest contribution was furnishing the elderly with a collective voice and identity" (Torres-Gil, p. 244).

Organized interest groups representing the elderly populations did not re-emerge for several decades. From the 1960s to the 1990s, the number of private interest groups focused on old age policy and concerns jumped from a handful to more than 100. Nearly half of these groups were founded in the 1970s (Van Tassel & Meyer, 1992). Despite their rapid growth, the power and homogeneity of purpose of these groups are often overestimated (Binstock, 1991).

> These old age interest groups became known collectively as the gray lobby and have been seen by the media and the public as monolithic in ideology and a very powerful force, called gray power, in Washington. Rather than being uniform in approach or powerful in influence, the gray lobby, in fact, has always reflected the diversity of the elderly and retired population, the varying circumstances of the groups' origins, and the efficacy of their differing structures. (Van Tassel & Meyer, 1992, p. xv)

These national groups can be broken down into three categories: mass membership organizations, advocacy organizations for special older constituencies, and professional and trade organizations (Binstock & Day, 1996; Hanna, 1981). The large national organizations include the American Association of Retired Persons (AARP), which has 35 million members; the National Council for Senior Citizens (NCSC), which has 5 million members; the National Committee to Preserve Social Security and Medicare (NCPSSM), which has 5 million members; the National Alliance of Senior Citizens, which has 2 million members; the National Association of Retired Federal Employees, which has 490,000 members; and the Gray Panthers, which has 40,000 members (Binstock & Day, 1996).

There is considerable diversity in the histories, goals, and positions on activism among these groups. For example, the NCSC had its roots in the labor-based Senior Citizens for Kennedy in 1960. Currently, its membership represents largely trade union retirees, and varied ethnic and religious groups. The NCSC maintains a political action committee that is very active on Capitol Hill and in state and local politics (Van Tassel & Meyer, 1992). The AARP, on the other hand, had its origins in a retired teachers' insurance organization rather than in political action, although it has become increasingly political in recent years (Hooyman & Kiyak, 1999). Because of its large bipartisan membership, it is both easy and difficult for the AARP to take strong stands on issues.

It is easy since there is always a percentage of the membership that will support any given side of an issue related to old age and retirement. It is difficult since there is always a segment of the membership that will oppose such a stand. (Van Tassel & Meyer, 1992, p. xvii)

The Gray Panthers is a cause-oriented organization that has been critical of the AARP for not using its membership strength more effectively. Reflecting its roots in the social movements of the 1960s and 1970s, the Gray Panthers espouse a wide range of causes from civil rights to world peace; they have also stressed the importance of working in coalitions and of intergenerational cooperation (Van Tassel & Meyer, 1992). The NCPSSM was founded in 1982 to mobilize retirees through direct mail campaigns to defend social security against budget cuts. This advocacy organization has since taken on the defense of Medicare and Medicaid, and the development of a national long-term care program (Van Tassel & Meyer, 1992).

Because these national organizations have not always represented the concerns of older people of color, low-income elderly people, old women, or elderly people with disabilities, advocacy organizations for these specific populations have emerged. These organizations include the National Caucus and Center on Black Aged, la Asociación Nacional Por Personas Mayores, the National Indian Council on Aging, the Older Women's League (OWL), the National Pacific/Asian Resource Center on Aging, Families USA Foundation (for low-income elderly people), and the Alzheimer's Association (Binstock & Day, 1996; Hanna, 1981). Some of these organizations, such as OWL, attempt to mobilize their membership for national legislative advocacy.

National professional and trade organizations that address the interests of elderly people are very numerous indeed. Some of the better known organizations in this category include the American Society on Aging, the Association for Gerontology in Higher Education, the Gerontological Society of America, the National Association of Area Agencies on Aging, the National Council on the Aging, the National Association of State Units on Aging, the National Association of Homes and Services for the Aging, and the National Senior Citizens Law Center (Binstock & Day, 1996; Hanna, 1981).

Although individual elderly people may find an activist role through one of these national interest groups, some of the more accessible and richest activist opportunities appear to exist in specific programs.

Programs That Promote Activism

A range of programs and projects have facilitated activism for older adults. There are programs that emphasize training in advocacy, programs that focus on community organizing, programs that facilitate activism specifically for very frail elderly people, and service programs that have an activist component.

Programs That Emphasize Training in Advocacy. The Joint Public Affairs Committee for Older Adults (JPAC) is a grassroots organization, founded in 1977, that has members from 200 diverse senior and community groups throughout metropolitan New York; it mobilizes older adults to effect positive change (Epstein, West, & Riegel, 2000). In 1994 the JPAC created a 10-week leadership training course—the Institute for Senior Action—to fulfill its mission of educating and empowering elderly people to participate in the public policy arena more effectively. Offered twice annually, the course consists of 10 all-day interactive sessions. The curriculum covers

- city, state, and federal budget and legislative processes
- voter registration and outreach
- senior policies, programs, and entitlements
- methods of organizing across the generations and within a multicultural community
- fundraising fundamentals
- techniques of social action
- volunteerism and mentoring
- effective meetings
- techniques for working with the media
- writing skills and techniques
- conflict resolution
- public speaking with confidence (Epstein et al., 2000).

Institute graduates not only replenish JPAC's senior leadership base, but also "return to their communities and organizations with new skills and a renewed sense of purpose and self-confidence" (Epstein et al., 2000, pp. 96–97). A survey of Institute graduates revealed that 75 percent had taken on leadership roles in their organizations since completing JPAC's training. Graduates advocate for the needs of communities throughout the city, doing things such as organizing tenants' associations, block groups, grandparent clubs, and social action committees. "From legislative issues such as the threat of privatizing social security, to local concerns such as the need to make post offices accessible to frail and disabled individuals, Institute-trained senior advocates are mobilizing community responses" (Epstein et al., 2000, p. 98).

Quotes from Institute graduates demonstrate how empowering activism can be for adults in their later years. "I expected to learn some new techniques. Instead, the Institute taught me to open my mind, to recognize the potential power we have to move mountains" (quoted in Epstein et al., 2000, p. 94), said one woman who graduated. "I feel rejuvenated, and the realization that I can still be productive to society gives me a feeling of new power" (quoted in Epstein et al., 2000, p. 95), remarked another. The Institute for Senior Action has been so successful that it has developed a Tool Kit to assist groups in replicating the training. (See the appendix for JPAC contact information.)

Although the Institute for Senior Action rightfully prides itself on the diversity of its participants in terms of race, gender, age, organizational affiliation, and geography (within the New York metropolitan area; Epstein, 2000), one group that has not been well represented—or at least not publicly identified—in organizations for elderly people has been lesbian, gay, bisexual, and transgender (LGBT) elderly people. Social and advocacy organizations for LGBT elderly people have now emerged in some of the largest cities in the United States. New York City's Senior Action in a Gay Environment (SAGE) is one of the most well-established of such organizations. One program offered by SAGE is Sage Voice/Sage Vote, which provides training in legislative advocacy for LGBT elderly people. (See the appendix for SAGE contact information.)

In March 2001 SAGE gathered 20 LGBT seniors from around New York state to go to the state capital of Albany and participate in a lobby day organized by a collaboration of 49 non-AIDS LGBT health and human services organizations throughout the state. These empowered elderly activists—many of whom had lived decades of their lives in the closet and who were representing the estimated 200,000 LGBT elderly people in the state—asked New York legislators for the following:

1. mandatory training for geriatricians, social workers, home health aids, and nursing home staff regarding the unique issues facing LGBT seniors and ways that staff might provide culturally competent services
2. support for the development of specific LGBT health and human services for the "old," in addition to housing and continuing care facilities
3. state-supported research on the demographics and needs of LGBT seniors (Washaw, 2001)

Legislative advocacy in state capitals is a vehicle for senior activism that has developed in various ways around the United States. In West Virginia, when the nonprofit Council for Senior West Virginians voiced its concerns that state legislators were not adequately addressing senior citizens' needs, elected officials pressured the state to withdraw funding from the organization (Crittenden, 1985). As a result, a new statewide lobbying group was established in 1976—the Coalition on Legislation for the Elderly (COLE). Because most COLE members were new to the advocacy arena, they educated themselves through meetings.

The monthly meetings were used for education as well as planning. Staff people from agencies such as the Public Service Commission, or what was then the Department of Welfare, were invited to the meetings to contribute insights and statistics. After they left, we would decide on strategy. (Crittenden, 1985, p. 55)

COLE has had many legislative successes since its inception. Each year, elderly people throughout West Virginia advocate for a variety of issues, such as improvements in home health services, rural transportation, and reductions in telephone base rates for low-income customers. As one elder West Virginian activist said, "We must encourage other seniors to become involved. Grassroots advocacy is super-important for getting things done. It's also a way for many seniors to realize their personal potential" (quoted in Crittenden, 1985, p. 56).

A more uniform model of legislative advocacy for senior citizens is the Silver Haired Legislature (SHL), first developed in Missouri in 1973 (Goeke & Wolfe, 1979) and now existing in many states (Hanna, 1981). The SHL was originally conceived by a state Senate leader in Missouri, who was concerned that many groups were speaking on behalf of elderly people, but they were not united in their support for legislation to improve the lives of older people. As a result of this concern, the Missouri Jaycees were given a grant to conduct an elderly people's legislature patterned after the Jaycees mock legislature (Goeke & Wolfe, 1979). Six years after the start of the SHL in Missouri, Goeke and Wolfe described its success:

> Perhaps the best thing that can be said about the Silver Haired Legislature is that "it works"! Over the past six years the session has grown in visibility and esteem. Legislative bills that bear the stamp "Silver Haired Priority" now have special significance in Missouri General Assembly and the Silver Haired track record speaks for this. In 1978, three of the five priority bills became law. In 1976 and 1977, four of the five priority bills passed. (p. 9)

With this model, which is now used in many states, elderly people elect other elderly people to be their representatives at a three- to five-day session, generally held during the summer recess in the state capital legislative chambers (Hanna, 1981). After winning their campaigns for office, representatives receive extensive training and participate in nearly everything that takes place in the regular legislative process. The Silver Haired representatives receive assignments to committees, debate bills, elect leadership, and pass a limited number of bills. As mentioned earlier, these bills are often introduced in the regular legislature with a high rate of success for passage (Hanna, 1981). (See the appendix for contact information regarding the SHL.)

Programs That Focus on Community Organizing. A classic case of community organizing that has facilitated senior activism is the Tenderloin Senior Outreach Project (TSOP) in San Francisco. The Tenderloin area is a 45-block section of the city with a reputation for high crime rates. It has long been recognized as a red light district, housing ex-offenders, prostitutes, and individuals coping with drug addiction and mental illness. It is also one of the country's largest "gray ghettos," with as many as 8,000 elderly people living in many of the single-room residence hotels (Minkler, 1986). In 1977 students of the University of California at Berkeley's School of Public Health established the TSOP. The Project had two major goals: (1) to improve the physical, mental, and emotional health of the elderly residents and (2) to facilitate an empowering process through which residents would identify common problems that they could individually or collectively work to solve. Three major theoretical areas have guided the Project: social support theory, Paulo Freire's education for critical consciousness, and Saul Alinsky's community-organizing techniques for effecting social change (Minkler, 1986).

In early TSOP discussions, crime arose as the problem of most concern to the elderly tenants in the Tenderloin district. The TSOP organized a meeting with the mayor that led to increased police patrols in Tenderloin neighborhoods and efforts by police to get to know the elderly residents. A second early success of the TSOP was the establishment of the Safehouse Project through which residents recruited local businesses, restaurants, bars, and agencies to be places of refuge where residents could go in times of danger or medical emergency (Minkler, 1986).

Although organizing this population has had many challenges—including ill health, very diverse backgrounds among the residents, and lack of leadership experiences—it has been empowering for many of the residents involved in the TSOP (Goldoftas, 1988). One elderly resident who had struggled with mental illness said of her experience with the TSOP, "I learned that it's possible to beat the system. . . . I've learned that it's possible for people of different ages and different backgrounds to work together and actually get something done" (quoted in Goldoftas,1988, p.19). Another tenant was also impressed by the power of collective action:

> I thought that when you're down like this, way below the poverty level, you're powerless. . . . but I realized that you can make the big shots stand up and listen. It was amazing to me to learn that if you work together you can do something. (quoted in Goldoftas, 1988, p. 19)

A second example of community organizing with the intent to increase senior citizen advocacy is the Chicago-based Metro Seniors in Action (MSA)—a coalition of 77 senior community and church groups (Reitzes & Reitzes, 1991). Like the Tenderloin Senior Outreach Project, MSA was originally based on the Saul Alinsky principle of commu-

nity power. It was founded in 1978 by an individual with training in community organizing. According to Reitzes and Reitzes, MSA was most successful in its early years under the leadership of its founder, who generated enthusiasm for MSA by establishing personal relationships with local leaders and by initiating confrontations and actions that ignited excitement for the organization. With the retirement of the MSA founder, organizational ties to local groups weakened, and the emphasis shifted from confrontations to lobbying, which further disengaged some membership groups. Although MSA failed to maintain its initial momentum, its early period proved that seniors engaged in protest actions are often very effective.

> Metro Seniors demonstrated early on that although seniors are a heterogeneous group, citywide issues can be developed that highlight shared interests. For example, seniors of all social class backgrounds benefited by Metro Seniors' efforts to make public transportation more accessible and comfortable. . . . Although Metro Seniors in Action may not survive, its experiences demonstrate the potential of a citywide senior organization. (Reitzes & Reitzes, 1991, p. 262)

Brown (1985) examined grassroots advocacy for and by elderly people in a four-county, rural region of northern Arizona. Through informant interviews, Brown examined what motivated people to advocate for increased services for elderly people in their rural towns. He discovered that the perception that one could personally benefit from increased services and programming prompted the most consistent involvement in grassroots efforts. Advocating for senior programs gave some elderly people a legitimate reason to keep active, or as one elderly activist said, it kept him "up and doing" (quoted in Brown, 1985, p. 419). Another motivating factor was a personal affinity for and desire to interact and work with other elderly people. "I just enjoy going to meetings and having a chance to visit with other old-timers in the community" (quoted in Brown, 1985, p. 419), remarked one community activist. Another informant told Brown about an elderly man who was, at first, unconvinced that there was a need for a senior citizen program in his community; when he attended a gathering of elderly people at which their needs were discussed, however, he enthusiastically took a leadership role in developing programs to serve local seniors. Also mentioned as a motivating factor in their advocacy work by a number of Brown's elderly informants was the personal recognition that being active brought to their lives. Evidently, active involvement in grassroots organizing enriches the lives of elderly people on many levels.

Programs That Facilitate Activism for Frail Elderly People. Although social workers may have experience advocating on behalf of frail elderly people, perhaps operating under the assumption that people who are very frail are unable to be personally involved in activism and to advocate for themselves, there are programs that prove otherwise. Two social workers employed in the Veterans Administration

Hospital in Bedford, Massachusetts, founded Living Is for the Elderly (LIFE) in 1972. Within 15 years, LIFE included residents of more than 100 nursing homes in the Greater Boston Area (Kautzer, 1988).

From the start, the primary goal of LIFE was to provide nursing home residents who previously had not had a voice in the State House with the opportunity to take on a political role. LIFE succeeded in activating nursing home residents through nurturing, encouragement, and considerable assistance from the staff (Kautzer, 1988). Political activities have included participating in demonstrations at the State House, making telephone calls and writing letters to legislators, and testifying at legislative hearings. Kautzer's investigation of the impact of this activism on nursing home residents identified three areas of change: self-image, social ties, and empowerment. The interviews with LIFE activists indicated that it is possible to lead an enjoyable and rewarding life in a nursing home, provided that an organization such as LIFE is available to mitigate the dehumanizing aspects of institutionalization and empower residents to pursue the respected and challenging role of activist.

The Minnesota Alliance of Health Care Consumers (MAHCC) also demonstrates the value of activism by nursing home residents. Developed in 1972 by a social worker interested in providing residents of nursing facilities with a forum for self-expression, self-control, and self-advocacy (Meyer, 1991), MAHCC uses strategies similar to those of LIFE: letter writing, testifying, and holding rallies. MAHCC also has experienced many successes, including the organization of resident and family councils in nursing homes throughout the state, the passage of numerous friendly legislative bills and regulations, and the defeat of unfriendly legislation. Meyer's study corroborated Kautzer's finding that professional organizers are essential in mobilizing and supporting frail elderly people in their activist activities. One MAHCC activist described how a social worker supported her work: "Pam and I got together and wrote a testimony which I just read. But I had my own ideas. I'm the one who lives here" (quoted in Meyer, 1991, p. 373). Meyer further suggested that, although frailty is generally viewed as a limitation in activist work, it can be a resource within particular contexts: "politicians are very reluctant to vote against the wishes of a frail constituency" (p. 375).

Both LIFE and MAHCC provide evidence that activism is both empowering and enjoyable for frail elderly people. As one informant in Kautzer's investigation of LIFE indicated: "LIFE gives you something to live for. You're not just sitting in a corner" (quoted in Kautzer, 1988, p.171). The successes of these organizations are a reminder that no one should underestimate the ability of elderly people, no matter how disabled, to remain actively engaged in their lives. In contrast, many advocacy groups decide to work *on behalf of* the frail elderly—thus placing the group that they serve in a less empowering position. For example, the Citizens for Better Care (CBC) in Nursing Homes in Detroit consciously chose not to include nursing facility residents or their families in their organization membership:

It was decided that the organization would attempt to represent the interests of nursing home patients, but would probably have few, if any, representatives from active patients. It was also deemed unwise to draw any substantial numbers from people who had parents or other relatives in nursing homes. The rationale was that both patients and relatives might fear retaliatory action, such as eviction by the nursing home. (Jacobson, 1977, p. 120)

Perhaps this exclusionary strategy is overly cautious and does a disservice to frail elderly people and their families, in that it does not provide an opportunity for older adults to develop and exercise control.

Service Programs That Have an Activist Component. As noted in chapter 5, volunteer work and community service can enrich the lives of elderly people. Some of these service programs have an activist component. For example, Experience Corps, the signature program of Civic Ventures, is an initiative mobilizing neighborhood retirees to help transform struggling inner-city schools. (See the appendix for contact information.) For some volunteers, the one-on-one work with children is a form of activism. One participant in Experience Corps, who in early adulthood had been active in the Civil Rights Movement and community organizing, sees his volunteer work as part of a larger social change effort:

Children think they are to blame in a lot of their situations. They need a lot of praise and love and recognition.

We also need to take the steps necessary to bring about more systemic kinds of change. The school system here has no money. Kids don't even have books. If more people were active and created a new awareness of these conditions, there would be change. There has to be a rebirth of involvement. . . . These kids are the potential organizers for change in the future. (quoted in Freedman, 2001, p. 23)

Intergenerational community service projects allow older adults and youths to work together to improve local conditions and practice activist skills. The Neighborhoods 2000 program—implemented in seven neighborhoods between 1987 and 1994—attempted "to engender an awareness that there are people of other age groups who have valuable insights into community life" (Kaplan, 1997, p. 214). One goal of the program was to instill a sense of active citizenship and to plant seeds of community activism. The program curriculum involves bringing young adolescents and senior adults from the same neighborhoods together in a school setting to work on a series of communication and neighborhood exploration activities. Participants became more competent in their advocacy skills; more aware of local issues; and more likely to contact public officials, agencies, and other residents about their concerns. One senior participant described how her awareness and sense of citizenship had grown through the Neighborhoods 2000 program:

Unlike other projects with which I volunteer, I have expanded my life by becoming more aware of the current issues facing our community. Like most seniors, I keep up with the news. However, becoming actively involved and getting to know the children makes the many problems facing the children and their parents personal issues for me. (Quoted in Kaplan, 1997, p. 221)

Environmental Alliance for Senior Involvement (EASI), another intergenerational program with an activist slant, sponsors more than 500 projects throughout the United States. Sponsored by the AARP and the Environmental Protection Agency, EASI projects have explicit activist goals, such as showing local gardeners how to reduce the use of pesticides and herbicides, promoting energy conservation, restoring natural habitats, and preventing pollution (Thompson, 2001). (See the appendix for contact information.)

Social Work Practice to Facilitate Activism among Elderly People

Clearly, activism can enhance and enrich the lives of elderly people, just as it does for people of all ages. Many older U.S. citizens are already politically active, and some have a connection to groups that encourage activism. Certainly, those individuals who have been activists throughout their lives will be likely to maintain those activities in their later years (Champlin, 1982), but other elderly people may need more encouragement to find their political voices. If they are to assist elderly people in developing their activist selves, social workers themselves must be both comfortable with activism and aware of opportunities for activism for their elder clients (Cox & Parsons, 1993). Fortunately, the increased emphasis on policy practice in schools of social work (for example, Haynes & Mickelson, 2000; Jansson, 1999) and the acknowledged importance of training social workers to influence state policy (see, for example, www.statepolicy.org) should sensitize newly trained social workers—no matter what their field of practice—to the power of activism for themselves and their clients. Activism, social change, and empowerment practice have a long history in the profession of social work (Simon, 1994), and promoting elder activism is clearly congruent with the values of the profession.

Micro Level Interventions

Social workers practicing at the individual and small-group levels are encouraged to consider the following techniques in their work with older clients to facilitate elder activism:

- Promote feelings of self-efficacy and the acquisition of an internal locus of control.
- Facilitate the understanding and awareness of collective experiences.
- Create opportunities for group identity and cohesiveness among elderly people.
- Obtain and share knowledge about the policy-making process and current policies that directly affect older clients.
- Connect clients to existing local opportunities for activism, such as state Silver Haired Legislatures, local legislative days for elderly people, or grassroots organizations

concerned with issues of importance to individual clients.
- Familiarize clients with national organizations that advocate activism and represent their interests, such as the Older Women's League, the National Caucus and Center on Black Aged, or the Gray Panthers.
- Assist and empower frail elderly people to express their needs and desires and to have their voices heard.

Macro Level Interventions

Social workers engaged in program planning, administration, community development, or policy change should consider the following practice principles and techniques in their efforts to promote elder activism:

- Ensure that elderly people have leadership roles in the planning of programs, organizations, and advocacy groups that serve their needs.
- Organize a state level Silver Haired Legislature if one does not currently exist.
- Create, with input from elderly people, a training institute that promotes senior activism. (The Institute for Senior Action has materials to assist in such efforts; see Joint Public Affairs Committee for Older Adults (JPAC) in the Appendix.)
- Organize a lobby day for elderly people at the State House.

Final Thoughts on Elder Activism and Productive Aging

The phrase "productive aging" has drawn criticism from some scholars for promoting a cultural ideal about appropriate roles and norms for elderly people in our society. For example, Holstein (1999) cautioned that an emphasis on productive aging appears to affirm the societal ideal that it "is good and desirable for U.S. culture to elevate productivity as a ruling metaphor for 'good' old age" (p. 359). As she suggested, productivity is generally linked to paid work, and it is a link that is hard to sever in our culture. Thus, a productive aging ideal could negatively influence patterns of dominance and oppression for women and people of color, if there were changing societal expectations about an extended employment life. On the other hand, she submitted that if we are able to cast productivity as a metaphor for self-respect, dignity, and social validation, then we can discover how to achieve those ends through avenues outside the paid labor market. Engaging in activism can be one such avenue to empowered and productive aging.

References

Berger, M. (1976). An orienting perspective on advocacy. In P. A. Kerschner (Ed.), *Advocacy and age* (pp. 1–16). Los Angeles: University of Southern California Press.

Binstock, R. H. (1991). Aging, politics and public policy. In B. B. Hess & E. W. Markson (Eds.), *Growing old in America* (4th ed., pp. 325–340). New Brunswick, NJ: Transaction Books.

Binstock, R. H. (1997). The 1996 election: Older voters and implications for policies on aging. *Gerontologist, 37,* 15–19.

Binstock, R. H., & Day, C. L. (1996). Aging and politics. In R. H. Binstock & L. K.

George (Eds.), *Handbook of aging and the social sciences* (pp. 362–387). San Diego: Academic Press.

Brown, A.S. (1985). Grassroots advocacy for the elderly in small rural communities. *Gerontologist, 25,* 417–423.

Champlin, L. (1982). Militant elderly: The wave of the present. *Geriatrics, 37,* 125–130.

Cox, E. O., & Parsons, R. J. (1993). *Empowerment-oriented social work practice with the elderly.* Pacific Grove, CA: Brooks/Cole.

Crittenden, B. (1985, March–June). West Virginia elderly people make a difference. *Southern Exposure,* pp. 52–56.

Epstein, D., West, A. J., & Riegel, D. G. (2000). The Institute for Senior Action: Training leaders for advocacy. *Journal of Gerontological Social Work, 33*(4), 91–99.

Estes, C. L. (1999). The aging enterprise revisited. In M. Minkler & C. L. Estes (Eds.), *Critical gerontology: Perspectives from political and moral economy* (pp. 135–146). Amityville, NY: Baywood.

Freedman, M. (2001). Anything but retired. *Hope Magazine, 25,* 21–23.

Goeke, M. L., & Wolfe, J. B. (1979). *Silver Haired Legislature: A model for senior legislative advocacy.* Washington, DC: NRTA/ American Association of Retired Persons.

Goldoftas, B. (1988). Organizing in a gray ghetto. *Dollars & Sense, 133,* 18–19.

Hanna, W. J. (1981). Advocacy and the elderly. In R. H. Davis (Ed.), *Aging prospects and issues* (3rd ed., pp. 297–316). Los Angeles: University of Southern California Press.

Haynes, K. S., & Mickelson, J. S. (2000). *Affecting change: Social workers in the political arena* (4th ed.). Boston: Allyn & Bacon.

Holstein, M. (1999). Women and productive aging: Troubling implications. In M. Minkler & C. L. Estes (Eds.), *Critical* gerontology: Perspectives from political and moral economy (pp. 359–373). Amityville, NY: Baywood.

Hooyman, N. R., & Kiyak, H. A. (2002). Social gerontology: A multidisciplinary perspective (6th ed.). Boston: Allyn & Bacon.

Jacobson, S. G. (1977). Consumer advocacy. In L. A. Baumhover & J. D. Jones (Eds.), Handbook of American aging programs (pp. 119–131). Westport, CT: Greenwood Press.

Jansson, B. S. (1999). Becoming an effective policy advocate: From policy practice to social justice. Pacific Grove, CA: Brooks/Cole.

Kaplan, M. (1997). The benefits of intergenerational community service projects: Implications for promoting intergenerational unity, community activism and cultural continuity. Journal of Gerontological Social Work, 28, 211–228.

Kautzer, K. (1988). Empowering nursing home residents: A case study of "Living is For the Elderly," an activist nursing home organization. In S. Reinharz & G. D. Rowles (Eds.), Qualitative gerontology (pp.163–183). New York: Springer.

Kuhn, M. E. (1976). What old people want for themselves and others in society. In P.A. Kerschner (Ed.), Advocacy and age (pp. 87–96). Los Angeles: University of Southern California Press.

Kuypers, J. A., & Bengtson, V. L. (1973). Social breakdown and competence: A model of normal aging. Human Development, 16, 181–201.

Long, D. D., & Holle, M. C. (1997). Macro systems in the social environment. Itasca, IL: F. E. Peacock.

Meyer, M. H. (1991). Organizing the frail elderly. In B. B. Hess & E. W. Markson (Eds.), Growing old in America (4th ed., pp. 363–376). New Brunswick, NJ: Transaction Books.

Minkler, M. (1986). Building support networks from social isolation. Generations, 10(2), 46–49.

Pratt, H. J. (1976). The gray lobby. Chicago: University of Chicago Press.

Reitzes, D. C., & Reitzes, D. C. (1991). Metro Seniors in Action: A case study of a city wide senior organization. Gerontologist, 31, 256–262.

Rice, F. P. (1992). Human development: A life-span approach. New York: Macmillan.

Simon, B. L. (1994). The empowerment tradition in American social work: A history. New York: Columbia University Press.

Thompson, A. (2001). Common bonds: Intergenerational programs unite young and old with surprising results. Hope Magazine, 25, 24–25, 71.

Torres-Gil, F. M. (1993). Interest group politics: Generational changes in the politics of aging. In V. L. Bengtson & W. A. Achenbaum (Eds.), The changing contract across generations (pp. 239–257). New York: Aldine de Gruyter.

Treas, J. (1995). Older Americans in the 1990s and beyond. Population Bulletin, 5(2). Washington, DC: Population Reference Bureau.

Trela, J. E. (1976). Status inconsistency and political action in old age. In J. F. Gubrium (Ed.), Time, roles and self in old age (pp. 126–147). New York: Human Sciences Press.

Trela, J. E. (1978). Social class and political involvement in age-graded and non-age graded associations. International Journal of Aging and Human Development, 8, 335–344.

Van Tassel, D. D., & Meyer, J.E.W. (1992). U.S. aging policy interest groups: Institutional profiles. New York: Greenwood Press.

Washaw, S. (2001, May). New York State Advocacy Day 2001. News & Events: SAGE, p. 3.

11

Physical Activity, Exercise, and Recreation

Melonie D. Grossman

Introduction

Physical activity, exercise, and recreation are critical to continued health and functioning for people of all ages. Research suggests that a physically active lifestyle is especially important for older people. Physically active seniors live longer, and they are at lower risk of many physiological changes associated with aging (Evans, 1995). Physical activity, exercise, and recreation are fundamental to productive aging because they add years of health, independence, well-being, and physical capability to the lives of seniors (Bortz, 1996; Mazzeo et al., 1998; Stewart, King, & Haskell, 1993).

Chronological age does not necessarily diminish participation in and enjoyment of a physically active life. For millions of older people in the United States today, leisure time physical activity is a continuation of healthy behaviors established earlier in life. For others, increased physical activity represents new behavior and change. But whether physical activity habits are long established or recently acquired, benefits extend not only to the healthy older population, but also to chronically ill, frail, and very old elderly people (Mazzeo et al., 1998). According to the Surgeon General's Office, no one is too old to enjoy the benefits of regular physical activity (U.S. Department of Health and Human Services, 1996).

Still, physical activity declines with age. Today, approximately 29 percent of the general population report no leisure time physical activity (Centers for Disease Control and Prevention [CDC], 2001). For older people, the numbers are far worse. According to three national data sets, 38 percent to 54 percent of people over age 70 are considered sedentary (U.S. Department of Health and Human Services, 1996). In ethnic minority populations, even higher percentages of older people may be sedentary (Rejeski & Brawley, 2000).

As more people live longer, knowledge about maintaining health, autonomy, and quality of life for older adults has expanded. Social workers in traditional mental health care, acute care, rehabilitation, and long-term care roles have always recognized the value of physical activity in helping older clients maintain a productive life. As the human life span continues to lengthen, the focus on wellness and prevention of disease will make information about physical activity increasingly indispensable to all social workers in every aspect of the field of gerontology.

Active Aging

"I exercise to stay fit, and not just spend my life in a reclining chair."

—An 80-year-old man

In 1999, 11,937 athletes ranging in age from 55 to 89 and representing a diversity of backgrounds competed in the 1999 National Senior Games, also known as the Senior Olympics (www. nsga.org). Organizations such as Elderhostel (www.elderhostel.org) offer seniors active adventures, with choices of light or moderate physical activity such as birding, boating, or walking tours. For those who prefer more vigorous activities, kayaking or hiking are also available. Other organizations such as the 50 Plus Fitness Association (www.50plus.org) promote health and fitness in older people, offering information, workshops, and physical activity events all across the United States.

Many older people in the United States today choose to participate regularly in energetic activities such as dancing, swimming, tennis, biking, or sailing—either on their own or in groups. Other older adults prefer home-based exercise or moderate walking, the most popular physical activity for seniors (Booth, Bauman, Owen, & Gore, 1997).

Local senior and community centers like the YMCA/YWCA offer vigorous group activities, such as square dancing, or more moderate activities, such as easy stretch, low-impact aerobics, tai chi, or chair exercises. As the benefits of strength building for older people are becoming more widely recognized, community colleges, senior centers, and even some long-term care facilities are offering classes in weight training (Youngquist, 1998).

For many older people, the main source of physical activity occurs through their daily activities, such as gardening, running errands, climbing stairs, or working. For people with medical issues, specially designed exercise programs, such as Sit and Be Fit, are available on television or through videos. The Arthritis Foundation, the National Institute on Aging, the American Diabetes Association, the American Heart Association, and other organizations offer booklets and Internet information (see appendix) on exercise for people with special health concerns—always with the proviso that exercise be undertaken only in conjunction with ongoing medical follow-up.

The image of men and women spending their golden years in rocking chairs is receding. Older adults of all ages who for generations were cautioned to "take it easy" are now being told to "use it or lose it!" Over the past 25 years, research in the fields of medicine, psychology, epidemiology, public health, and behavioral sciences has led the CDC to recommend physical activity and exercise as a means of promoting physical health, maximizing psychological health, and preventing some of the functional declines that often accompany aging (Fletcher et al., 1992).

New CDC guidelines recommend 30 minutes or more of moderate-intensity physical activity on most, preferably all, days of the week for older people (Friede, O'Carroll, & Nicola, 1997). These guidelines are good news for seniors, because they are more likely to exercise moderately than vigorously (Sallis et al., 1986). Moderate activities, such as walking or swimming, have now been shown to achieve many of the benefits once thought achievable only through vigorous exercise (Kushi et al., 1997; Manson et al., 1999; Martinsen & Stephens, 1994; U.S. Department of Health and Human Services [DHHS], 1996; Wannamethee, Sharper, & Walker, 2000).

The new guidelines have another advantage for older people. It is now believed that exercise can be done in short bouts (10 minutes at one time). Physical activity interspersed throughout the day is thought to be just as beneficial as continuous exercise done during one time period (U.S. Department of Health and Human Services, 1996). Seniors who are pressed for time or who cannot sustain long periods of exercise because of pain or other health problems can meet the guideline of performing 30 minutes of physical activity on most days of the week by pacing themselves and spreading their activities over a longer period of time throughout their day.

A well-balanced regimen that includes a combination of physical activities to enhance strength, endurance, flexibility, and balance is considered ideal (Mazzeo et al., 1998). To avoid injury or soreness in beginning a physi-

cal activity regimen, the Office of the Surgeon General (DHHS, 1996) recommended that individuals start slowly and gradually build up to meet physical activity guidelines. People with chronic health problems, such as high blood pressure or diabetes, should always consult a physician before making changes in their physical activity levels. Also, men over age 40 and women over age 50 who are planning vigorous physical activity should consult a physician first to rule out heart disease or other health problems.

Benefits of Physical Activity

Longevity and Disease Prevention

"I wasn't going to let sitting around kill me off."

—An 81-year-old woman

Some of the strongest evidence for the positive relationship between physical activity and longevity came out of a longitudinal study that has followed an initial 3,978 Harvard alumni since 1960 (Paffenbarger & Hyde, 1988). The study showed an inverse association between physical activity and mortality. An active lifestyle exerts its effect largely because physical activity reduces the rate of age-associated deterioration in cardiovascular functions, leading to longer life for both men and women (Hakim et al., 1998; Manson et al., 1999). In addition to playing a role in primary prevention, physical activity and exercise are also important secondary prevention measures for those who already have heart disease. Recent studies have shown that the rate of mortality decreases in men and women who have survived their first heart attack if they participate in regular physical activity (for example, Steffen-Batey et al., 2000).

Another health benefit of a physically active lifestyle is the accompanying reduction of blood pressure and cholesterol levels, which contributes to a lower risk of strokes in active seniors (Seals, Hagberg, Hurley, Ehsani, & Holloszy, 1984). Physically active men and women are also at lower risk for some cancers, especially colon or colorectal cancer (Graham, Cannuscio, & Frazier, 1997). Even a light- to moderate-intensity walking program has been shown to reduce the risk of many of these diseases (Kushi et al., 1997; Manson et al., 1999).

Functional Capacity and Independence

"You aren't going to get better by just sitting around."

—A 75-year-old man

Muscle mass is critical to all aspects of physical functioning, such as walking, climbing stairs, sitting, and standing. After age 30, muscle density decreases, and fat increases, producing a gradual loss of muscle fiber that is directly related to a decrease in strength (Evans, 1995). Exercise and physical activity can modify age-related physiological changes, even in very old people (Fiatarone & Evans, 1993), such as muscle weakness and stiffness, that decrease mobility and reduce independence.

Age-related declines in posture, flexibility, and balance are positively associated with frequency of falling, especially in women (Tinetti, Ducette, Claus, & Marttoli, 1995). Fear of falling can lead older people to restrict their activity (Lawrence et al., 1998),

increasing their risk of falls. Stretching activities, such as tai chi and yoga, increase range of motion, improve posture, and promote better balance; thus, they lead to increased functioning and independence in older people (Mazzeo et al., 1998).

Management of Chronic Diseases and Pain

"The more you do the better you feel."

—A 79-year-old woman

Many chronic diseases respond favorably to physical therapy, supervised physical activities, and even simple home-based exercise regimens—although as noted earlier, people with chronic diseases should consult a physician before increasing their physical activity and exercise. Physical activity can lower glucose insulin levels and reduce hypertension, obesity, and bone loss in older people (Ebrahim, Thompson, Baskaran, & Evans, 1997; Kirwan, Kohrt, Wojta, & Holloszy, 1993). Regularly performed exercise, strength training, and sometimes a simple program of brisk walking can offset age-associated declines in bone density and reduce the risk of bone fractures (Mazzeo et al., 1998; Prior, Barr, Chow, & Faulkner, 1996).

In some instances, increased physical activity and conditioning can control chronic pain, which frequently increases with age (Ferrell, 1991, 1995). Nonpharmacological pain management strategies include physical therapy, strength training, and supervised fitness walking (Agre, Pierce, Raab, McAdams, & Smith, 1988; Ferrell, Josephson, Pollan, Loy, & Ferrell, 1997). Osteoarthritis accounts for the majority of chronic pain complaints among older people, and it often responds well to physical activity, which reduces pain and keeps joints limber (Agre et al., 1988; Sharpe et al., 1997).

Mental Health

"I know if you are feeling a little depressed, if you get out and walk or become active, that helps you."

—A 77-year-old woman

Major depression affects more than 19 million adults in the United States, 10 percent of whom are over age 65 (National Academy on an Aging Society, 2000). Epidemiological studies show an inverse relationship between physical activity and depression (Schoenborn, 1986). Intervention studies are now providing evidence that exercise is at least as effective as standard pharmacotherapy in the treatment of depression (Blumenthal et al., 1999; Martinsen & Stephens, 1994). In addition, those who exercise may be less likely to relapse into depression than those who receive standard medication (Babyak et al., 2000).

Physical activity has also been shown to be effective in treating various forms of anxiety, including panic disorder and agoraphobia (Tkachuk & Martin, 1999). Studies focusing on older populations with these conditions have yet to be conducted, however. A large prospective study recently concluded in Canada found physical activity to be associated with lower risks of cognitive impairment, Alzheimer's disease, and dementia of any type (Lauren, Verreault, Lindsay, MacPherson, & Rockwood, 2001). Still, a causal link between physical activity and improved cognitive capacity has still not been definitively established (Spirduso, 1995). Finally, exercise is an effective method of reducing stress and improving overall psychological well-being in seniors (McAuley & Rudolph, 1995), an important finding for social workers who work with older clients.

Theory

Although the physical and mental health benefits of exercise and physical activity are well-known, sustaining or increasing physical activity levels in older people is often far from simple. Knowledge of the theoretical underpinnings of behavior maintenance and change can be useful, both in terms of supporting successfully aging seniors in remaining active and encouraging sedentary or underactive seniors to increase their levels of leisure time physical activity. Continuity theory (Atchley, 1993) and social cognitive theory (Bandura, 1977b) are especially helpful in understanding the relationships among activity, change, and aging. The transtheoretical model of behavioral change (Prochaska et al., 1994) is also useful, especially in working with less active clients interested in making changes in their physical activity levels.

Continuity theory suggests that unique patterns of behaviors and traits characterizing the individual show considerable stability across the lifespan (Atchley, 1989). By the time people reach middle-age, they have usually developed clearly identifiable patterns of behavior and thinking that involve values, preferences, competencies, habits, knowledge, and skills. These patterns tend to persist over time, kept in place by internal and external pressures and by expectations for behaviors that are established and familiar (Atchley, 1993).

Because people do indeed make changes, even when they are older, Atchley (1993) hypothesized that change occurs as a gradual evolution of behavior in which new directions come from past successes, competencies, and preferences. A continuity perspective suggests that increases in physical activity levels are most likely to occur in activities that the individual prefers and in areas in which the individual already has some interest, knowledge, or competence. In clinical applications of continuity theory, Fry (1992) suggested an approach that considers adaptive strategies related to an individual's previous strengths and preferences. For example, activities such as walking that relate to successes in the present or even the past have a better chance of increasing exercise levels.

Social cognitive theory offers insights into the specific mechanisms by which behaviors are maintained or changed. According to Bandura (1977b), behavior is mediated through cognitive processes, especially through the use of language, which facilitates the use and storage of information; through vicarious processes, such as observing others (role modeling); and through self-regulatory processes, which occur when the individual generates cognitive supports for behavior (goals, self-reinforcement, and self-evaluation).

Expectations of personal efficacy play a central role in an individual's willingness to try new behaviors, according to Bandura (1977a). A belief in one's ability to perform mediates not only whether new behavior is initiated, but also how much effort is expended in trying to master the behavior and how long the behavior is sustained in the face of barriers and adverse experiences. Bandura (1986) described four sources of efficacy that are especially pertinent to physical activity and exercise: (1) personal mastery; (2) vicarious experience, such as watching the success of others; (3) verbal persuasion; and (4) expressions of confidence from others. The individual's physiological or psychological state can influence efficacy because a person who feels weak, anxious, or fearful has lower expectations of efficacy and is unlikely to try to change behavior.

Bandura's (1977a, 1986) theories may explain why it is difficult to introduce new behaviors to people who are feeling ill, are depressed, or lack self-confidence. Social work practices such as providing information, focusing on strengths, reinforcing successes, modeling, offering support, and marshaling the support of existing formal and informal networks are some of the techniques that social cognitive theory suggests would be helpful in working with older adults on physical activity issues.

The transtheoretical model of behavioral change has been advanced as a conceptualization of motivation and change that can be generalized across a range of problematic behaviors, such as smoking, alcohol dependence, and drug addiction (Prochaska et al., 1994). The model has been used successfully in physical activity research with interventions designed to decrease sedentary behaviors (Marcus & Owen, 1992; Marcus & Simkin, 1994). Prochaska and colleagues described a series of five "stages" experienced by most people in the course of making changes:

1. precontemplation. Need for change is denied, and no change is considered.
2. contemplation. Change is considered, and pros and cons are weighed.
3. preparation. Change is seriously considered, and groundwork is done.
4. action. Overt changes occur, and commitment to continued change is made.
5. maintenance. Change behavior is stabilized, and relapse prevention is implemented.

The transtheoretical model suggests tailoring interventions to the needs of people at different stages of change. For example, it may be necessary to address feelings of ambivalence in a person at the contemplation stage, whereas a relatively active person who is in the maintenance stage, but is facing new health problems, may need help overcoming these new barriers and preventing a relapse into sedentary behavior.

Motivation is viewed within the transtheoretical model as a state of "readiness" for change or an acceptance of stasis that results from the barriers to change. Both of these arise from the interaction of internal and external circumstances (Miller & Rollnick, 1991). Understanding and addressing internal and external motivation and barriers can be an important step toward increasing readiness to change.

Motivation

"I want to continue to be in good health, because I want to see those grandkids grow up."
                    —A 76-year-old woman

Relatively little research has been done on physical activity motivation in older people. Research is more likely to explore associations between physical activity and other variables, such as gender and age. In large epidemiological studies (Schoenborn, 1986; Stephens, Jacobs, & White, 1985), education is positively associated with physical activity, age is negatively related, and income shows only a modest positive correlation. Although in general people are less likely to be physically active as they age, one longitudinal survey of community-dwelling adults showed that age and gender were not factors for the adoption of moderate activity, such as walking (Sallis et al., 1986).

In addition to the relatively immutable demographic variables mentioned earlier, there are a number of subjective factors associated with physical activity. Informal social support for exercise from family and friends has been linked to increases in physical activity in older people (Hovell et al., 1989; Wolinsky, Stump, & Clark, 1995). Physician support or recommendation is also positively related to physical activity (Calfas et al., 1996; Damush, Stewart, Mills, King, & Ritter, 1999). Wolinsky, Stump, and Clark (1995) also found that older people who perceived their health to be poor were less likely to exercise. It is not surprising that a knowledge of health issues and a belief in the value of exercise are also associated with physical activity behavior (Ferrini, Edelstein, & Barrett-Connor, 1994; Sallis et al., 1986). Finally, self-efficacy has been positively associated with physical activity (Hovell et al., 1989; McAuley, 1993).

In studying motivation directly, Smith and Storandt (1997) asked athletes who participated in the Senior Olympics National Finals and older nonexercisers to select and rate reasons for exercising from a list of possible motivations. The most frequently chosen motivations for exercising for both groups were to comply with a recommendation from a doctor and to feel better physically. The study also found that senior athletes selected a greater variety of motivations for exercising than did nonexercisers, such as improving mood and being with friends.

In a qualitative study using in-depth interviewing with subjects who were age 75 and older (mean age 80), motivational factors in increasing physical activity levels that were most often mentioned were health and fitness (Grossman, 1999). Other motivations were improved appearance and weight loss, maintenance of independence, family support, and continued quality of life. Independence, including staying in one's own home, was especially important to people over age 80.

In studies that used focus groups to explore physical activity attitudes and motivations in African American and Hispanic men and women (Grossman, McLellan, Gillis, & Stewart, 2000; Grossman et al., 2001), health was the most frequently mentioned motivator. Mental health benefits and enjoyment were also important. Lehr (1992), who interviewed older exercisers in Germany, found that participants stressed "expressive" motivations, such as "just for the fun of it," over "instrumental" motivations, such as "to stay in shape." Lehr concluded that as people age, health maintenance alone would not lead them to participate in sports and active recreational pursuits.

Barriers to Physical Activity

"I don't have enough time to get everything done that I want to do."

—A 79-year-old woman

Lack of time is the most frequently reported obstacle to exercise and recreational activities in all age groups, including elderly people (Dishman, Sallis, & Orenstein, 1985; Shephard, 1994). Health problems are another important barrier for older people (Booth et al., 1997; Kriska et al., 1986). In qualitative interviews, Grossman (1999) found that health presents the main barrier to physical activity in older people, in addition to fatigue, lack of energy, and, for people over age 80, failing eyesight.

Some older people fear that exercise may create health problems, such as a heart attack, or exacerbate existing conditions, such as arthritis (Cousins, 2000; Shephard, 1994). Fear of falling keeps some older people from exercising or enjoying physically active recreation (Lachman et al., 1998; Lawrence et al., 1998). In African American and Hispanic focus groups, participants mentioned a lack of sustained motivation and commitment (Grossman et al., 2000, 2001). Environmental barriers include lack of access to facilities, lack of transportation, unsafe sidewalks, and poor weather (Clark, 1996; Dishman, 1994; Grossman, 1999; Shephard, 1994). Neighborhood safety, which King and colleagues (1992) proposed as a barrier to physical activity for seniors in low socioeconomic status communities, has not been studied extensively and was not found to be significant in the African American and Hispanic focus groups studied by Grossman and colleagues (2000, 2001).

Social and cultural barriers to physical activity for seniors have received scant attention, although they would be of particular interest to social workers. Lee (1993) argued that older women had fewer opportunities to participate in active sports when they were young, so they had acquired fewer physical activity skills that they could use in later life. The importance of physical activity for girls and women also has been downplayed in the past, making it difficult for older women to place value and priority on exercise today.

The Hispanic and African American women in the focus groups held by Grossman and colleagues (2000, 2001) appeared to agree that physical activity was important, especially for its physical and mental health benefits. Hispanic women named family obligations as a barrier, however, while African Americans saw their tradition of service to others as receiving priority over self-care. As one African American woman put it, "I'm always doing stuff for others, but sometimes I forget about me."

For Hispanic older men, "image" or appearance sometimes get in the way of exercising. As one man in the focus groups said, "I go to the gym and I try to stay out of the groups because I get ashamed, because some guys are lifting these gigantic weights, and I can only lift about two pounds." Very little is known about the attitudes of older African American men toward physical activity, and recruiting them for focus groups and other studies has been difficult.

Shephard (1990) argued that the belief that "old age is a time to slow down and take a well earned rest" continues to act as a barrier to physical activity in older people. Although this particular belief was not evident in qualitative interviews (Grossman, 1999), the "wear and tear" theory of aging was apparent when an 81-year-old man noted: "Your body's getting older, too. It's just like an automobile or anything else. Things start to wear out."

Although many elderly people today are knowledgeable about the importance of physical activity and exercise (Grossman et al., 2000, 2001), lack of information continues to be a barrier. Older people are frequently unsure of how to get started, how much they should do to receive benefits, and which exercises are best for their particular situation. Finally, many under-active seniors believe that they get all the exercise that they need by performing their daily routine and thus feel that increasing their physical activity would not bring them added benefits (Clark, 1995).

Social Work Practice Roles

"I don't want to give in just because I'm old."

—An 84-year-old woman

Helping older people to remain active and productive is an important social work role today. As the baby boomers continue to age, this role is likely to become more common. Sustaining an active lifestyle despite physical changes brought on by aging can be a challenge for some older adults. Changing a sedentary lifestyle to an active one is even more challenging. One expanding role for social workers is to foster decision making about the adoption of new behavior by older adults, to help them overcome barriers to new behavior, and to support the maintenance of healthy behavior. But social work roles must go beyond working with the individual.

To implement population level increases in the number of elderly people who are physically active, a multilevel approach will be necessary. Because of the diversity in the age, gender, marital status, income, racial–ethnic background, geography, education, health, attitudes, and physical ability of our older population, "one size fits all" interventions are unlikely to be successful. The National Blueprint for Increasing Physical Activity among Adults Age 50 and Older (Chodzko-Zajko, 2001) conceptualizes the various multilevel approaches as upstream, midstream, and downstream interventions.

Upstream or Macrosystem Level Interventions

"You got TV programs, radio, newspapers, magazines, all touting exercise and fitness, and it's a good idea I think."

—A 78-year-old man

Macrosystem level interventions strengthen social norms regarding the value of physical activity, exercise, and recreation for older people. They also encourage public policies that support healthy behaviors through funding for increased research and services, as well as through improved environments in which these behaviors can flourish. Some of the upstream interventions that social workers, either as individuals or as a profession, can address include national public education campaigns, professional education, the

creation of economic incentives in support of healthy behaviors, and the removal of institutional barriers to physical activity for seniors (McKinlay, 1995).

There is some evidence that our culture and institutions are beginning to recognize the value of physical activity for seniors. The National Institutes of Health, through the National Institute on Aging and the National Institute of Mental Health, have supported research on physical activity and aging. The American College of Sports Medicine, the American Heart Association, the Centers for Disease Control and Prevention, the Office of the Surgeon General, the President's Council on Physical Fitness and Sports, and many others have published national guidelines for exercise and physical activity. The Arthritis Foundation, the American Diabetes Association, the National Osteoporosis Foundation, the American Association of Retired Persons, the National Institute on Aging and others offer Web sites and free or inexpensive materials designed to help older people stay physically active. (See the appendix for a complete list of resources.)

Despite the success of many physical activity initiatives for seniors, fragmentation of services and policies at a national level continues (Chodzko-Zajko, 2001). Incentives for physical fitness services remain vague. Legislation to authorize even small reductions in Medicare premiums for physical activity participation or to reimburse health care professionals, including social workers, for physical activity assessment, education, and counseling would help to raise awareness of the importance of physical activity in older people.

As a matter of public policy, high-quality programs and facilities should be made available to every older adult, including those living in rural and low-income areas. One predictor of exercise participation is a short travel distance to reach exercise facilities (Sallis, Hovell, Hofstetter, & Elder, 1990). Policies that support local physical activity classes and transportation to the classes for elderly people are needed. Because walking is the most frequently chosen physical activity for seniors (Booth et al., 1997), and those over age 80 prefer walking close to their homes (Grossman, 1999), policies ensuring safe sidewalks in both urban and rural areas would help to keep very old individual more active.

Subsidizing the redesign of public buildings and senior housing complexes in ways that facilitate the use of stairs over elevators or that provide indoor and outdoor walking paths would also be helpful. Policies to address liability issues for senior housing developments and other facilities (including churches and schools) that offer physical activity programs are also needed (Chodzko-Zajko, 2001).

Midstream or Mesosystem
Level Interventions

"I think people are aware now that exercise is important in older years, and people are supportive."

—A 78-year-old man

Social workers execute midstream interventions when they work with defined populations at the community level. The fragmentation of physical activity resources in the community frequently creates barriers that the development of coalitions (a process familiar to many social workers) on the local, state, and national levels may overcome (Stewart, 2001). Parks and recreation departments, county commissions, state agencies, community centers, senior housing associations, wellness programs, transportation agencies, adult education programs, senior centers, and community colleges represent a wide range of agencies that can capitalize on common goals and the sharing of expertise and resources.

One example of a midstream program that fostered change on a community and state level through the use of coalitions is On the Move! (Cassady, Jang, Tanjasiri, & Morrison, 1999). In this program, the California Department of Health Services funded nine sites to serve ethnically diverse adults, promoting physical activity through local coalitions that fit the cultural, social, economic, and geographic characteristics of each community. Another example of a successful midstream program is America Walks (www.americawalks.org), a coalition of 22 groups from around the United States dedicated to promoting walkable communities by linking grassroots participants to government, media, and institutional resources.

Social workers also affect mesosystems when they directly encourage the widening of programs and coalitions in the agencies where they work. Promoting good quality strength-building classes for older people in day programs, senior centers, and nursing homes can lead to a reduction in the incidence of falls (Jette et al., 1999) and an increase in functional capacity for older people (Fiatarone et al., 1994).

Changing agency policies regarding physical activity, networking with other agencies, overcoming agency ambivalence, and addressing barriers within their own agencies are midstream interventions that social workers can undertake.

The Commission on Aging (COA) office in Marin County, California, successfully expanded its own services, for example. The COA increased public awareness of the benefits of strength training for seniors, presented workshops on strength training at nursing homes and adult day health centers throughout the county, created a video to be used in nursing homes, and established four community strength-training classes open to all older adults (Youngquist, 1998). This project was accomplished through collaboration with the California Active Aging Project.

Downstream or Microsystem
Level Interventions

"Sometimes seniors feel that they can't do this, or that's for young people."

—A 77-year-old woman

Social workers are in an ideal position to support productive aging through the maintenance or increase of physical activity, exercise, and recreation on the individual level. They have expertise in supporting healthy behaviors, solving problems, and helping people make changes in their lives. They are also expert at making referrals to appropriate agencies and working closely with those agencies. Social workers are not physical activity experts, however, and they must work with physicians, physical therapists, exercise physiologists, and others who have the necessary knowl-

edge to make specific physical activity recommendations. The social work role at the individual level is to educate clients, assess their needs, help resolve issues of their health behaviors, and when appropriate, to refer them to suitable physical activity resources.

Continuity theory suggests strategies that may be helpful in maintaining or increasing physical activity in older people; for example, it is often helpful to review earlier exercise experiences to link present recommendations to preferences and past successes. Some elderly people without much physical activity experience must go all the way back to childhood to remember being physically active (Grossman, 1999). One older woman chose a water aerobics class as part of her physical activity regimen because of fondly remembered family visits to a lake as a child. An 85-year-old woman who had very negative physical activity associations, but who had enjoyed and valued intellectual pursuits all her life, chose to listen to books on tape while she exercised on a treadmill at home.

Behavioral approaches that may be helpful include setting concrete goals; teaching self-monitoring skills (such as the use of logs and diaries); and mobilizing social support through family, friends, and professionals (King et al., 1992; Stewart et al., 1997; Stewart et al., 2001). Choosing an activity that is fun and enjoyable also encourages participation (King, Taylor, Haskell, & Debusk, 1988; Lehr, 1992). Providing support and encouragement, setting achievable goals, breaking down complex target behaviors into more manageable components, developing concrete measures of progress, modeling, and connecting new behaviors to previous skills and successes can all increase physical activity efficacy (Stretcher, DeVellis, Becker, & Rosenstock, 1986).

Intervention strategies developed by Miller and Rollnick (1991), known as motivational interviewing and based on the transtheoretical model, can also be helpful. Social workers using a motivational interviewing approach first assess the client's readiness to change. Then they tailor their physical activity intervention or referral to the client's current "stage of change." A precontemplator, for example, will not start exercising immediately, but explaining the risks of a sedentary lifestyle may cause the precontemplator to start thinking about changing some behaviors. Motivational interviewing also concentrates on resolving ambivalences, listening reflectively, clarifying goals, enhancing choices, assisting with problem solving, partnering with the client, and preventing relapse (Rollnick & Miller, 1995).

Making appropriate referrals can also facilitate safe, sustainable physical activity choices. Because seniors generally name their physician as the preferred source of specific guidance for physical activity and exercise (Booth et al., 1997), encouraging clients to talk with their physician about physical activity can be very helpful. Damush and colleagues (1999) found that physicians are less likely to talk about physical activity with patients who are over age 75 or who are not already thinking about changing their physical activity behaviors (precontemplators). Physicians and health care workers may need to know that their older patients may

also respond to physical activity counseling if it is handled appropriately.

Social workers may follow up referrals for physical activity classes such as those found at senior centers, the YMCA/YWCA, community centers, and parks and recreation departments with a telephone call to see if there are any problems and, ideally, to resolve any that have arisen. Encouraging physical activity instructors to reach out to participants can also help. Personal attention from program staff was perceived as the most helpful aspect of a community-based physical activity program in one recent study (Gillis, Grossman, McLellan, King, & Stewart, 2002). Older people appreciate instructors who give personal encouragement, who leave time to answer questions, or who follow up with participants having difficulty with attendance.

The Community Healthy Activities Model Program for Seniors (CHAMPS) is a successful downstream individual level program (Stewart, 2001). The CHAMPS program was designed to increase the sustainable lifetime physical activity levels of seniors. It encourages participants to develop a personal physical activity regimen that takes into account their health, preferences, ability, and other factors. Participants can join existing exercise classes in the community or develop an exercise regimen that they can do on their own or with friends. CHAMPS has also been adapted and established in low-income and ethnic minority communities.

Conclusion

"Don't be a couch potato."

—An 83-year-old woman

How can it be that it has taken so long for science to prove that physical activity is good for older adults? Although the benefits of physical activity, exercise, and recreation are significant and interest in physical activity for seniors is growing, both community-dwelling and institutionalized elderly people need more physical activity opportunities, information, encouragement, and support.

For physical activity interventions to succeed, whether at the community or the individual level, they must occur over time and in a context that is meaningful to both the community and the individual. The social work practice of "starting where the client is" (or working with the client or community wherever their physical, mental, or political circumstances happen to be) provides a good strategy for encouraging older people to maintain or increase their physical activity levels. Any amount of individual physical activity or community interest can provide a base from which to build.

Although it is true that change takes time, it is also true that times are changing. As one 84-year-old woman put it: "There's been a change in the whole general attitude toward older people, not feeling that the poor dears should just stay home and rest." The baby boomers will rewrite the definition of what it means to grow old. Social workers have a major role to play in realizing the promise of a more active, productive future for our older population.

References

Agre, J. C., Pierce, L. E., Raab, D. M., McAdams, M., & Smith, E. L. (1988). Light resistance and stretching exercise in women: Effect upon strength. *Archives of Physical Rehabilitation, 69,* 273–276.

Atchley, R. C. (1989). A continuity theory of normal aging. *Gerontologist, 29,* 183–190.

Atchley, R. C. (1993). Continuity theory and the evolution of activity in later life. In J. R. Kelley (Ed.), *Activity and aging: Staying involved in later life* (pp. 5–16). Newbury Park, CA: Sage Publications.

Babyak, M., Blumenthal, J. A., Herman, S., Khatri, P., Doraiswamy, M., Moore, K., Craighead, W. E., Baldewicz, T. T., & Krishnan, K. R. (2000). Exercise treatment for major depression: Maintenance of therapeutic benefit at 10 months. *Psychosomatic Medicine, 62,* 633–638.

Bandura, A. (1977a). Self-efficacy: Toward a unifying theory of behavioral change. *Psychological Review, 84,* 191–215.

Bandura, A. (1977b). *Social learning theory.* Englewood Cliffs, NJ: Prentice Hall.

Bandura, A. (1986). *Social foundation of thought and action.* Englewood Cliffs, NJ: Prentice Hall.

Blumenthal, J. A., Babyak, M., Moore, K. A., Craighead, W. E., Herman, S., Khatri, P., Waugh, R., Napolitano, M. A., Doraiswamy, P. M., & Krishnan, K. R. (1999). Effects of exercise training on older adults with major depression. *Archives of Internal Medicine, 159,* 2349–2356.

Booth, R. L., Bauman, A., Owen, N., & Gore, C. J. (1997). Physical activity preferences, preferred sources of assistance, and perceived barriers to increased activity among physically inactive Australians. *Preventive Medicine, 26,* 131–137.

Bortz, W. M. (1996). *Dare to be 100.* New York: Fireside.

Calfas, K. J., Long, B. J., Sallis, J. F., Wooten, W. J., Pratt, M., & Patrick, W. (1996). A controlled trial of physician counseling to promote the adoption of physical activity. *Preventive Medicine, 25,* 225–233.

Cassady, D., Jang, V. L., Tanjasiri, S. P., & Morrison, C. M. (1999). California gets "On the Move!" *Journal of Health Education, 30*(Suppl. 2), 6–12.

Centers for Disease Control and Prevention. (2001). Physical activity trends, 1990–1998. *Morbidity and Mortality Weekly Report, 50,* 166–169.

Chodzko-Zajko, W. J. (Ed.). (2001). National blueprint: Increasing physical activity among adults 50 and over. *Journal of Aging and Physical Activity* [Special issue], *9,* 13–24.

Clark, D. O. (1995). Racial and educational differences in physical activity among older adults. *Gerontologist, 35,* 472–480.

Clark, D. O. (1996). Age, socioeconomic status, and exercise self-efficacy. *Gerontologist, 36,* 157–164.

Cousins, S. O. (2000). "My heart couldn't take it": Older women's beliefs about exercise benefits and risks. *Journal of Gerontology: Psychology, 55B,* P283–P294.

Damush, T. M., Stewart, A. L., Mills, K. M., King, A. C., & Ritter, P. L. (1999). *Journal of Gerontology: Medical Sciences, 54A,* M423–M427.

Dishman, R. K. (1994). Motivating older adults to exercise. *Southern Medical Journal, 87,* S70–S82.

Dishman, R. K., Sallis, J. F., & Orenstein, D. R. (1985). The determinants of physical activity and exercise. *Public Health Reports, 100,* 158–171.

Ebrahim, S., Thompson, P. W., Baskaran, V., & Evans, K. (1997). Randomized placebo-controlled trial of brisk walking in the prevention of postmenopausal osteoporosis. *Age and Aging, 26,* 253–260.

Evans, W. (1995). Effects of exercise on body composition and functional capacity of the elderly. *Journal of Gerontology, 50A,* 147–150.

Ferrell, B. A. (1991). Pain management in elderly people. *Journal of the American Geriatric Society, 39,* 64–73.

Ferrell, B. A. (1995). Pain evaluation and management in the nursing home. *Annals of Internal Medicine, 123,* 681–687.

Ferrell, B. A., Josephson, K. R., Pollan, A. M., Loy, S., & Ferrell, B. R. (1997). A randomized trial of walking versus physical methods for chronic pain management. *Aging Clinical and Experimental Research, 9,* 99–105.

Ferrini, R., Edelstein, S., & Barrett-Connor, E. (1994). The association between health beliefs and health behavior change in older adults. *Preventive Medicine, 23,* 1–5.

Fiatarone, M. A., & Evans, W. J. (1993). The etiology and reversibility of muscle dysfunction in the aged [Special issue]. *Journal of Gerontology, 48,* 63–77.

Fiatarone, M. A., O'Neill, E. F., Ryan, N. D., Clements, K. M., Solaris, G. R., Nelson, M. E., Roberts, S. B., Kehayias, J. J., Lipsitz, L. A., & Evans, W. J. (1994). Exercise training and nutritional supplementation for physical frailty in very elderly people. *New England Journal of Medicine, 330,* 1769–1775.

Fletcher, G. F., Blair, S. N., Blumenthal, J., Caspersen, C., Chaitman, B., Epstein, S., Falls, H., Sivarajan-Froelicher, E. S., Froelicher, V. F., & Pina, I. L. (1992). Statement on exercise: Benefits and recommendations for physical activity programs for all Americans. *Circulation, 86,* 2726–2730.

Friede, A., O'Carroll, P. W., & Nicola, R. M. (Eds.). (1997). *CDC prevention guidelines: A guide for action.* Baltimore: Williams & Wilkins.

Fry, P. W. (1992). Major social theories of aging and their implications for counseling concepts and practice: A critical review. *Counseling Psychologist, 29,* 246–329.

Gillis, D. E., Grossman, M. D., McLellan, B. Y., King, A. C., & Stewart, A. L. (2002). Participants' evaluations of program components of a physical activity promotion program for seniors (CHAMPS). *Journal of Physical Activity and Aging, 10,* 336–353.

Graham, A. C., Cannuscio, C. C., & Fazier, A. L. (1997). Physical activity and reduced risk of colon cancer: Implications for prevention. *Cancer Causes and Control, 8,* 649–667.

Grossman, M. D. (1999). *Increasing physical activity in previously underactive seniors: Viewing change from a 75+ perspective.* Unpublished doctoral dissertation, Bryn Mawr College, Bryn Mawr, PA.

Grossman, M. D., McLellan, B., Gillis, D., & Stewart, A. L. (2000). Physical activity beliefs and preferences in older Hispanics [Abstract]. *Annals of Behavioral Medicine, 21,* S092.

Grossman, M. D., Pruitt, L., Gillis, D., McLellan, B., Castrillo, M., Stewart, A. L., & Harris, M. (2001). Physical activity perceptions, preferences and barriers in older African Americans [Abstract]. *Annals of Behavioral Medicine, 23,* S109.

Hakim, A. A., Petrovitch, H., Burchfiel, C. M., Ross, W., Rodriguez, B. L., White, L. R., Yano, K., Curb, J. D., & Abbott, R. D. (1998). Effects of walking on mortality among nonsmoking retired men. *New England Journal of Medicine, 338,* 94–99.

Hovell, M. F., Sallis, J. F., Hofstetter, C. R., Spry, V. M., Faucher, P., & Caspersen, C. J. (1989). Identifying correlates of walking for exercise: An epidemiological prerequisite for physical activity promotion. *Preventive Medicine, 18,* 856–866.

Jette, A. M., Lachman, M., Giorgetti, M. M., Assman, S. F., Harris, B. A., Lenenson, C., Wernick, M., & Krebs, D. (1999). Exercise—It's never too late: The Strong-for-Life program. *American Journal of Public Health, 89,* 66–72

King, A. C., Blair, S. N., Bild, D. E., Dishman, R. K., Dubbert, P. M., Marcus, B. H., Oldridge, N. B., Paffenbarger, R. S., Powell, K. E., & Yeager, K. K. (1992). Determinants of physical activity and interventions in adults. *Medicine and Science in Sports and Exercise, 24,* 221–236.

King, A. C., Taylor, C. B., Haskell, W. L., & Debusk, R. F. (1988). Strategies for increasing early adherence to and long-term maintenance of home-based exercise training in healthy middle-aged men and women. *American Journal of Cardiology, 61,* 628–632.

Kirwan, J., Kohrt, J., Wojta, K., & Holloszy, J. (1993). Endurance exercise training reduces glucose-stimulated insulin levels in 60- to 70-year-old men and women. *Journal of Gerontology: Medical Sciences, 48,* M84–M90.

Kriska, A. M., Bayles, C., Cauley, J. A., Laporte, R. E., Sandler, R. B., & Pambianco, R. G. (1986). A randomized exercise trial in older women: Increased activity over two years and the factors associated with compliance. *Medicine and Science in Sports and Exercise, 18,* 557–562.

Kushi, L. H., Fee, R. M., Folsom, A. R., Mink, P. J., Anderson, K. E., Sellers, T. A. (1997). Physical activity and mortality in postmenopausal women. *JAMA, 227,* 1287–1292.

Lachman, M. E., Howland, J., Tennstedt, S., Jette, A., Assmann, S., & Peterson, E. W. (1998). Fear of falling and activity restriction: The survey of activities and fear of falling in the elderly. *Journal of Gerontology: Psychology, 53,* P43–P50.

Lauren, C., Verreault, R., Lindsay, J., Mac-Pherson, K., & Rockwood, K. (2001). Physical activity and risk of cognitive impairment and dementia in elderly persons. *Archives of Neurology, 58,* 498–504.

Lawrence, R. H., Tennstedt, S. L., Kasten, L. E., Shih, J., Howland, J., & Jette, A. M. (1998). Intensity and correlates of fear of falling and hurting oneself in the next year. *Journal of Aging and Health, 10,* 267–286.

Lee, C. (1993). Factors related to the adoption of exercise among older women. *Journal of Behavioral Medicine, 16,* 323–334.

Lehr, U. M. (1992). Physical activity in old age: Motivation and barriers. In S. Harris, R. Harris, & W. S. Harris (Eds.), *Physical activity, aging, and sports* (Vol. 2, Practice, program, and policy, pp. 44–50). Albany, NY: Center for the Study of Aging.

Manson, J. E., Hu, F. B., Rich-Edwards, J. W., Colditz, G. A., Stampfer, M. J., Willett, C. C., Speizer, F. E., & Hennekens, C. H. (1999). A prospective study of walking as compared with vigorous exercise in the prevention of coronary heart disease in women. *New England Journal of Medicine, 341,* 650–658.

Marcus, B. H., & Owen, N. (1992). Motivational readiness, self-efficacy, and decision-making for exercise. *Journal of Applied Social Psychology, 22,* 3–16.

Marcus, B. H., & Simkin, L. R. (1994). The transtheoretical model: Applications to exercise behavior. *Medicine and Science in Sports and Exercise, 26,* 1400–1404.

Martinsen, E. W., & Stephens, T. (1994). Exercise and mental health in clinical and free-living populations. In R. K. Dishman (Ed.), *Advances in exercise adherence* (pp. 55–72). Champaign, IL: Human Kinetics.

Mazzeo, R. S., Cavanagh, P., Evans, W. J., Fiatarone, M., Hagberg, D., McAuley, E., & Startzell, J. (1998). ACSM position stand on exercise and physical activity for older adults. *Medicine and Science in Sports and Exercise, 30,* 992–1008.

McAuley, E. (1993). Self-efficacy and the maintenance of exercise participation in older adults. *Journal of Behavioral Medicine, 16,* 103–113.

McAuley, E., & Rudolph, D. (1995). Physical activity, aging, and psychological well-being. *Journal of Aging and Physical Activity, 3,* 67–96.

McKinlay, J. B. (1995). Population-based health promotion model. In E. Heikkinen, J. Kursinen, & I. Ruoppila (Eds.), *Preparation for aging.* London: Plenum Press.

Miller, W. R., & Rollnick, S. (1991). *Motivational interviewing: Preparing people to change addictive behavior.* New York: Guilford Press.

National Academy on an Aging Society. (2000, July). Depression: A treatable disease. In *Challenges for the 21st century: Chronic and disability conditions.* Available from www.agingsociety.org/agingsociety/pdf/depression/pdf

Paffenbarger, R. S., & Hyde, R. T. (1988). Exercise adherence, coronary heart disease, and longevity. In R. K. Dishman (Ed.), *Exercise adherence: Its impact on public health* (pp. 41–73). Champaign, IL: Human Kinetics.

Prior, J. C., Barr, S. I., Chow, R., Faulkner, R. A. (1996). Physical activity as therapy for osteoporosis. *Canadian Medical Association Journal, 155,* 940–944.

Prochaska, H. O., Velicer, W. F., Rossi, J. S., Goldstein, M. G., Marcus, B. H., Rokowski, W., Fiore, C., Harlow, L. L., Redding, C. A., Rosenbloom, D., & Rossi, S. R. (1994). Stages of change and decisional balance for 12 problem behaviors. *Health Psychology, 13*, 39–46.

Rejeski, W. J., & Brawley, L. R. (2000). *Physical activity in older adults* (White paper prepared for the Robert Wood Johnson Foundation).

Rollnick, S., & Miller, W. R. (1995). What is motivational interviewing? *Behavioral and Cognitive Psychotherapy, 23*, 325–334.

Sallis, J. F., Haskell, W. L., Fortmann, S. P., Vranizan, K. M., Taylor, C. B., & Solomon, D. S. (1986). Predictors of adoption and maintenance of physical activity in a community sample. *Preventive Medicine, 15*, 331–341.

Sallis, J. F., Hovell, M. F., Hofstetter, C. R., & Elder, J. P. (1990). Distance between homes and exercise facilities related to frequency of exercise among San Diego residents. *Public Health Reports, 105*, 179–185.

Schoenborn, C. A. (1986). Health habits of U.S. adults: The "Alameda 7" revisited. *Public Health Reports, 101*, 571–580.

Seals, D., Hagberg, J., Hurley, B., Ehsani, A., & Holloszy, J. (1984). Effects of endurance training on glucose tolerance and plasma lipid levels in older men and women. *JAMA, 252*, 645–679.

Sharpe, P. A., Jackson, K. L., White, C., Vaca, V. L., Hickey, T., Gu, J., & Otterness, C. (1997). Effects of a one year physical activity intervention for older adults at congregate nutrition sites. *Gerontologist, 37*, 208–215.

Shephard, R. J. (1990). The scientific basis of exercise prescribing for the very old. *Journal of the American Geriatrics Society, 38*, 62–70.

Shephard, R. J. (1994). Determinants of exercise in people aged 65 years and older. In R. K. Dishman (Ed.), *Advances in exercise adherence* (pp. 343–360). Champaign, IL: Human Kinetics.

Smith, C., & Storandt, M. (1997). Physical activity participation in older adults: A comparison of competitors, noncompetitors, and nonexercisers. *Journal of Aging and Physical Activity, 5*, 98–110.

Spirduso, W. W. (1995). *Physical dimensions of aging.* Champaign, IL: Human Kinetics.

Steffen-Batey, L., Nichaman, M. Z., Goff, D. C., Frankowski, R. F., Hanis, C. L., Ramsey, D. J., & Labarth, D. R. (2000). Change in level of physical activity and risk of all-cause mortality or reinfarction. *Circulation, 102*, 2204–2209.

Stephens, T., Jacobs, D. R., & White, C. C. (1985). A descriptive epidemiology of leisure-time physical activity. *Public Health Reports, 100*, 147–58.

Stewart, A. L. (2001). Community-based physical activity programs for adults aged 50 and older. *Journal of Physical Activity and Aging, 9*, S71–S91 .

Stewart, A. L., King, A. C., & Haskell, W. L. (1993). Endurance exercise and health-related quality of life in 50–65 year old adults. *Gerontologist, 33*, 782–789.

Stewart, A. L., Mills, K. M., Sepsis, P. G., King, A. C., McLellan, B. Y., Roitz, K., & Ritter, P. L. (1997). Evaluation of CHAMPS, a physical activity promotion program for older adults. *Annals of Behavioral Medicine, 19*, 353–361.

Stewart, A. L., Verboncoeur, C. J., McLellan, B. Y., Gillis, D. E., Rush, S., Mills, K., King, A. C., Ritter, P., Brown, B. W., & Bortz, W. M. (2001). Physical activity outcomes of CHAMPS II: A physical activity promotion program. *Journal of Gerontology: Medical Sciences, 56A*, M465–M470.

Stretcher, V. J., DeVellis, B. M., Becker, M. H., & Rosenstock, I. M. (1986) The role of self-efficacy in achieving health behavior change. *Health Education Quarterly, Spring, 13*, 73–92.

Tinetti, M. E., Ducette, J., Claus, E., & Marttoli, R. M. (1995). Risk factors for serious injury during falls by older persons in the community. *Journal of the American Geriatric Society, 43,* 1214–1221.

Tkachuk, G. A., & Martin, G. L. (1999). Exercise therapy for patients with psychiatric disorders. *Professional Psychology: Research and Practice, 33,* 275–282.

U.S. Department of Health and Human Services. (1996). *Physical activity and health: A report of the Surgeon General.* Atlanta, GA: U.S. Department of Health and Human Services, Centers for Disease Control and Prevention, National Center for Chronic Disease Prevention and Health Promotion.

Wannamethee, S. G., Sharper, A. G., & Walker, M. (2000). Physical activity and mortality in older men with diagnosed coronary heart disease. *Circulation, 102,* 1358–1363.

Wolinsky, F. D., Stump, T. E., & Clark, D. O. (1995). Antecedents and consequences of physical activity and exercise among older adults. *Gerontologist, 35,* 451–462.

Youngquist, R. (Ed.). (1998). *Marin County Task Force on strength training for seniors.* (Available from Marin County Division on Aging, 10 North Pedro Road, San Rafael, CA 94903)

12

Productive Aging: Personal and Professional Reference Points

Carter Catlett Williams and T. Franklin Williams

The connotation of the term "productive," as generally used in the United States today, implies income-producing, and the term "productive aging" suggests a concern with what older people accomplish in terms of potentially salable goods or in terms of volunteer hours worked in the family and the community as measured by converting their efforts to money values. The corollary implication is that whatever elderly people are doing that is not economically productive is of less value and importance. We believe, however, that "productivity" must encompass many describable, but not necessarily measurable, aspects of meaningful life, including relationships, creativity, expression of lifelong values in different forms, and explorations of both the interior and exterior worlds. Most important, our own personal and professional experiences show us that this encompassing productivity potential is clearly present in elderly people with all degrees of functional limitations, as it is in all those who are "healthy."

The proclivity toward weighing the value of a life in terms of material productivity is an ugly specter lurking just below the surface of society. From Nazi Germany, where many old people considered useless in narrow productivity terms were eliminated, to Thomas More's *Utopia*, this specter raises its ugly head. More, according to Fortunati (1998), "assigns an important role and function to old people, but when he confronts the problem of self-insufficient decrepitude, the common good prevails over that of the individual. Thus old people either stoically decide to commit suicide, or will be convinced to do so by the priests" (p. 80). Such extreme views are no longer expressed overtly, but many negative comments—slurs about older people—are all too common today. Yet, the value of a human life cannot be weighed and measured by the scales of material productivity.

There is an additional overall question to be addressed. Is any significant gain or possible injury likely to result from separating out the last years of life to put them under the microscope? Why are these years set apart from the rest of life? Are we different beings once we cross the 75-, 80-, 85-, or 90-year marks? Are we dismissed with a failing grade if we do not meet somebody else's standards of "productivity" or "success"? We think the answers to these questions are cultural and systemic. We have come of age in a culture that, at best, holds old age at arm's length and, at worst, denigrates it and seeks to avoid it and any sign of it at all costs.

But suppose we had the blessing of growing up in a society that celebrated the wholeness of life, both vertically and horizontally. Vertical growth begins in infancy, childhood, and adolescence; continues through the young adult and middle years; and culminates as part of old age. Horizontally, growth occurs in all ages, too, from the probing of toddlers to explore all their surroundings, to the excitement of teenagers and young adults in wrestling with new ideas and mastering new skills, through the assumption of responsibility and the desire for significance of work in the middle years, to the freedom to share learning and experience and to explore new territory in old age. Elderhood offers time to make sense of one's life. Each stage of life is intermeshed with the others; no one stage stands alone. And there is always a new frontier to experience for those who are open to the possibilities.

Our own career experiences have been in working with old people who have chronic limitations, from whom we have learned much about full and purposeful living. We have associations with many other elderly people as well—family; friends; those in public,

academic, and religious work—who present a full spectrum of health, capabilities, and contributions. We have learned much from these associations, and continue to learn; our own aging enhances that learning and deepens understanding. Most important, we have learned and continue to learn from each other.

T. Franklin Williams

As I begin my own reflections, I realize that I see my life, from early years on, as a series of opportunities—opportunities that have come my way thanks to family, friends, and living and academic settings. I have not "earned" these opportunities, but they have given me the chances to have experiences of meaning to me and to others, in particular, the meanings and challenges of aging.

Although I did not think at the time of what my childhood and young adult years would be teaching me about aging, I am sure that my own education in this field began in my close relationship with my grandparents. From age 12, I lived with my mother and her parents (after the early death of my father from a heart attack—he was a heavy smoker) in a small North Carolina town with other close relatives nearby. One enjoyable treat was making the rounds of two or three of the other homes on Sunday afternoons to sample their Sunday desserts. The family included individuals of all ages, with a full range of health and limitations.

In my college years at the University of North Carolina, I was caught up in the excitement of science, particularly chemistry, and acquired a lifelong commitment to working to bring the findings of science to the benefit of people. At the same time, I found myself concerned with and involved in the social and political issues of the times. My summer jobs and life had a great influence on me, as I traveled with a distinguished history professor who was preparing a biography of Theodore Roosevelt. I was his typist, copying material that he wanted from collections in New York and New England. His personal conceptions and convictions ran counter to many of the everyday world and forced me to examine my own and in some ways to modify them—a good, lasting lesson in keeping an open mind.

After a brief year in graduate school in organic chemistry at Columbia University and then almost three years on active duty on a naval cruiser in the battles in the western Pacific, I chose to take advantage of the G.I. Bill and the opportunity to enter Harvard Medical School. I saw the medical profession as the way that I might best bring my commitment and capabilities in science to bear on the health problems of people. It was in those years that Carter and I met and began building our lives together—the greatest opportunity of my life! She, with her roots in social service and knowledge in the field, quickly pointed out to me that I needed to give more attention to the social aspects and issues in medical care. She introduced me to the writings of Dr. Richard Cabot and Ida Cannon, the founders of medical social service right there in Boston, and she was glad that I also learned more about another Bostonian, Dr. Francis Weld Peabody, whose famous

statement, "The secret of the care of the patient is in caring for the patient," has become recognized worldwide as the epitome of medical care (Peabody, 1939; T. F. Williams, 1950).

My pathway into aging and special attention to the care of older people led through 18 years of training, teaching, patient care, and research in internal medicine with special attention to the challenges of diabetes. Again, not only did my background and interest in chemistry make diabetes a natural choice as a field of study, but also what I had learned and acquired in terms of understanding the social problems of patients with chronic conditions such as diabetes led me to work with others to develop a more comprehensive, multidisciplinary approach to helping patients manage their diabetes and overall lives more effectively. We had the good fortune to obtain one of the first federally funded grants for health services research to carry out this undertaking. In those years, I was also deeply involved in the Civil Rights Movement locally, as well as being a member of the Southern Regional Council.

It was from this background that I was invited, in 1968, to move to Rochester, New York, to develop one of the first medical school programs for the study and care of patients with chronic illnesses of all types. Its base was at Monroe Community Hospital, a setting devoted to the care of people with chronic disabilities of all ages. It was here that I began to recognize the widespread and special needs and challenges of older people, began to learn about what was known and what was not known about aging and geriatric medicine, and began to build educational and research programs in this field. With the help of many others, we developed one of the first clinics for the comprehensive, multidisciplinary evaluation and care of older persons with multiple chronic conditions. A team of physician, nurse, social worker, and rehabilitation specialist shared in the thorough evaluation of the patient's condition and, together with the patient and family, developed a comprehensive medical and social care plan. Again with a research design, we documented that this approach could improve overall function and quality of life, as well as reduce the need for acute care such as hospitalizations. We also had the opportunity to train a number of physicians who have moved on to lead geriatric programs around the United States.

In 1983, I was invited to become the second Director of the National Institute on Aging at the National Institutes of Health, and we moved to Bethesda, Maryland, for eight years. It was an exciting time to be involved in aging research. Our institute, as distinct from other institutes there, had from the beginning a section on social and behavioral aging, as well as sections on the biological, clinical, and dementing aspects of aging. I had opportunities to call attention to the essential partnerships of research and care (T. F. Williams, 1988). It was also a time for visiting and becoming long-term friends with others working in all of these areas of aging, both in the United States and around the world.

Back in Rochester since 1991—although technically retired—I have had the opportunity to continue teaching geriatric medicine, mentoring and working with others in the care of patients, offering advice about aging research, and helping to select promising candidates who merit special support for academic careers. I have also been able to work with the Veterans Administration, the Programs for All-Inclusive Care of Elderly (PACE) models, our Community Consortium for Long-Term Care, and other programs aimed at reaching more effectively those who need more comprehensive, continuing help in long-term care. This "stage" of my life seems to be the time for me to continue to learn and to share my experiences with others and to help them learn about aging in all aspects. There is more than enough to keep me busy and interested for some time to come.

Throughout these years of rich experience, I have learned much about the tremendous varieties of aging experiences—from those of very healthy aging post-100 years to those of people with infirmities that may have beset them early in life, but have not prevented them from living in various degrees of satisfaction and productivity into later years. I know how much more we need to learn about the life courses of aging itself and of the social and medical challenges and opportunities to be faced. I have learned that we must think truly comprehensively whenever we want to consider what any individual older person may desire and what the potentials are for helping that person achieve what means the most to her or him: That will be the definition of productivity for that person.

Carter Catlett Williams

In my experience of aging, the personal and professional are very much interwoven. I, like Frank, grew up in a three-generation household in the rural and small-town South of the Great Depression years. Two of the elderly people in my household had severe functional limitations—one thought to be from heart disease, the other from Parkinsonism. I was acquainted on an intimate and daily basis with the caregiving responsibilities of my mother, aunt, and the paid companion for my great aunt.

After I earned my master's degree from the Simmons College School of Social Work in 1949, I held positions in the social work departments of teaching hospitals. After five years, I interrupted formal employment and gave my time over to child rearing, participation in the Civil Rights Movement in North Carolina, and advocacy in other social justice arenas. In addition, I gave support to Frank, who carried a very heavy workload, both professional and volunteer.

At 51, I re-entered the field of social work by answering an advertisement in the newspaper, responding chiefly because the ad described a part-time position. So it was quite by chance that in 1974 I landed in the field of aging—as social worker for an innovative day program initiated by the Jewish Home of Rochester, New York, for elderly people who were still living in their own homes, but whose ability to do so was threatened by social isolation and loss of function. I also became consultant for several proprietary nursing homes and, a few years later, joined the staff of the downtown Lutheran Church of the Reformation.

My training in medical social work, my experience in three teaching hospitals, and my volunteer advocacy work—even my year of work in a rural county welfare department before I began my professional education—all enriched my approach to elderly people, both those in their homes and those in institutions. At first glance, this patchwork of jobs looked like a helter-skelter situation, but it proved, instead, to have exposed me to a rich slice of life with elderly people, ranging over the whole spectrum of health and economic challenges, as well as varieties of living settings.

Some of the things revealed by this slice of life grieved me deeply. I had the benefit of knowing people initially in their own homes and, through the varied community services then available in Rochester, could often help them remain at home—pushing the envelope very far sometimes. However, there were instances in which admission to a nursing home became unavoidable. Placed in sterile, hospital-like physical surroundings with no control over their daily lives, surrounded by people who did not know them, many elderly people who were my clients declined dramatically. The physical restraint, so freely applied in those days, became for me the concrete symbol of this decline. Forty percent of elderly people living in U.S. nursing homes were at that time tied down some or all of their days and nights (Evans & Strumpf, 1990).

By 1983, when we moved to Washington, DC, for a period of eight years,

I despaired of any change in this situation. Not only were the people in restraints suffering, but also the nursing staff who had to apply the restraints were becoming numb. Furthermore, in my mind, there was the question of the ethics of social workers helping people to "adjust to the nursing home," as so many referrals requested, when these elderly people lived in circumstances that denied them choice and decision making, dignity, and self-respect. This concern, coupled with what I was soon to learn abroad, combined to make me conclude that systems change was needed, and that I had to work for such change.

Happily, the move to Washington and Frank's work and encouragement gave me splendid opportunities to learn from other cultures. A visit with him to Sweden in 1987 opened my eyes to restraint-free care and gave me hope about changing the experience of long-term care in the United States. In Gothenburg, I saw a nursing home that—even though caring for elderly people at the same functional level as those in our nursing homes—never tied anyone down. The administrator/director of nursing of Graberg Nursing Home, Ulla Turemark, explained that this was achieved through attention to "the many details of daily life," over which residents of this home exercised a great deal of control. I came home knowing that I had to bear witness to what I had seen (C. C. Williams, 1989).

One of Frank's Swedish colleagues, Dr. Alvar Svanborg, had guided me to the restraint-free nursing home. Back in the United States, another of Frank's colleagues, Doris Schwartz, eminent retired faculty member of the Cornell School of Nursing, steered me to Drs. Lois Evans and Neville Strumpf, nurses on the faculty of the University of Pennsylvania School of Nursing, who were engaged in research on the effects of physical restraint. The pathway for my work has been highly interdisciplinary.

At this point, the personal and the professional intersected. My life and professional experiences combined to give me a confidence and surety that I had never had before. On the eve of official elderhood, age 64, I began to speak out at every opportunity about the physical, psychological, and spiritual destructiveness of physical restraint and the attainability of restraint-free care. With the words of one of my clients ringing in my ears—"It's a terrible thing to lose your freedom!"—and with Frank's support in many practical as well as intangible ways, I spoke in at least half of the 50 states over the next seven years, joining a rising chorus of voices on this subject. We were immensely aided by the passage of the Nursing Home Reform Law of 1987 (P.L. 100-203).

In the past five years, the work to attain restraint-free care has grown and has undergone a transformation to a far larger vision—that of changing the culture of long-term care and, indeed, the culture of aging itself. This vision is now embodied in the work of the Pioneer Network of which I am honored to be the Convener. The Network, which can be found at www.pioneer network.net, aims for deep systems change in our society.

In this work, I have found my voice. When a leader in the field of geriatrics said to me with puzzlement in his voice, "I visited that same nursing home in Sweden, but I didn't see the things you saw," I knew that my social work and personal eyes had a contribution to make. The derision and skepticism that met my proposals, as well as similar proposals of other speakers in many audiences, were simply to be expected when familiar care habits were challenged.

While I was still engaged in a busy professional schedule, my own mother developed ever more pressing care needs. I began to have experiences like those of my clients and their families, and I learned firsthand that mere knowledge is no substitute for living those experiences. In making preparations to help my mother carry out her decision to enter a nursing home, I soon found my own neglected feelings of sorrow and loss pushing to the surface so insistently that I had to write about them in an effort to understand them (C. C. Williams, 1992).

Writing has increasingly become a path to understanding my own aging (Williams, 1993, 1994, 1995). But it has gone far beyond that. Using a treasury of some 400 previously unread letters from my father to his parents, as well as some of theirs to him, I am, for the first time, claiming the family life of my first two years. In my eighth decade, I am not only gaining a completely new perspective, but also getting to know the father of whom I had no conscious memory (C. C. Williams, 2001).

So it is that, in my own later life, I am experiencing a re-orientation and a growth far beyond reasonable expectation. If, at age 78, I do not explore, when will I? For the first time, I am giving priority to these personal explorations, reducing professional work to a

few hours a week, and gratefully accepting Frank's help with some of the household tasks that formerly have been chiefly mine. Writing requires uninterrupted time and space, and there was neither time, nor inclination, to set aside and protect undistracted periods earlier in life. Family, community, and professional interests kept me in a constant balancing act. Nor had I lived long enough to want to look back, not knowing that you have to look back in order to look forward with equanimity. But those simply were not the seasons of my life when such activity called me. Now is the season, and the call is not to be denied.

I see two elements as fundamental to social work practice with elderly people: first, a recognition of the capacity for growth and well-being in all elderly people, regardless of their limitations, and second, an approach that builds on their strengths. All elderly people, no matter where they are on the health scale—and all are vulnerable to back-and-forth shifting on that scale—have a capacity for growth, development, and the continued search for meaning. We all have the need and right to be known for who we are, without the mask of illness robbing us of our uniqueness. The social worker is the person particularly equipped to capture our unique stories and, when need be, as in an institutional setting, to interpret them to others.

The "new aged," described by Kaye (L. W. Kaye, personal communication, March 16, 2001) as "those older adults who are more mobile, active, healthy, economically secure, educated, and politically sophisticated than any previous generation of older persons," may nevertheless be poorly equipped to traverse the territory of old age. The cultural messages of our society value youth, energy, and activity, and they do not communicate to us at any age the special opportunities that the later years bring. It is through growth in these years that elderly people can begin to make sense of their lives and find meaning as they advance farther into elderhood.

Frank and I can offer firsthand testimony to the important role that a social worker has played in our development. Over the last five years, beginning at ages 75 and 73, respectively, we have sought her help in understanding and dealing with a range of questions: concerns for our children and our relationships with them in this stage of our lives, our own growing into different life and professional roles, our future living plans, and most critically, my search for my father in which Frank has accompanied me all the way.

Conclusion

We are convinced that it is through strengths-based practice that social workers can best help elderly people. Such practice is in clear contrast to the problem-oriented approach of our medical colleagues. Helping elderly people to identify strengths that they have built over the years, rather than focusing foremost on the problems and pathologies that beset them, equips them to negotiate the new terrain of old age and not feel strangers to themselves. As the "new aged" face the inevitable breakdowns in health, they will be well served by the social worker who has known them before the breakdowns occur. If dementia develops over the course of time, if there is a diagnosis of cancer, or if arthritis increasingly limits function, the social worker will be in a good position to help the elderly people to hold on to those things that give meaning to their lives, or to construct new pathways to meaning. This requires imagination, creativity, the resource of a relationship established over time, and a strengths-based approach.

References

Evans, L. K., & Strumpf, N. E. (1990). Myths about elder restraint. *Image: The Journal of Nursing Scholarship, 22*(2), 124–128.

Fortunati, V. (1998). Aging and Utopia through the centuries. *Aging Clinical and Experimental Research, 10*, 77–82.

More, T. (1975). *Utopia*. New York: W. W. Norton. (Original work published 1516)

Nursing Home Reform Law of 1987, Subtitle C, Omnibus Budget Reconciliation Act of 1987 (P.L. 100–203).

Peabody, F. W. (1939). Doctor and patient. In *Papers on the relationship of the physician to men and institutions* (pp. 56–57). New York: Macmillan.

Williams, C. C. (1989). The experience of long-term care in the future. *Journal of Gerontological Social Work, 14*, 3–18.

Williams, C. C. (1992). Reclamation. *Aging and the Human Spirit, 2*(2), 2–3

Williams, C. C. (1993). Salsify and sacrament: Discovering gifts of the aging spirit. *Aging and the Human Spirit, 3*(1), 10–11.

Williams, C. C. (1994). Child of Tidewater: Belonging and exile. *Aging and the Human Spirit, 4*(1), 6–7, 10–11.

Williams, C. C. (1995). Family portrait: The baby and the dream. *Aging and the Human Spirit, 5*(2), 6–7, 11.

Williams, C. C. (2001). Voyage in time. In R. Atchley & S. McFadden (Eds.), *Aging and the meaning of time* (pp. 113–129). New York: Springer.

Williams, T. F. (1950). Cabot, Peabody and the care of the patient. *Bulletin of the History of Medicine, 24*, 462–481.

Williams, T. F. (1988). Research and care: Essential partners in aging. *Gerontologist, 28*, 579–585.

Appendix A

Resources for Practitioners to Facilitate Productive Aging

Jennifer Campbell and Fontaine H. Fulghum

The list of resources in this appendix provides sources of assistance and inspiration to social workers who are planning programs and activities to facilitate productive aging. Although the available resources are too numerous to catalogue fully here, this listing can be a starting point for gathering ideas and finding further information on the subjects covered in this book. The list includes organizations, Web sites, and periodicals.

Contact information for each resource is listed, including Web site address and telephone number and postal address, as well as a brief description of each resource. The resources are organized alphabetically. Because many resources apply to more than one of the areas covered in the book, a summarizing table of all resources listed is included at the end of the section to provide an overall view of the resources and their associated subject areas.

The department of the federal government charged with establishing a network of aging services across the United States is the Administration on Aging (AoA), which in turn calls on each state to designate a statewide network of community agencies. The local Area Agency on Aging, which is listed in the blue pages of every telephone book, is thus a good place to begin to explore resources and opportunities that support productive aging. Practitioners can also contact the AoA for a referral to their local Area Agency on Aging.

The authors would like to thank the following for their contributions to this appendix: E. Michael Brady, Sandra S. Butler, Roberta Greene and Melonie D. Grossman.

Administration on Aging (AoA)

Telephone:	(202) 619-7501
	(800) 677-1116 (Eldercare locator)
Address:	330 Independence Avenue, SW
	Washington, DC 20201
Web site:	www.aoa.dhhs.gov
Description:	The AoA is responsible for programs funded under the Older Americans Act, which forms the core of the aging network. This aging network includes the AoA's 10 regional offices, 57 offices on aging at the state and territorial level, 655 Area Agencies on Aging, and 230 Native American Title IV Aging programs. The Web site includes "Aging Program Resources" for professionals seeking information on a variety of programming needs, as well as an Eldercare locator service linking callers to resources in the area where the older consumer lives. In addition, the site has demographic and family caregiving information, including information on grandparenting issues.

Adult Education Quarterly (periodical)

Telephone:	(800) 818-7243 or (805) 499-9774
Contact:	SAGE Publications, Inc.
	2455 Teller Road
	Thousand Oaks, CA 91320
Web site:	www.sagepub.com/
Description:	The primary research vehicle of the American Association for Adult and Continuing Education, *Adult Education Quarterly* contains empirical research studies and critical essays in all areas of adult education and adult learning.

AgingStats.Gov

Telephone:	(301) 458-4440
Web site:	www.agingstats.gov
Description:	AgingStats.Gov is the Web site of the Federal Interagency Forum on Aging-Related Statistics. The forum encourages collaboration among its member federal agencies, including the (U.S.) Administration on Aging, the Bureau of Labor Statistics, the U.S. Bureau of the Census, the Health Care Financing Administration, the National Institute on Aging, the Office of Management and Budget, the Social Security Administration, and others producing or using statistics on aging. A recent forum report, *Older Americans 2000: Key Indicators of Well-Being*, encompasses five subject areas— population, economics, health status, health risks and behaviors, and health care. A hard copy of the report is available. Also available at this site are census-generated statistics, estimates, and projections of age distribution across the United States.

Alliance for Retired Americans

Telephone: (800) 333-7212
Address: 888 16th Street, NW
Washington, DC 20006
Web site: www.retiredamericans.org
Description: The Alliance for Retired Americans was launched in 2001 by a national coalition of unions affiliated with the American Federation of Labor–Congress of Industrial Organizations (AFL-CIO) and community-based organizations dedicated to economic and social justice. It serves as a voice for retirees and older U.S. residents in national, state, and local policy making.

America Walks

Telephone: (617) 367-1170
Address: Old City Hall
45 School Street, 2nd floor
Portland, OR 97296
Web site: www.americawalks.org
Description: America Walks is a coalition of local advocacy groups dedicated to promoting walkable communities around the United States. The Web site contains a list of existing groups and offers advice on how to start a local grassroots effort for increased planning, resources, and rights for walkers and bicyclers in U.S. cities and towns.

American Association of Retired Persons (AARP)

Telephone: (800) 424-3410
Address: 601 E Street, NW
Washington, DC 20049
Web site: www.aarp.org
Description: The AARP, the widely known membership organization for persons 55 and older, not only provides membership offerings and services, but also is a key advocacy and lobbying organization. Its Web site includes a listing of articles on career choices, financial planning, and consumer issues, as well as online information on the social security system. The Web site also includes extensive listings on volunteering, with links and state pages showcasing available volunteer opportunities. AARP also offers information on health care and wellness, and it has a number of publications, including the well-known periodical, *AARP: The Magazine,* and the *AARPBulletin.*

American Diabetes Association

Telephone: (800) 342-2383
Address: 1701 North Beauregard Street
                 Alexandria, VA 22311
Web site: www.diabetes.org
Description: The American Diabetes Association offers books on exercise and diabetes, which are available by telephone and over the Internet. The Web site has safety tips and information about getting started with an exercise regimen and suggestions about staying motivated under its "Healthy Living/Exercise" page. In addition, the Web site offers free pamphlets on exercise and diabetes. Practitioners can also contact regional offices for more information and materials.

American Heart Association

Telephone: (800) 242-8721
Address: 7272 Greenville Avenue
                 Dallas, TX 75231
Web site: www.americanheart.org
Description: The American Heart Association offers booklets, an exercise diary, and other materials on physical activity by telephone and through the Internet. A catalogue of English and Spanish language materials is available by telephone. Online, two exercise programs are available: "JustMove" (www.justmove.org), with tips on staying motivated, an interactive exercise diary, and information on who should contact a physician before starting an exercise regimen, and "Choose to Move" (www.choosetomove.org), a physical activity program for women. Both programs have some print material available by telephone. In addition, there are advocacy opportunities.

America's Job Bank

Web site: www.ajb.dni.us
Description: Professionals working with older populations facing work-life transitions, as well as such older people themselves, can access America's Job Bank, a Web site developed through a partnership between the U.S. Department of Labor and the state-operated public employment services.. This Internet database is updated nightly with more than 5,000 new jobs received from the states each day. Most jobs are in the private sector; included are professional, technical, managerial, blue collar, and clerical positions.

Arthritis Foundation

Telephone: (800) 283-7800
Addresst: P.O. Box 7669
Atlanta, GA 30357
Web site: www.arthritis.org
Description: Free pamphlets from the Arthritis Foundation, including "Exercise and Arthritis," are available by telephone. Spanish speakers are available by telephone. English and Spanish books and videos can be ordered by telephone or online. Also available online, a free "Connect and Control" program features an 18-week self-management course with goal setting, contracting, an exercise diary, prompting, and e-mail reminders for 52 weeks. In addition, there are advocacy opportunities related to arthritis.

Asociación Nacional Pro Personas Mayores (ANPPM)

Telephone: (213) 487-1922
Address: 3325 Wilshire Boulevard, Suite 800
Los Angeles, CA 90010
Web site: www.buscapique.com/latinusa/buscafile/oeste/anppm.htm
Description: The ANPPM was founded to inform policy makers and the general public regarding the status and needs of low-income elderly Hispanics and other low-income elderly persons. The organization provides direct social services, conducts national research, provides training and technical assistance to community groups, and produces and distributes bilingual information on the Hispanic elderly population.

BlackWomensHealth.com

Web site: www.blackwomenshealth.com
Description: Health and wellness information for African American women is available at BlackWomensHealth.com. This online site includes information on general exercise, fitness, strength training, weight loss, and exercise that can be combined with specific diseases, especially type II diabetes. An online personal trainer locator is also available, as is information on spirituality issues.

Center for Mental Health Services

Telephone: (800) 789-2647
Address: P.O. Box 42557
Washington, DC 20015
Web site: www.mentalhealth.org
Description: The Center for Mental Health Services offers mental health information with access to free publications, referral information and links to mental-health related topics.

Civic Ventures and Experience Corps

Telephone: (415) 430-0141
Address: 425 Second Street, Suite 601
San Francisco, CA 94107
Web site: www.civicventures.org
Description: A California-based nonprofit organization, Civic Ventures works to expand the contributions of older U.S. residents to our society and to promote individual and social renewal as our society ages. It publishes a newsletter "Coming of Age," and sponsors initiatives in 18 states.

Experience Corps, the organization's signature program [www/experience.org], operates in 15 cities across the United States, mobilizing adults 55 and over in meaningful service projects in their local communities. Established in 1995, the program has initially focused on involving older adults in the school systems and in youth-serving organizations to improve academic performance and support youth development. A list of those cities where projects are located is available through the organization's home page.

Educational Gerontology: An International Journal (periodical)

Telephone: (800) 354-1420, ext. 216
Contact: Journals Customer Service Manager
Taylor and Francis
325 Chestnut Street, Suite 800
Philadelphia, PA 19106
Web site: www.taylorandfrancis.com
Description: *Educational Gerontology* is a scientific journal published eight times a year. It addresses a wide range of issues related to the intersection of aging and education.

Elderhostel, Inc.

Telephone: (877) 426-8056
Address: 11 Avenue de Lafayette
Boston, MA 02111
Web site: www.elderhostel.org
Description: Elderhostel is a not-for-profit organization offering educational experiences for adults 55 and older at its local, national, and international sites. The Web site can be searched through location, activity, or special interest. The Elderhostel mission of lifelong learning includes the "Active Outdoor Program," which offers trips built around physical activities.

Environmental Alliance for Senior Involvement (EASI)

Web site: www.easi.org

Description: The mission of the EASI is to build, promote, and use the environmental ethic, expertise, and commitment of older persons to expand citizen involvement in protecting and caring for our environment for present and future generations.

FIRSTGOV for Workers

Web site: www.workers.gov

Description: This is a government Web site that provides information on job searches, related services, and employment rights and protection for all U.S. workers or prospective workers. There is some emphasis on aging-related issues, such as age discrimination in employment, estate planning, and money management in retirement. Information on volunteering and learning is also included.

Forum on Religion, Spirituality, and Aging (FORSA)

Telephone: (415) 974-9600

Contact: American Society on Aging (ASA)
833 Market Street, Suite 511
San Francisco, CA 94103

Web site: www.asaging.org/networks/index.cfm?cg=FORSA

Description: Founded a decade ago, FORSA constitutes a large multidisciplinary, interfaith, nondenominational community of professionals across the United States who are concerned with examining the spiritual dimension of human existence and its role in the aging process. Working closely with its parent organization, ASA, the Forum sponsors networking opportunities among its 8,500 members and publishes a quarterly members' newsletter, *Aging and Spirituality,* as well as the journal, *Generations,* and a bimonthly newspaper, *Aging Today.*

Gerontology and Geriatrics Education (periodical)

Telephone: (800) 429-6784

Contact: The Haworth Press, Inc.
10 Alice Street
Binghamton, NY 13904

Web site: www.haworthpressinc.com

Description: Published quarterly, *Gerontology and Geriatrics Education* deals with a broad set of issues in aging and education. Issues covered include intergenerational tutoring, the interdisciplinary team teaching of a gerontology course, learning theory and Elderhostel, and improving rural health care to elders. Educators in a variety of settings, including higher education and health care, are the target audience.

Grandparent Place: A Grandparenting Resource
Web site: www.grandparentplace.com
Description: Grandparent Place has a list of resources and Web links to grandparenting resources, including information about family relationships, different styles of grandparenting, and grandparents who are raising grandchildren.

Grandsplace
Web site: www.grandsplace.com
Description: For the more than 2 million grandparents who are raising one grandchild or more, Grandsplace provides support, education, and resources for caregiving.

Gray Panthers
Telephone: (800) 280-5362
Address: 733 15th Street, NW, Suite 437
                Washington, DC 20005
Web site: www.graypanthers.org
Description: Gray Panthers is an intergenerational advocacy organization. Members refer to themselves as "Age and Youth in Action" activists, working together for social and economic justice.

Jewish Community Centers, National Headquarters
Telephone: (212) 532-4949
Address: 15 East 26th Street
                New York, NY 10010
Web site: www.jcca.org
Description: The Jewish Community Center programs and services cover a wide range of education, health and exercise, volunteer, and family enrichment opportunities. The National Headquarters can refer callers to local Jewish Community Centers. All denominations are welcome.

Joint Public Affairs Committee for Older Adults (JPAC)
Telephone: (212) 273-5261
Address: 132 West 31st Street, 15th floor
                New York, NY 10001
Web site: www/jpac.org
Description: The JPAC trains elderly people to be activists through a twice yearly program called "Institute for Senior Action."

Journal of Aging and Physical Activity (periodical)

Telephone: (800) 747-4457

Contact: Human Kinetics Publishers, Inc.
P.O. Box 5076
Champaign, IL 61825

Web site: www.humankinetics.com

Description: The *Journal of Aging and Physical Activity* is the official journal of the European Group for Research into Elderly and Physical Activity. The authors who contribute to the journal are from a variety of disciplines. The articles explore the dynamic relationship between physical activity and the aging process.

Medicare Rights Center

Telephone: (212) 869-3850

Address: 1460 Broadway, 17th floor
New York, NY 10036

Web site: www.medicarerights.org

Description: A not-for-profit organization, the Medicare Rights Center is dedicated to ensuring that older adults and people with disabilities receive good, affordable health care. The Web site offers assistance and reliable Medicare information.

National Caucus and Center on Black Aged (NCBA)

Telephone: (202) 637-8400

Address: 1220 L Street, NW, Suite 800
Washington, DC 20005

Web site: www.ncba-aged.org

Description: The NCBA, founded in 1970, is a national organization dedicated to improving the quality of life for elderly African Americans.

National Center for Health Statistics

Telephone: (301) 458-4000

Address: 3311 Toledo Road
Hyattsville, MD 20782

Web site: www.cdc.gov/nchs/agingact.htm

Description: The Web site of the National Center for Health Statistics affords access to the federal government's principal source of health statistics, including information on health status, lifestyle, onset and diagnosis of illness and disability, and the use of health care by all U.S. residents.

National Council on Aging (NCOA)

Telephone: (202) 479-1200
Address: 300 D Street, SW, Suite 801
                 Washington, DC 20024
Web site: www.ncoa.org/about/index.html
Description: The NCOA is an association of organizations and professionals
                 seeking to promote the dignity, well-being, self-determination,
                 and contributions of older U.S. residents through both public
                 policy and program initiatives. Although a key focus of the
                 organization is on frail, disadvantaged, and ethnic minority
                 elderly people, the NCOA remains concerned more broadly with
                 vital aging among the general populace. The organization's Web
                 site includes information on research and demonstration
                 projects, workforce development, publications, and membership.

National Hispanic Council on Aging

Telephone: (202) 429-0787
Address: 1341 Connecticut Avenue, NW
                 Washington, DC 20009
Web site: www.nhcoa.org
Description: Founded in 1980, the National Hispanic Council on Aging is
                 dedicated to improving the quality of life for Hispanic elderly
                 people, families, and communities. Their advocacy work in-
                 cludes developing educational materials, technical assistance,
                 and capacity building. Their active membership is focused on
                 strengthening families, building community, and enhancing
                 policy analysis and research.

National Indian Council on Aging (NICOA)

Telephone: (505) 292-2001
Address: 10501 Montgomery Boulevard, NE, Suite 210
                 Albuquerque, NM 87111-3846
Web site: www.nicoa.org/
Description: The NICOA was formed by a group of tribal chairpersons in 1976
                 as an advocacy agency for the nation's elderly American Indians
                 and Alaska Natives. It strives to better the lives of the nation's
                 indigenous elderly population through advocacy, employment
                 training, dissemination of information, and data support.

National Institute on Aging (NIA)

Telephone: (301) 496-1752

Address: Building 31, Room 5C27
31 Center Drive, MSC 2292
Bethesda, MD 20892

Web site: www.nih.gov/nia

Description: The NIA was established in 1974 as part of the National Institutes of Health. It supports and conducts research and disseminates information to the public, including information on demographics related to health. In addition, the NIA has free publications about health and fitness for older adults.

National Osteoporosis Foundation

Telephone: (202) 223-2226

Address: 1232 22nd Street, NW
Washington, DC 20037

Web site: www.nof.org

Description: Information on exercise and its critical role in the well-being of the elderly is available through the National Osteoporosis Foundation. The Web site offers the organization's official video, "Be BoneWise," which focuses on weight-bearing and resistance exercises for people with osteoporosis. The Web site's "Prevention" page offers articles on falls and how to avoid them.

National Senior Games Association

Web site: www.nationalseniorgames.org

Description: The National Senior Games Association supports senior athletes interested in competing at a local, state, or national level. It sponsors summer and winter games and promotes healthy lifestyles for seniors through education, fitness, and sports. The Web site offers links to other Web sites with physical activity information for seniors, including the latest publications on physical activity benefits.

Older Women's League (OWL)

Telephone: (800) 825-3695

Address: 1750 New York Avenue, NW, Suite 350
Washington, DC 20006

Web site: www.owl-national.org

Description: OWL is a national grassroots membership organization that focuses on the needs of women as they age. Advocacy activities are conducted through a local chapter network.

President's Council on Physical Fitness and Sports

Telephone: (202) 690-9000

Contact: Department W
200 Independence Avenue, SW, Room 738 H
Washington, DC 20201

Web site: www.fitness.gov

Description: The President's Council on Physical Fitness and Sports high-lights the benefits of and encourages physical fitness for U.S. residents of all ages. "Pep up Your Life," a free exercise booklet for older adults developed in partnership with the AARP, can be requested by telephone. It can also be downloaded from the Web site. The Web site's "Reading Room" page offers numerous articles, including "Fitness Fundamentals" and "Guidelines for Personal Exercise Programs."

Senior Action in a Gay Environment (SAGE)

Telephone: (212) 741-2247

Address: 305 7th Avenue
New York, NY 10001

Web site: www.sageusa.org

Description: SAGE was founded in 1977 and is the nation's oldest and largest social service and advocacy organization dedicated to lesbian, gay, bisexual, or transgendered senior citizens. This organiza-tion trains elders to be activists through their program SAGE Voice/SAGE vote. In addition, educational opportunities are offered.

Senior Community Service Employment Program (SCSEP)

Telephone: (202) 693-3842

Contact: Division of Older Worker Programs
U.S. Department of Labor, Employment and Training
200 Constitution Avenue, NW, Room N-4641
Washington, DC 20210

Web site: www.wdsc.doleta.gov

Description: The SCSEP Web site provides information on part-time employ-ment for low-income persons age 55 and over. Program partici-pants work at community and government agencies and may receive training and use their participation as a bridge to other employment. Additionally, other national organizations de-voted to older workers can be accessed through this site. These include the Senior Job Bank, the National Urban League, the National Caucus and Center on the Black Aged, the National Indian Council on Aging, the National Asian-Pacific Center on Aging, and Asociación Nacional Pro Personas Mayores.

Senior Corps

Telephone: (202) 606-5000

Contact: Corporation for National and Community Service
1201 New York Avenue, NW
Washington, DC 20525

Web site: www.seniorcorps.org/

Description: The Senior Corps comprises three different national programs: the Foster Grandparent Program, the Retired Senior Volunteer Program (RSVP), and the Senior Companion Program. Local volunteer opportunities are available through each of these programs.

SeniorNet

Telephone: (415) 495-4990

Address: 121 Second Street, 7th floor
San Francisco, CA 94105

Web site: www.seniornet.org

Description: A nonprofit organization, SeniorNet offers adults over the age of 50 an opportunity to learn about computers through access to computers and technology education. It then provides volunteer opportunities for sharing computer information with others.

Silver Haired Legislature

Telephone: (918) 682-7891

Contact: Oklahoma Development District Area Agency on Aging
P.O. Box 1367
Muskogee, OK 74401

Web site: www.shls.org

Description: Silver Haired Legislatures exist in many states and consist of seniors, age 60 and over, who are elected by their peers to represent them and who work closely with elected state legislators around state legislative initiatives that would improve conditions for elderly people. The organization's Web site is coordinated by the Oklahoma Silver Haired Legislature.

Sit and Be Fit

Telephone: (509) 448-9438
Address: P. O. Box 8033
                 Spokane, WA 99203
Web site: www.sitandbefit.com
Description: The Sit and Be Fit program offers exercises developed by a nurse that promote functional fitness in older adults and physically limited individuals. Most exercises foster strength and flexibility and can be done from a sitting position. The Web site lists schedules for Sit and Be Fit programs on Public Television on a state-by-state basis. Videos are also available, as are videotapes for specific medical conditions such as Parkinson's disease, chronic obstructive pulmonary disease, and osteoporosis. Less expensive audiotapes with illustrated booklets are also available. Spanish video is available.

U.S. Census Bureau

Telephone: (301) 763-4636
Address: U.S. Census Bureau
                 Washington, DC 20233
Web site: www.census.gov
Description: Sponsored by the National Institute on Aging, this database provides information from government-sponsored surveys and statistics about the older population.

YMCA, National Headquarters

Web site: www.ymca.net
Description: The YMCA Web site is useful for locating centers and services offered in a given locale. The YMCA offers educational classes, as well as exercise programs. Services vary, but many locations offer exercise programs for older adults, including endurance exercises, strength training, water exercises, tai chi, and dance. In addition, there are opportunities for volunteering and pursuing learning opportunities.

Table A-1

Resources for Practitioners to Facilitate Productive Aging

Agency, Organization or Name of Resource	Demographics	Work Life	Volunteerism	Family Life	Personal Growth Spirituality	Leisure	Life Time	Activism	Physical Exercise
Administration on Aging	✓			✓					
Adult Education Quarterly (periodical)	✓				✓		✓		
AgingStats.gov									
Alliance for Retired Americans								✓	
America Walks								✓	✓
American Association of Retired Persons (AARP)		✓	✓	✓	✓		✓	✓	✓
American Diabetes Association									✓
American Heart Association								✓	✓
America's Job Bank		✓							
Arthritis Foundation									
Asociación Nacional Pro Personas Mayores (ANPPM)							✓	✓	
BlackWomensHealth.com	✓								
Center for Mental Health Services			✓	✓					
Civic Ventures and Experience Corps					✓	✓	✓	✓	
Educational Gerontology (periodical)					✓	✓	✓		
Elderhostel, Inc.									✓
Environmental Alliance for Senior Involvement (EASI)			✓					✓	
FIRSTGOV for Workers		✓	✓		✓		✓		
Forum on Religion, Spirituality, and Aging (FORSA)									
Gerontology and Geriatrics Education (periodical)									
Grandparent Place				✓					
Grandsplace				✓				✓	
Gray Panthers								✓	

Table A-1

Resources for Practitioners to Facilitate Productive Aging (continued)

Agency, Organization or Name of Resource	Demographics	Work Life	Volunteerism	Family Life	Personal Growth Spirituality	Life Time Leisure	Activism	Physical Exercise	Universal
Jewish Community Centers			✓	✓	✓	✓	✓	✓	
Joint Public Affairs Committee for Older Adults (JPAC)				✓	✓	✓	✓		
Journal of Aging and Physical Activity (periodical)								✓	
Medicare Rights Center							✓		
National Caucus and Center on Black Aged (NCBA)	✓								
National Center for Health Statistics				✓	✓		✓		
National Council on Aging (NCOA)		✓					✓		
National Hispanic Council on Aging				✓	✓				
National Indian Council on Aging (NICOA)	✓	✓		✓	✓		✓		
National Institute on Aging (NIA)	✓							✓	
National Osteoporosis Foundation								✓	
National Senior Games Association								✓	
Older Women's League (OWL)							✓		
President's Council on Physical Fitness and Sports								✓	
Senior Action in a Gay Environment (SAGE)			✓				✓		
Senior Community Service Employment Program (SCSEP)		✓	✓						
Senior Corps			✓			✓			
SeniorNet				✓		✓			
Silver Haired Legislature							✓		
Sit and Be Fit								✓	
U.S. Census Bureau	✓				✓	✓			
YMCA				✓	✓	✓	✓	✓	

Appendix B

Strengths Assessment Interview Guide

1. What makes a day a *good* day for you? What do you hope for at the start of a new day?

2. What are the things you do, each day or each week, because you really want to—not because you have to? Where you get totally absorbed, forget about everything else, and the time seems to fly?

3. What are you good at? What kinds of things did you used to be good at? What about yourself has always given you confidence or made you proud?
NOW
PAST

4. What kinds of exercise do you do regularly? What kinds <u>could</u> you do to help you feel better?
<u>DO</u>
<u>COULD</u> DO

5. What kinds of help, service, or assistance do you <u>give</u>? To whom? What help or service would you like to give?
<u>GIVE</u>
<u>WOULD LIKE TO GIVE</u>

6. When you get out, what do you like to do? Where do you like to go? What <u>would</u> you like to do? Where <u>would</u> you like to go?
LIKE TO DO/GO
WOULD LIKE TO DO/GO

7. What lessons have you learned about how to cope with life from day to day? Are there ways you wish you could cope better?
   LESSONS/COPE
   COPE BETTER

8. Who are the people that are especially important to you these days? Tell me about these relationships.

9. What physical things or objects do you have, that are most precious to you? What things do you save? Or take special care of? If you had to relocate, what few things would you take with you?

10. [To interviewer: What additional strengths, values, commitments, skills, or assets do you know (from whatever source) that this person has?].

Source: Kivnick, H. Q., & Murray, S. V. (2001). Life strengths interview guide: Assessing elder clients' strengths. *Journal of Gerontological Social Work, 34*(4), 7–32. © The Haworth Press. Reprinted with permission.

Index

A

AARP (American Association of Retired Persons), 73, 182, 227
    environmental programs, 190
    Foundation Project on Successful Aging and Adaptation, 5, 6
    Public Policy Institute survey, 85
    qualities of older workers study, 68
    unions and, 74
Activism, 177–193
    barriers to, 180
    community organizing programs, 186–188
    empowerment-oriented practices, 179–190, 184
    facilitating with social work practice, 190–191
    frail elderly and, 188–189
    old age interest groups, 181–183
    political behavior of elderly, 180–181
    productive aging and, 191–192
    programs promoting, 183–186
    service programs and, 189–190
    social breakdown syndrome/reconstruction theory, 178–179
Activity programs, 144
Activity theory, 13–14, 40–41
Adaptation, 4, 42, 47, 125, 133
    families and, 114
    natural coping mechanisms, 115
Adjustment, 39–40
Adler, Alfred, 156, 157

Administration on Aging (AoA), 85, 165, 225, 226
Adult Education Quarterly, 226
Advocacy, 180
AFL-CIO, 74
African Americans
    extended families and, 110
    physical activity and, 202, 203
    poverty rates of, 64
    social networks of, 51
    spirituality/religion and, 51
    vital involvement and, 130
Age Discrimination in Employment Act (ADEA), 69, 71, 72, 78
Aging
    older Americans as resource, 37–38
    fear of consequence of, 28–29
    predictors of successful, 6
    of U.S. society, implications of, 107
Aging and society paradigm, 89
AgingStats.Gov, 226
Agoraphobia, 199
Albert, M., 4
Alcohol use, 153
Alinsky, Saul, 186, 187
Alliance for Retired Americans, 227
Alzheimer's Association, 183
Alzheimer's disease, 153, 199
American Association of Retired Persons (AARP). *See* AARP (American Association of Retired Persons)
American Council on Education, 171

American Diabetes Association, 228
American Heart Association, 228
American Music Conference, 140
America's Job Bank, 228
America Walks, 205, 227
Antonovsky, A., 115
Anxiety, 199
Apocalyptic demography, 28
Arthritis Foundation, 229
Arts programs, 140, 142–43
Asociación Nacional Pro Personas Mayores
  (ANPPM), 183, 229
Assessment(s), 134–36
        geriatric health care and, 110–111
        multilevel, 113
        obtaining full client story, 135
        planning/implementing intervention
          with, 136
        primary foci, 134
        rethinking approach to, 117
        spiritual needs, 158
Assistive technology, 29
Atchley, R. C., 115, 200
Attitude(s)
        adjustments, 150
        on aging, 108, 109, 157, 160
        disease prevention and, 152
Autonomy, 49–50

B

Baby boomers
        demographics and, 21–23, 62
        family life and, 108
        post-retirement work plans, 64, 66,
          68, 85
        productivity and, 38
        retirement and, 108–109
        social security system and, 70
Bandura, A., 200
Behavioral change, transtheoretical model
  of, 199–201
Bengtson, V. L., 178
Bereavement counseling, 74
Birth cohorts, 22–25
Birth rates, 19–20
Bisexual elderly, 184–185
Bismarck, Otto von, 65–66
BlackWomensHealth.com, 229
Blau, Z., 41
Bloom, M., 4
Bodily-kinesthetic intelligence, 167

Boszormenyi-Nagy, I., 111
Bradley, Don E., 19
Brady, E. Michael, 163
Breaking the Rules of Aging (Lipschitz), 4
Brody, E., 111
Brown, A. S., 187–188
Bulka, R. P., 155, 156
Bush, George W., 158
Butler, Robert, 12
Butler, Sandra S., 177

C

Cabot, Richard, 217
Campbell, Jennifer, 225
Cannon, Ida, 217
Carden, Melinda, 83
Career transitions, 71
Caregiving, 75, 110–12, 111–113
Cattell, R. B., 166–67
Center for Mental Health Services, 229
Centers for Disease Control, 196–197
Change, stages of, 200
Child care programs, 138–139
Children
        activism on behalf of, 189–190
        dependent parents of adult, 111
        raised by grandparents, 110
Citibank, 75
Citizens for Better Care, 189
Civic Ventures, 189, 230
Client triage, 117
Clinebell, H., 158
Coalition on Legislation for the Elderly
  (COLE), 185
Cognitive function, 153, 166
Cohen, H. J., 152
Cole, T. R., 45
Commission on Aging, 206
Commonwealth Fund survey, 85, 86
Communication network societies, 25
Community Healthy Activities Model
  Program for Seniors (CHAMPS), 207
Community involvement, 9, 139
        community organization programs,
          186–88
        intergenerational projects, 190
        religious congregations, 154, 159–160
Competence, 47
        individual, 48–50
        system-level interventions and, 52–53
Computer skills, 29, 71–72, 172

Continuity theory, 42, 88–89, 115, 199–200, 206
Continuous care communities, 144
Continuums of care, 117, 118
Control, 49–50
    social reconstruction theory and, 178–179
    transaction control, 50
Coopers and Lybrand, 75
Coping needs/strategies, 4, 169
Corporation for National Service, 95
Council for Senior West Virginians, 185
Council for Social Work Education, 157
Counseling programs, 75
Cowger, C. D., 134, 135
Cox, E. O., 179–180
Crime, 186–187
Crisis intervention, 74
Crisis of meaning, 45–46
Critical gerontology, 43–45
"Crystallized" intelligence, 167
Cultural stereotypes, 72
Cumming, E., 41

D

Damush, T. M., 207
Dance Exchange, 140
Day treatment, 144
Death rates, 20–21
Dementia, 199
Demographic imperative, 28
Demographics, 19–36
    age categories, 23–24
    aging of population, 37, 61
    birth cohorts, 22–25
    demographic transition theory, 19–21
    economic status, 27
    education, 26–27
    family structures, 27–28, 109
    fear of consequence of population aging, 28–29
    fluctuations in population growth, 21–22
    health, 25–26
    life course perspective, 22–23
    modernization theory, 22–23
    productivity of Third Age, 29–34
    racial/ethnic diversity, 27
    Third and Fourth Ages, 24
    workforce trends, 62–64, 68, 70
    world population aging, 19

Depression, 199
Diagnostic and Statistical Manual of Mental Disorders, 158
Diet, 7
Disability, 14, 15
Discrimination, age, 11, 15, 61, 65
    formal complaints of, 73–74
    in workplace, 65, 69, 78
Disease
    Alzheimer's, 153
    avoiding, 4, 115, 152–153
    effect of, on learning ability, 168
    health care services and, 111
    heart disease, 29
    prevention, physical activity and, 197–199
Disengagement theory, 41
Diversity, 27
    families and, 110
    in workforce, 64–65
Divorce, 110
Dowd, J. J., 41–42
Downsizing, 72
Dychtwald, K., 4
Dynamic balance of opposites principle, 125, 127

E

Early eligibility age, 65
Ecological perspective, 113
Economic security, 51
Economic status, 27
Economy, 12
Educational gerontology, 164
Educational Gerontology: An International Journal, 230
Education and learning, 14, 42, 163–176
    demographics and, 26–27
    learning ability, 166–168
    lifelong learning, 163–164
    multidimensional intelligence, 166–168
    needs and motivation, 168–171
    noncognitive or environmental factors, 168
    older learner preferences, 171
    productivity and, 33–34, 52
    public policy and older adult education, 165–166
    selected programs, 171–174
    social work and older adult education, 174–175

Education for critical consciousness, 186
Efficacy, 200
Eldercare, 75
Elderhostel, Inc., 170, 172–173, 196, 230
Ellor, James W., 149
Employment, 10, 30–32
Empowerment, 44–45, 130
    activism and, 177–178, 179–190, 184
    control and, 49
    environmental changes and, 50–51
    individual competence and, 49
Environment
    adaptation and, 47
    autonomy and control beliefs and, 50
    economic security, 51
    empowerment and, 50–51
    person-environment theoretical
        perspective, 47–48
    social breakdown syndrome and, 178
Environment, human behavior and. *See*
    Human behavior and social environment
    (HBSE)
Environmental Alliance for Senior Involve-
    ment (EASI), 95, 190, 231
Environmental press, 47, 48
Environmental Protection Agency, 190
Epidemiological transition, 20
Equal Employment Opportunity Commis-
    sion (EEOC), 69
Erikson, Erik H., 4, 38, 124
Erikson, J. M., 4
Estes, C. L., 180
Ethnic diversity, 27
Evans, Lois, 220
Exchange theory, 41–42, 44
Exercise. *See* Physical activity
Experience Corps, 91, 95, 98, 189, 230
Expressive learners, 169–170

F

Falling, fear of, 198, 202
Families USA Foundation, 183
Family First Program, 86
Family Friends, 93
Family life, 42, 107–22
    augmenting social work's practice
        base, 112–114
    caregiving and, 110–112, 111–112
    changing nature of, 107–108
    family roles, 27–28
    geriatric social work and, 114

    intervening with families of later
        years, 114–115, 117
    new family forms, 109–110
    resilience and, 115, 117
Family Medical Leave Act of 1993, 76
Federal Council on Aging, 165
Federal Interagency Forum on Aging-Related
    Statistics, 226
Feminist perspectives, 44
Fengler, A. P., 88
50 Plus Fitness Association, 196
Financial planning, 76
FIRSTGOV for Workers, 231
Flex-time jobs, 76
"Fluid" intelligence, 167
Fortunati, V., 215
Forum on Religion, Spirituality, and Aging
    (FORSA), 231
Foster Grandparents Program, 87, 95, 98
Fountain of Age, The (Friedan), 38
Fourth Age, 24
Frankl, V., 155–157
Freedman, M., 88
Freire, Paulo, 186
Freud, Sigmund, 156
Friedan, Betty, 38
Fries, J. F., 26
Fry, P. S., 168
Fry, P. W., 200
Fulghum, Fontaine H., 225

G

Gardner, H., 167–168
Gay elderly, 184–185
GE Capital Services, 75
Geistig, 155, 156
Gender, dynamic balance of opposites and, 127
Generations of Hope, 94
Generativity, 38
Genetics, 4, 150, 152
Germany, retirement in, 65
Gerontology, 39
    industrial, 76
    instrumental, 45
Gerontology and Geriatrics Education, 231
GI Bill, 26
Giddens, A., 46
Goeke, M. L., 186
Graberg Nursing Home, 220
Grandparent Place: A Grandparenting
    Resource, 232

Grandparents, 110
Grandsplace, 232
Gray Panthers, 177, 182, 183, 232
Great Depression, 182
Greene, Roberta R., 107, 109
Green Thumb, 77
Grossman, Melonie D., 195, 202

H

Harvard alumni study, 197
Harvard Study of Adult Development, 4
Havighurst, Robert, 40
Hazen Paper Co. v. Biggins, 71, 73
Health. *See also* Physical activity
    demographics of, 25–26
    disabled elderly, 28–29
    disease prevention, 152–153
    education level and, 26
    longevity and, 26
    mental health, 199
    productivity and, 14, 33
    social support groups, 154, 158–159
    trends, in older Americans, 83–84
    volunteerism/service and, 87–88
Health care costs, 70
Health insurance, 68
Health issues, in workplace, 72, 74
Heart disease, 29, 198
Henry, W. E., 41
Heterogeneity, 110
Hispanics, 27
    physical activity and, 202, 203
    poverty rates of, 64
Holism, 157–158
Holstein, M., 192
HomeFriends, 94
Hooyman, Nancy R., 37
Horn, J. L., 166–67
Hospital-based social work, 141–144
Houle, C., 168–169
Household activities, 30–32
Housing, 133, 144
Human behavior and social environment
    (HBSE), 123, 124

I

Independent Sector survey, 85
Individual competence, 47
Individualism, 25
Influence, ability to, 170

Information-based economy, 25
Institute for Retired Professionals, 173
Institute for Senior Action, 184
Institutional ageism, 52
Institutional capacity, productive engage-
    ment and, 90–91
Instrumental gerontology, 45
Interest groups, 181–183
Intergenerational projects, 190
Internet use, 22
Interpersonal intelligence, 167
Interventions. *See* Social work interventions
Intrapersonal intelligence, 167

J

Jewish Community Centers, 232
Job sharing, 76
Johns Hopkins University, 95
Joint Public Affairs Committee for Older
    Adults (JPAC), 183–184, 191, 232
Journal of Aging and Physical Activity, 233

K

Kahn, R. L., 152
Kautzer, K., 189
Kaye, Lenard W., 3, 221
Kivnick, Helen Q., 4, 123, 135
Klein, W. C., 4
Koenig, H. G., 151, 152
Kuhn, Maggie, 177
Kuypers, J. A., 178

L

Labor force participation, 14
    adults ages 55 and older by gender, 63
    alternative work arrangements, 77
    benefits of, 66–68
    diversity in, 64–65
    emotional-social fulfillment, 68
    legislation/social policy and, 65–66
    matrix model for, 66–79
    organizational barriers, 72–73
    organizational benefits, 68–69
    organizational interventions, 76–78
    personal barriers, 71–72
    personal interventions, 74–76
    projections to 2008, 69
    ratio of younger workers to older
        retirees, 70

Labor force participation *(continued)*
    social/cultural benefits, 69–71, 73–74
    social/cultural interventions, 78–79
    social work interventions, 74
    women and, 63
    workforce demographic trends, 62–64
Laslett, P., 38
Latino families, 110
Lauerman, J. F., 3–4
Leadership, 170
Learning. *See* Education and learning
Lee, C., 203
Legislation, retirement age/older workers, 61, 65–66
Leisure *vs.* productivity, 42
Lerman, Liz, 140
Lesbian, gay, bisexual, and transgender (LGBT) elderly, 184–185
Libraries, 172
Life cycle development theory
    dynamic balance of opposites, 125, 127
    process in time, 125, 126
    vital involvement, 127–130
Life expectancy, 25–26, 37, 40, 83, 123
Life-long learning institutes (LLIs), 173
Lifestyle, wellness and, 152
Linguistic intelligence, 167
Lipschitz, David, 4–5
Living arrangements, 27–28
Living Is for the Elderly (LIFE), 188–189
Living standards, 63–64
Logical-mathematical intelligence, 167
Logotherapy, 155–157
Longer Life Foundation, 87n
Longevity
    family structures and, 109–110
    genetic predisposition to, 4
Longino, Charles F. Jr., 19
Long-term care insurance, 75
Lowy, L., 175

M

MacArthur, Douglas, 149
MacArthur Foundation Study of Aging, 85, 115
Manheimer, R., 170
Martin Marietta Corporation, 69
Maslow, Abraham, 152
Masunaga, H., 165–166
McClusky, Howard Yale, 165, 169–170

McKhann, G. M., 4
Meadowood Health Center, 142
Meaning, in life, 45–47, 156–157, 170. *See also* Spiritual and religious life
Medical benefits, 68
Medicare, 77
Medicare Rights Center, 233
"Me" generation, 24
Mental health, 199
Metro Seniors in Action (MSA), 187
Meyer, J. E. W., 182, 189
Microsoft Corporation, 77
"Middle-aged" employees defined, 65
Miller, W. R., 207
Minkler, M., 129
Minnesota Alliance of Health Care Consumers, 188–189
Minority groups, 110
    physical activity and, 195
    poverty rates of, 64–65, 67
Modeling of the ideal, 158
Modernization theory, 22–23
Moody, H. R., 45–46, 164, 175
Moral economy of aging, 45
Mor-Barak, Michàl E., 61
More, Thomas, 215
Morrow-Howell, Nancy, 83
Morstain, B. R., 169
Mortality rates, 20
Motivation
    education and, 168–169
    physical activity and, 201–202
Multiculturalism, 25
Multidimensional intelligence theory, 166–168
Murray, S. V., 135
Muscle mass, 198
Muse Workshops, 139–40
Music, 140
Musical intelligence, 167

N

National Alliance of Senior Citizens, 182
National Association of Retired Federal Employees, 182
National Blueprint for Increasing Physical Activity Among Adults, 204
National Caucus and Center on Black Aged (NCBA), 183, 233
National Center for Health Statistics, 233
National Committee to Preserve Social Security and Medicare, 182, 183

National Council for Senior Citizens, 182
National Council on Aging (NCOA), 93, 234
National Hispanic Council on Aging, 234
National Indian Council on Aging (NICOA), 183, 234
National Information and Resource Clearinghouse for the Aging, 165
National Institute on Aging (NIA), 218, 235
National Institutes of Health, 218
National Osteoporosis Foundation, 235
National Pacific/Asian Resource Center on Aging, 183
National Senior Games Association, 196, 235
Naturalist intelligence, 167
Neighborhoods 2000 program, 190
Neugarten, B. L., 23
"New aged," 133
Noölogical dimension, 155
Nursing Home Reform Law, 220
Nursing homes, 219–20
    Citizens for Better Care (CBC), 189
    LIFE program, 188–189
    social workers and, 141

O

OASIS Intergenerational Tutoring Program, 96
O'Connor, D., 175
Office of Faith-Based and Community Initiatives, 158
Older Americans 2000: Key Indicators of Well-Being, 226
Older Americans Act of 1965, 165
Older Americans Comprehensive Services Amendments of 1973, 165
"Older" employees defined, 65
Older Women's League (OWL), 183, 235
On the Move!, 205
Operation Reach Out, 140
"Opportunistic downsizing," 72
Osher, Bernard, 174
Osher Lifelong Learning Institute, 173–174

P

Pain, chronic, 198–199
Panic disorder, 199
Parent care, 111
Pargament, K., 158
Parsons, R. J., 179–180

Peabody, Francis Weld, 217
Perls, T. T., 3–4
Personal assistance technologies, 29
Personal growth, 112, 149–150
    life cycle development and, 124–132
    strengths-based perspective, 130–131
Person-environment theoretical perspective, 47–48
"Personhood," 44–45
Peter D. Hart Research Associates, 85
Peterson, D. A., 165–66
Physical activity, 4, 195–213
    active aging, 196–197
    barriers to, 202–203
    behavioral approaches to, 206–207
    benefits of, 197–199
    guidelines, 197
    motivation, 201–202
    social work practice roles, 203–207, 208
    theory, 199–201
Physical limitations, workplace issues, 72
Pioneer Network, 220
Polaroid Corporation, 77
Policy formation, 107, 165–166
Policy practice, 191
Political behavior, 180–81. *See also* Activism
Political economy, 43–45
Popenoe, D., 107
Population. *See* Demographics
Positive aging, 150
Positive attitude, 152
Poverty rates, 64, 67
Practical knowledge, 38
Practice perspective, 3–17
    defining terms, 3–10
Pratt, H. J., 181
Prescription drugs, 77
President's Council on Physical Fitness and Sports, 236
Prevention programs, 10
Primary control, 49
Problem focus, 130–132, 145
Prochaska, H. O., 200
Productive aging, 37–57
    critical gerontology, 43–45
    defending emphasis on, 8–10
    defined, 12, 38–39
    demographic mandate, 10–12
    environmental changes and, 50–53
    facts illustrating, 14
    human service programs for, 9
    individual competence and, 48–50

Productive aging *(continued)*
    meaning/purpose and, 45–47
    mental/physical exercise and, 4
    multiple dimensions of, 13
    personal/professional reference
       points, 215–223
    person-environment theoretical
       perspective, 47–48
    profile, 33
    seniors as valuable resource, 84
    social work skill sets and, 12
    theoretical models, 39–43
Productive engagement, 89–91
Productivity
    activities of productive seniors, 31
    defined, 38–39
    education and, 33–34
    environment and, 51
    health and, 33
    household activities, 30–32
    measures of, 30–31
    Third Age population profile,
       29–34
Programs Across Ages, 93
Prussian Empire, 65

R
Racial diversity, 27
Reciprocation, 42
Recreation, 38, 42. *See also* Physical activity
Reitzes, D. C., 187
Religion. *See* Spiritual and religious life
Repair and maintenance activities, 30, 32
Residential locations, 133
Resilience, 115, 117
Resources for practitioners, 225–240
Retirement
    age, legislation/social policy and,
       65–66
    baby boomers and, 108–109
    communities, 42
    company subsidizing of, 70
    early retirement trend, 44, 70, 72, 78
    gradual/incremental plans, 77
    income sources, 27
    phased retirement, 76
    planning, 76
    time and, 37–38
Rice, F. P., 178
Robert Wood Johnson Foundation, 93
Role discontinuity, 40

Role theory, 40
Rollnick, S., 207
Roots & Branches Theatre, 140
Rosenblatt, R., 5
Rowe, J. W., 152

S
Safehouse Project, 187
Safety, 202
Salutogenesis orientation, 114–115
Schaie, K. W., 168
Schwartz, Doris, 220
Secondary control, 49
Selective optimization, 49
Self-actualization, 164
Self-determination, 130
Self-esteem, 49, 125, 127
Self-identity, 46
Self-transcendence, 155–156
Senior Action in a Gay Environment
    (SAGE), 185, 236
Senior centers, 42
Senior College, 173–174
Senior Community Service Employment
    Program (SCSEP), 236
Senior Companion Program, 87, 98
Senior Corps, 237
SeniorNet, 237
Senior Olympics, 196
Senior service programs. *See* Volunteerism
    and service
Seniors for Childhood Immunization, 96
Seniors for Schools, 94
Service. *See* Volunteerism and service
Shephard, R. J., 203
Sherraden, Michael, 83
Silver, M. H., 3–4
Silver Haired Legislature, 185–186, 191, 237
Silverstone, B., 109
Sit and Be Fit, 238
Smart, J. C., 169
Smith, C., 201–202
Smoking, 29, 153
Social breakdown syndrome, 178
Social clock, 40
Social cognitive theory, 199
Social creation of dependency, 43
Social exchange theory, 41–42
Social gerontological theory, 42
Social involvement, 115
Socializing, 14

Social policy, 37, 61, 65–66
Social reconstruction theory, 177, 178–179
Social Security Act, 65, 182
Social Security system, 70
Social support, 186
    programmatic interventions and, 52
Social workers
    alternative perspective for working
      with older adults, 7–8
    geriatric, with older adults and their
      families, 114
    gerontological, 99
    longevity revolution and, 107–112
    older adult education and, 174–175
Social work interventions, 75–76
    labor issues, 74–75, 78–79
    traditional fields of concern, 131–132
    vital involvement and, 136
    volunteerism/service and, 99, 102
Spark, G., 111
Spatial intelligence, 167
Spiritual and religious life, 4, 115, 149–161
    holistic view of later life, 151–152
    intrafaith approaches, 160
    logotherapy, 155–157
    model for positive aging program-
      ming in clinical setting, 151
    positive aging in counseling, 157–159
    positive aging programming, 159–160
    religion, defined, 150
    religion *vs.* spirituality, 150–151
    religious coping, 153
    spirituality, defined, 151
    successful aging and, 152–157
St. Croix River Valley Arts Council, 140
State policy, 191
Stereotyping, 15
Storandt, M., 201
Storytelling, 145
Strengths-based perspective, 130–131, 158
    traditional *versus,* 131–132
Stress reduction, 152, 153
Stretching activities, 198
Structural lag theory, 42, 91
Strumpf, Neville, 220
Successful aging, 150, 152
    components, 115, 116
    major factors of, 115
    men's *vs.* women's views of, 5
    and productive aging compared, 39
    social systems and, 41
Svanborg, Alvar, 220

T
Technological skills, 71–72, 73
Technology, assisted living and, 29
Tenderloin Senior Outreach Project (TSOP),
    186
Theater programs, 140
Third Age, 24, 37–38, 133
*Third Age: the National Survey of Families and
    Households,* 29–30
Tillich, P., 155
Time Slips, 145
Townsend Movement, 182
Transaction control, 50
Transcendence, 155–56, 170–171
Transgender elderly, 184–185
Trela, J. E., 181
Trends
    early retirement, 70, 72, 78
    labor force participation, 62–64
    living alone, 23
    retirement, 37
    volunteerism and service, 83
Turemark, Ulla, 220

U
Unions, 74
U.S. Census Bureau, 238
Utopia (More), 215

V
Vaillant, George, 4
Values, personal, 24–25, 133–134
Van Tassel, D. D., 182
Varian Medical Systems, 77
Vital involvement, 127–130, 133–144
    agency programming, 138–141
    assessment, 134–136
    case work with individuals, 136–138
    defined, 127–128
    gerontological social services and,
      133–144
    hospitals/nursing homes and, 141–144
    housing and day treatment, 144
    intervention, 136
Volunteerism and service, 14, 52, 83–105
    activism and, 189–90
    areas of, 85–86
    challenging roles in, 91–92
    educational aspects of, 170
    effects of, on older adults, 87–88

Volunteerism and service *(continued)*
    Elderhostel and, 172–173
    extent of, 84–86
    factors associated with, 86–87
    senior service programs, 92–101
    service as an emerging institution,
       92–99
    social work roles, 99, 102
    theoretical perspectives on later-life,
       88–92
Voting, 180

W

Walsh, F., 109, 114, 115
Wellness programs, 10, 74, 117, 144, 150,
   152
Westburg, 157
White House Conference on Aging, 165
Williams, Carter Catlett, 141, 215, 217,
   219–122
Williams, T. Franklin, 215, 216–118

"Will to meaning," 156
Wilson, Steve, 61
Wisdom, 38
Wolfe, J. B., 186
Women
    effects of volunteerism/service on
       health of, 87
    life expectancy of, 25–26
    lifestyle choices of elderly, 28
    perception of successful aging, 5
    physical activity and, 203
    poverty rates of, 64–65, 67
    social networks of African American,
       51
    vital involvement of, 130
Workforce. *See* Labor force participation
Workforce Investment Act of 1998, 77–78

Y

YMCA, National Headquarters, 238
Yuppies, 24

About the Editor

Lenard W. Kaye, PhD, is professor of social work at the University of Maine School of Social Work and director of the UMaine Center on Aging. During the 2000–2001 academic year, he was the Visiting Libra Professor in the University of Maine's College of Business, Public Policy, and Health. Previously, he was professor of social work and social research and director of the doctoral program at the Graduate School of Social Work and Social Research at Bryn Mawr College, Bryn Mawr, Pennsylvania.

A prolific writer in the field of social gerontology, Dr. Kaye has published approximately 100 journal articles and book chapters and 11 books on specialized topics in aging, including rural social work practice, older men, home health care, family caregiving, controversial issues in aging, support groups for older women, and congregate housing.

Dr. Kaye is the co-principal investigator of the Maine Primary Partners in Caregiving Project funded through the U.S. Administration on Aging, the principal investigator of the Hartford Geriatric Social Work Curriculum Infusion Project at the University of Maine School of Social Work, and principal investigator of the Maine Parenting Relatives Mental Health and Substance Abuse Project.

Dr. Kaye is the former chair of the National Association of Social Workers's Section on Aging, sits on the editorial boards of *Social Work Today*, the *Journal of Gerontological Social Work*, and *Geriatric Care Management Journal*, and is a Fellow of the Gerontological Society of America. He is currently a member of the National Advisory Committee on Rural Health and Human Services of the U.S. Department of Health and Human Services.

About the Contributors

Don E. Bradley, PhD, is visiting assistant professor, Wake Forest University, Winston-Salem, North Carolina.

E. Michael Brady, PhD, is professor, adult education, and research fellow, Osher Lifelong Learning Institute, University of Southern Maine, Portland.

Sandra Sue Butler, PhD, is associate professor, School of Social Work, University of Maine, Orono.

Robert N. Butler, MD, is president and chief executive officer, International Longevity Center, New York, New York.

Jennifer Campbell, MS, is instructor, Graduate School of Social Work and Social Research, Bryn Mawr College, Bryn Mawr, Pennsylvania.

Rev. James W. Ellor, PhD, Dmin, DCSW, GCP, is director, Institute for Gerontological Studies, Baylor University, Waco, Texas.

Fontaine H. Fulghum, MSW, ABD, is lecturer, School of Social Work, Rutgers, The State University of New Jersey, Camden.

Roberta Greene, PhD, MSW, is Louis and Ann Wolens Centennial Chair in Gerontology and Social Welfare, School of Social Work, University of Texas, Austin.

Melonie D. Grossman, PhD, LCSW, is research associate, Institute of Health and Aging, University of California, San Francisco.

Nancy R. Hooyman, PhD, is dean emerita, School of Social Work, and professor of social work, University of Washington, Seattle.

Helen Kivnick, PhD, is professor, School of Social Work, University of Minnesota, St. Paul.

Charles F. Longino, PhD, is director, Reynolds Gerontology Program, and professor, Department of Sociology, Wake Forest University, Winston-Salem, North Carolina.

Michál E. Mor-Barak, DSW, is professor, School of Social Work and Marshall School of Business, and chair, industrial/occupational social work, University of Southern California, Los Angeles.

Nancy Morrow-Howell, PhD, is professor of social work, George Warren Brown School of Social Work, Washington University, St. Louis.

Carter Catlet Williams, ACSW, is a social worker and consultant on aging, Rochester, New York.

T. Franklin Williams, MD, is former director, National Institute on Aging and professor of medicine emeritus, School of Medicine and Dentistry, University of Rochester, Rochester, New York.

Steve Wilson, MSW, is lecturer, California State University, Long Beach, and doctoral student, School of Social Work, University of Southern California, Los Angeles.